Morton Paglin

Three Essays on

THE STATE OF ECONOMIC SCIENCE

Three Essays on
THE STATE OF
ECONOMIC SCIENCE

TJALLING C. KOOPMANS

Professor of Economics
Yale University

McGRAW-HILL BOOK COMPANY, INC.

New York   Toronto   London

1957

THREE ESSAYS ON THE STATE OF ECONOMIC SCIENCE

Library of Congress Catalog Card Number 57-8008

8 9 10 11 12 – MP – 1 0 9 8 7

35337

To T. W. K.

PREFACE

I am not now writing a treatise, but simply prefacing a somewhat peculiar narrative by observations very much at random. [EDGAR ALLAN POE, *The Murders in the Rue Morgue*]

This bundle of essays is the result of an opportunity to spend more than a year in reading and reflection about economics in the present phase of its development. It is by no means intended as a diagnosis of that phase, or as a set of recommendations for future research. What is offered is one man's explanations of some recent developments in economic theory, his comments and perplexities about the character and basis of economic knowledge, and his intuitions about possible directions of future work in theory and in empirical investigations. In keeping with the unsystematic nature of this undertaking, the essays reflect the particular preoccupations and limitations of their author at least as much as they reflect the current state of economic science. These preoccupations concern broadly the parallel and connected development of economic theory and economic observation and measurement in order to increase man's understanding and society's control of economic conditions, advancement, and well-being. More in particular, they concern the development and the use of mathematical and statistical concepts and tools for these purposes.

At the Atlantic City meeting of the American Economic Association, held in January, 1947, Professor J. M. Clark appealed to mathematical economists to communicate their results to the general economist. In the subsequent issue of *Econometrica* he elaborated on his plea for communicability and made it more specific. The first essay of this book is an attempt to communicate the logical content, and some of the underlying reasoning, of certain recent developments in mathematical economics. It is the longest of the three essays, and requires relatively the highest degree of concentration from the reader. It argues that, with the help of more fundamental mathematical tools, the common logical structure of received economic theories of quite diverse origin

can be brought out. The descriptive theory of competitive equilibrium
—the word "descriptive" is used at the rather abstract level indicated
by the postulates of the theory—and the normative theory of the use of
prices for the efficient allocation of resources appear as two sides of
one coin. In addition, the recent advances in computing methods for
the allocation or programming problems of a single organization are
seen as another offshoot from the same mathematical stem. Finally,
the derivation of all results from prime postulates throws a clear light
on the limits of their applicability. No attempt is made, however, to
offer a rounded survey of significant recent work in mathematical
economics. Important contributions to the literature are not mentioned
unless they have a direct connection with the subjects selected for
presentation.

If the first essay attempts to respond to Professor Clark's appeal,
the second addresses a plea of its own to the general economist. It
urges a clearer separation, in the construction of economic knowledge,
between reasoning and recognition of facts, for the better protection
of both. It recommends the postulational method as the principal instrument by which this separation is secured. Thereafter it goes on to
explore various directions in which the postulates of economic theory
could be modified and refined in order to recognize more aspects of
reality.

The third essay considers the interaction between tools of analysis
and choice of problems in economics. It examines in particular four
recent and current tool developments and seeks to perceive some of their
implications for future research, particularly in regard to the problems
of achieving a stable rate of growth of the economy. If it is felt that
the latter discussion is somewhat speculative, it may be said in defense
that tools are of interest more in their promise than in their achieve-
ment. Perhaps the inhibitions we feel against committing our intuitions
to the printed page in substantive discussion should not be allowed to
impede us to the same extent when we discuss choices of tools and of
problems.

The three essays, concerned with questions of substance, of method,
and of tools, respectively, can be read separately or in any desired
order. Nevertheless, a common thread runs through all three. Thus the
substantive developments reported in the first essay serve as examples
in the discussions of method and of tools. The connecting thread of the
volume is an emphasis on explicit formal model construction both in

theory and in empirical research. This emphasis derives from a belief that in the present period economics as a practical art is ahead of economics as a science. At this stage most of us prefer to see the advising of government economic policies entrusted to the experienced intuitive economist. But the task of providing him over time with better, more explicit, and more transferable knowledge requires, I believe, an approach somewhat different from his usual habits of thought. To argue this case is a common purpose of the three essays.

The book, then, is primarily addressed to the general economist. In addition, it may have value to the social scientist, the philosopher, the statistician, or the mathematician who seeks information about or an appraisal of the actual and potential use of mathematical and other tools in the current phase of economics.

When the manuscript for this book was in an advanced state of preparation, two books appeared with in part similar objectives: Professor J. R. Hicks's *A Reconsideration of Demand Theory*, and Professor Sidney Schoeffler's *The Failures of Economics*. At that point it seemed preferable not to delay the present book by an attempt to respond in its pages to the important contributions made by these authors.

I am indebted to many friends and colleagues, and in particular to Kenneth J. Arrow, Carl Christ, Gerard Debreu, William J. Fellner, Carl G. Hempel, Leonid Hurwicz, Lawrence R. Klein, Edmond C. Malinvaud, Alan S. Manne, Harry Markowitz, Lionel McKenzie, Richard Ruggles, Leonard J. Savage, and James Tobin, who have read portions of the manuscript and given me the benefit of highly valued criticism and comment. While the interrelated research of many of these has made an account like the present volume possible, it will be understood that the author is solely responsible for the use made of their published ideas and of the further discussions and advice he has received.

I am indebted to the Rockefeller Foundation and to Yale University for the opportunity to concentrate on the studies that have crystallized in these essays, and to the Cowles Foundation for Research in Economics at Yale University for permission and encouragement to use the further time required to complete them.

I wish to thank Mrs. Truus W. Koopmans, Miss Anne W. Koopmans, Mrs. Ellen Ryan, and Mrs. Natalie Sirkin for their help in reading proof and in preparing the Index.

T. C. K.

CONTENTS

I

ALLOCATION OF RESOURCES
AND THE PRICE SYSTEM

It must be admitted that in many areas of mathematical economics very substantial abstractions are being used, so that one can hardly speak of a good approximation to reality. But it should be remembered that, on the one hand, mathematical economics is a very young science and, on the other, that economic phenomena are of such a complicated, involved nature that far-reaching abstractions must be used at the start merely to be able to survey the problem, and that the transition to more realistic assumptions must be carried out step by step. [ABRAHAM WALD, "ON SOME SYSTEMS OF EQUATIONS OF MATHEMATICAL ECONOMICS," TRANSLATED, *Econometrica*, VOL. 19, NO. 4, OCTOBER 1951, P. 369]

ALLOCATION OF RESOURCES
AND THE PRICE SYSTEM

1. POINT SETS, LINEAR FUNCTIONS, AND THE DECENTRALIZATION OF ECONOMIC DECISIONS

1.1   NEW TOOLS FOR OLD PROBLEMS

In the Introduction to *Foundations of Economic Analysis*,[1] Professor Paul A. Samuelson points to the formal similarities in a wide variety of problems arising in diverse parts of economic theory. To bring out the common logical structure of these problems is the principal purpose and accomplishment of his book.

[1] Harvard University Press, Cambridge, Mass., 1948 (2d ed.). To be quoted hereafter as *Foundations* . . . .

The similarities arise from wide application, in the description of economic behavior and in the recommendation of economic actions, of the idea of maximization under constraints. For instance, it is postulated that the entrepreneur in his role of production manager minimizes the cost of whatever is produced, within a given range of technological possibilities. It is further assumed that as a market agent he chooses the amount and composition of his output in such a way as to maximize profit from its sale. Other models postulate that the consumer maximizes, within the bounds of his income and/or wealth, a quantity, called a *utility function*, which expresses how his satisfaction varies when his consumption varies. Discussions of economic policy or of the programming of government activities[1] recommend that the policy makers seek to maximize some target function of variables regarded as social objectives, subject to given restraints of technology, of resource limitations, or of international intercourse. In all these cases, it is either assumed or recommended that an index of the degree of attainment of some objective is or be maximized under given constraints.

It is not the purpose of the present essay to appraise the realism of this assumption or the appropriateness of the recommendation. We accept the fact that a large body of economic thought has taken off from such premises. What we propose to do is to pursue Samuelson's purpose a step further into the realm of tools of analysis.

In recent years, mathematical tools of a more basic character have been introduced into economics, which permit us to perceive with greater clarity and express in simpler terms the logical structure of important parts of economic theory. Parallel with this change in tools, there has been a change in emphasis as between various aspects of the theories in which the tools are applied. Traditionally, mathematical economics has emphasized models that describe the formation of prices and quantities in competitive markets through unique, or at least locally determinate, solutions of equation systems. Such models have also been used to study how these solutions respond to changes in technological knowledge, in consumers' preferences, in governmental policies, or in

---

[1] See for instance, J. Tinbergen, *On the Theory of Economic Policy*, North-Holland Publishing, Amsterdam, 1952; and Marshall K. Wood and George B. Dantzig. "The Programming of Interdependent Activities," in T. C. Koopmans (ed.), *Activity Analysis of Production and Allocation*, Cowles Commission Monograph 13, Wiley, New York, 1951, chaps. I and II, (pp. 15–32).

"external conditions" such as weather or foreign demand. Calculus and the theory of implicit functions have formed the main mathematical tools for this type of analysis.

The new tools allow us to shed new light on older and perhaps also more fundamental problems. The emphasis is shifted to the specification of conditions under which decentralization of economic decisions through a price system is compatible with efficient utilization of resources. It is not suggested that these classical problems were at any time lost out of sight. The "new welfare economics" has made them its special concern. However, the tools referred to were inadequate for the purpose in question. In the first place, they did not permit recognition of restraints on choice that require expression by inequalities rather than by equations. Owing to this limitation of the tools in use, the literature of an entire period almost completely ignored such simple facts as the impossibility of consuming negative quantities of goods or of rendering negative quantities of labor, or the impossibility of running production processes in reverse. Secondly, the calculus, used in the way it was used to scan the (restricted) domain of the target function for a maximum position, is a myopic instrument. It served only to compare the would-be-maximum position with alternative positions in its immediate neighborhood. For this reason, the problem of formulating conditions under which a position could stand comparison with more distant rivals was not faced.

As a result, the conditions for optimal allocation of resources formulated by the new welfare economics lacked necessity because of the first-mentioned defect of the tools used, and lacked sufficiency because of the second defect—thus ending up with no assured connection with optimality. Fortunately, as often happens, the intuitions that had originally led to the theories in question were better than the first attempts at their mathematical expression. It has now become apparent that propositions of the kind aimed at in the new welfare economics can be formulated more succinctly, and can be established by reasoning both simpler and more compelling, with the help of a few elementary concepts and theorems borrowed from the mathematical theory of *linear spaces*. At the same time, the basic unity of welfare economics with the descriptive theory of competitive equilibrium is brought out more clearly by these formulations.

In the present Section 1 of this essay, we shall first explain the concept of a linear space and its use in describing any commodity bundle by a point in such a space. Since a restraint on choice is then suitably described by a *set of points*, we shall thereafter review a few concepts and theorems about point sets in linear spaces that have been found useful in economic theory, and illustrate their application by examples designed to bring out the essential character of the services they render. The first concept to be discussed, that of *summation of sets*, provides a tool for translating restraints on individual choices into limitations on their aggregate effects, and for showing that profit maximization at given uniform prices can under suitable conditions be decentralized. The second concept, that of *convexity* of a point set, allows us to formulate conditions with regard to technology and preferences that ensure the existence of a price system which sustains decentralized optimizing production and consumption decisions.

In the subsequent sections these concepts will then be used in combination for the description of competitive equilibrium and the analysis of its optimality properties (Section 2), for the further study of productive efficiency under constant returns to scale and its relation to the price system (Section 3), and for the study of allocation of resources over time (Section 4).

1.2 THE COMMODITY SPACE

Any choice we shall consider can be represented as a choice of a commodity bundle. On the basis of a numbered list of commodities, a commodity bundle is given by specifying a sequence of n numbers, $a_1, a_2, \ldots, a_n$, each number representing the amount of the corresponding commodity in the bundle. Depending on the application, these amounts may be interpreted as rates of flow per unit of time, maintained at a constant level for an indefinite period; or each number a_k may be regarded as a quantity made available during just one specified period out of a number of successive periods. In the latter interpretation, each commodity is characterized not only by its qualitative characteristics but also by the period during which it is regarded as available.

The following meaning is to be attached to the (positive or negative) sign of an amount of a commodity: If the bundle represents the results of a productive activity, we shall give a positive sign to each output or rate of output and a negative sign to each input (rate), whereas a zero amount indicates that the commodity in question is not involved in the activity in question, either as output or as input. If the bundle represents the choice of a consumer, the amounts or rates of his consumption are represented by positive numbers, those of the various kinds of labor supplied by him by negative numbers.

Two operations on commodity bundles are important. The first consists of the joining of two bundles $(a_1, a_2, \ldots, a_n)$ and $(b_1, b_2, \ldots, b_n)$ into a new one $(s_1, s_2, \ldots, s_n)$, and is carried out by addition of corresponding amounts,

$$s_1 = a_1 + b_1, \qquad s_2 = a_2 + b_2, \qquad \ldots, \qquad s_n = a_n + b_n.$$

If all amounts involved are positive, the operation describes simply the putting together of two bundles of commodities. If some amounts are negative, for instance because the bundles represent the results of productive activities, the operation gives the net results of the two processes, obtained possibly by using some of the outputs of one process as inputs for the other and conversely. The second operation consists of multiplying all amounts in a commodity bundle $(a_1, \ldots, a_n)$ by a common factor of proportionality, a real number or *scalar* λ, to result in a new bundle $(\lambda a_1, \ldots, \lambda a_n)$. We shall see later that this operation is important in expressing the idea of constant returns to scale in production.

By taking each of the amounts $a_1, \ldots, a_n$ of a bundle as a Cartesian coordinate of a *point* or *vector*[1] a, commodity bundles are represented by points in an n-dimensional Euclidean space. The joining of two bundles is then represented by *addition* of the two representing vectors, as illustrated for bundles of two commodities in Figure 1.1. Geometrically, in any number of dimensions, the sum s of two vectors a and b is found as the fourth vertex of a parallelogram having the origin and the vectors a and b as the other vertices. It is denoted by $s = a + b$. *Scalar multiplication* of a vector a by a number λ results in another vector (denoted λa) of the same direction if λ is positive, opposite in direction if λ is negative, coincident with the origin if λ is zero, and in all these cases having a length[2] $|\lambda|$ times that of a, as illustrated in Figure 1.2.

---

[1] The terms *point* and *vector* are used synonymously in a linear space.

[2] $|\lambda|$ denotes λ if λ is positive or zero, $-\lambda$ if λ is negative, and is called the *absolute value* of λ.

Because of the formal properties of addition and scalar multiplication,[1] the Euclidean space we are employing is an example of a linear space. The latter concept also includes spaces with an infinite number of dimensions, relevant to economic models involving an infinite number of future periods; or a continuous treatment of time over a period of finite duration; or a continuous treatment of locational coordinates; or

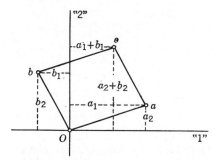 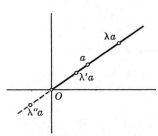

FIGURE 1.1. The sum s of two points a and b.

FIGURE 1.2. Scalar multiplication of a vector a ($\lambda > 1$; $0 < \lambda' < 1$; $\lambda'' < 0$).

other types of continuous quality variation. While most of the propositions we shall study carry over into the infinite-dimensional case,[2] we shall here consider only finite-dimensional spaces (except in Section 4 below).

1.3 SUMMATION OF OPPORTUNITY SETS AND DECENTRALIZED PROFIT MAXIMIZATION

Most of the properties of point sets in linear spaces that have been found useful to the economist are highly elementary to the mathematician. For this reason, it is difficult to find a text that spells them out in a manner and selection most useful to the economist. However, because the properties that concern us appeal strongly to geometrical intuition, our subject can be elucidated by diagrammatic illustrations based on

[1] Commutative and associative laws of addition, existence of a null bundle 0 (the origin) such that $a + 0 = a$ for all a; existence of a negative of each a, i.e., a vector $(-a)$ such that $a + (-a) = 0$; distributive and associative laws of scalar multiplication; $\lambda a = 0$ if $\lambda = 0$ and $\lambda a = a$ if $\lambda = 1$. For further details see, for instance, Paul R. Halmos, *Finite Dimensional Vector Spaces*, Princeton University Press, Princeton, N.J., 1948, chap. I.

[2] See Gerard Debreu, "Valuation Equilibrium and Pareto Optimum," *Proceedings of the National Academy of Sciences*, vol. 40, no. 7, July 1954, pp. 588–592, quoted hereafter as "Valuation Equilibrium . . . ."

elementary geometry, while confining occasional indications of proofs or references to methods of proof to footnotes.

A *set A* of points in a space is defined by any rule or criterion which allows us unambiguously to determine for every point x in the space whether it belongs to A or does not belong to A. Given any two sets A and B, their *intersection* is defined as the set of all points belonging to

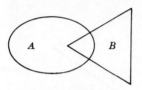 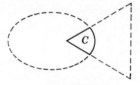 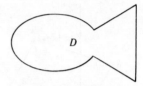

FIGURE 1.3a. Two point sets A and B.   FIGURE 1.3b. Their intersection C.   FIGURE 1.3c. Their union D.

both A and B, while their *union* is the set of all points belonging to either A or B (or both). These concepts are illustrated in Figures 1.3a–c. More important for our present purposes than the union is the notion of the sum of two sets A and B. This is defined as the set S of all points

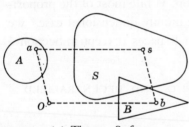

FIGURE 1.4. The sum S of two sets A and B.

$s = a + b$ that can be formed by taking the sum of any point a belonging to A and any point b belonging to B. This construction is illustrated in Figure 1.4.

Each of the operations of intersection, union, or summation can, of course, be applied in succession to any finite number of sets A, B, C, . . . , and the resulting set is in each case independent of the order in which the sets A, B, C, . . . are taken up.

The relation of the concept of summation of sets to the decentralization of allocative decisions has probably already occurred to the reader. Let the restrictions of technology and resource availability applicable to one producer be expressed by the statement that he can simultaneously realize the rates of net output of various commodities represented by the coordinates of any point a of a set A, called a *production set*, but not rates of net output represented by any point not in A. Let another producer be similarly restricted to a production set B. Then their pooled net output possibilities are represented by a set S found as the sum of A and B.

One implication of this construction needs emphasis. It is assumed that the range of alternatives open to one producer does not depend on the choice actually made by another. Whenever this assumption of non-interaction between choices can be made, the summation of sets is the appropriate mathematical tool for studying the aggregation of individual opportunities. Its use may be illustrated by a simple discussion of decentralized profit maximization at given prices.

Let a bundle of n commodities, represented by a point

$$x = (x_1, x_2, \ldots, x_n)$$

in n-dimensional space, be the result of a productive activity. At given prices, $p_1, p_2, \ldots, p_n$, the profit obtained from that activity will be a *homogeneous linear function* $l(x) = p_1 x_1 + p_2 x_2 + \ldots + p_n x_n$ of the coordinates of the point x, with the prices as coefficients. In the normal case where all prices are positive,[1] the terms $p_1 x_1, p_2 x_2, \ldots$ corresponding to outputs represented by positive numbers $x_1, x_2, \ldots$, will be positive and add up to the total value of output, while the terms $p_i x_i, \ldots$ corresponding to inputs, represented by negative numbers $x_i, \ldots$ will serve to subtract cost of inputs. The function is called homogeneous because it does not contain a "constant term." For this reason, if our bundle x is itself the sum $x = a + b$ of two bundles a and b, then its value $l(x)$ at the given prices is, of course, the sum $l(a) + l(b)$ of the values of the constituent bundles.

In the special case of only two commodities, a linear function $p_1 x_1 + p_2 x_2$ can be easily pictured by a set of parallel lines, on each of which the function is constant (Figure 1.5a). The common slope of the lines is determined by the coefficients p_1, p_2, of the function (the prices of the goods) in such a manner that, if a normal to the set of parallel lines is drawn through the origin, the coordinates of any point on this normal are proportional to the corresponding coefficients p_1, p_2, of the linear function. If a suitable unit of length is selected on this normal, it can serve as a new coordinate axis along which the profit function is meas-

---

[1] The possibility of negative prices is discussed at the end of Section 2.4 of this essay.

ured.[1] (Figure 1.5b). If the prices are positive, the positive direction of the normal points into the first (the positive) quadrant. Similar statements can be made with regard to linear functions of more than two variables.

The clue to our discussion is a simple theorem[2] relating to the maximization of a linear function on a sum of sets. We shall formulate it

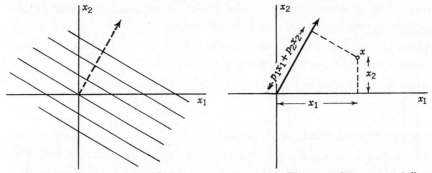

FIGURE 1.5a. Representation of a linear function of two variables.

FIGURE 1.5b. The same (homogeneous) linear function measured along a new axis.

for the sum S of only two sets, A and B, although it applies to any finite number of sets. The theorem consists of two statements which are converse to each other and which we shall number separately.

THEOREM I.1. If a linear function defined on a linear space reaches its maximum on a set A in a point a of A, and its maximum on a set B in a point b of B, then this function reaches its maximum on the sum set S of A and B in the point $s = a + b$.

THEOREM I.2. If a linear function defined on a linear space reaches its maximum on a set S, which is the sum of two sets A and B, in a point s, and if a and b are points of A and B, respectively, such that $s = a + b$, then this function reaches its maximum on A in a and its maximum on B in b.

[1] Because the profit function is homogeneous, the zero point on the new axis falls again in the origin. It might be thought that the concept of a normal should not or could not be used in a space of which the coordinates are subject to arbitrary choices of units of measurement. If the unit of commodity "1" is doubled, the number x_1 is cut in half, it is true; but at the same time the price p_1 is doubled, thus preserving the numerical value of the function $p_1x_1 + p_2x_2$. Hence, after a change of units, the (new) value axis is again normal to the (new) lines on which the profit function is constant. Properly, the value axis (or price vector) and the constant profit lines belong to different spaces which for convenience we have superposed.

[2] For ease of quotation, we shall refer to mathematical theorems as "theorems," and to economic theorems as "propositions."

These statements, to be referred to together as Theorem I, are illustrated in Figure 1.6. They assert the interchangeability of the two operations: summation of sets, and maximization of a linear function.[1] Trivial to the mathematician, this theorem is a basic tool for the economist. Some of its most useful services are rendered in conjunction with other theorems, as will become apparent in the next few chapters. But it may help us here to consider one somewhat artificial application that will bring out the nature of its contribution in isolation and may also impart a sense of its obviousness to a reader who mistrusts abstract formulations.

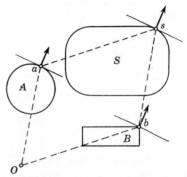

FIGURE 1.6. Illustration of Theorem I.

Consider a plant with departments between which intermediate products can be moved at zero cost. Let the possibility exist for each primary input, intermediate product, or final output of the plant to be either bought or sold, at the same given and constant price, at a location for which transportation cost to and from the plant is zero. Let the range of productive activities available to each department be represented, in the space of all commodities involved, by a point set which is called the *production set* of that department, and let this set be independent of the choices made by other departments. Then, so says Theorem I.1, if each department head acting independently chooses the productive activities of his department so as to maximize the profit on its net output bundle, this will ensure profit maximization for the plant as a whole. Conversely, says Theorem I.2, if by whatever means the activities of all departments have jointly resulted in the maximum achievable profit for the plant as a whole, then

---

[1] PROOF OF I.1. Let $l(x)$ denote the linear function in question after subtracting a constant to make it homogeneous. Assume that s' is any point of S. Then there exist, by the definition of set summation, points a' of A and b' of B such that $s' = a' + b'$. But then $l(s') = l(a') + l(b')$ and $l(s) = l(a) + l(b)$ because $l(x)$ is linear and homogeneous. Also $l(a') \leqq l(a)$ and $l(b') \leqq l(b)$ because of the premises of I.1. Hence $l(s') \leqq l(s)$.

PROOF OF I.2. Assume that, for some point a' of A, $l(a') > l(a)$. Then the point $s' = a' + b$ is in S by the definition of set summation, and $l(s') = l(a') + l(b) > l(a) + l(b) = l(s)$, contradicting the premise of I.2. In the same way one proves the impossibility of $l(b') > l(b)$ for a point b' of B.

each department necessarily operates so as to achieve the maximum profit available to it. The reason is obvious: the assumptions of noninteraction between the productive activities of departments and of the availability of a market with a constant price for each commodity have made the departments entirely independent of each other. Hence total profit is the sum of the profits of all departments, and the sum is at its maximum attainable value if and only if each component is at its maximum.

For later reference, we record this simple result of our reasoning in economic terminology.

> PROPOSITION 1. If each of m production sets describes the choices open to one of m agents (entrepreneurs or production managers) independently of the choices made by the other agents, and if prices of all inputs and outputs are independent of the choices made, the maximization of aggregate profit implies maximization of individual profits and conversely.

Of the many questions not answered by Theorem I, one may be taken up for some comment. Neither part of the theorem says that a maximum of the given linear function exists on the sum set S, or on its component sets A, B, . . . , either for every conceivable set of prices, or even for only some one given set of prices. With respect to any particular model of production possibilities, therefore, the question for what prices (if any) profit maximization is possible is entirely open. Two more mathematical concepts will enable us to specify one class of models for which the answer to that question is definite.

A point set is called *bounded*[1] if one can specify a square (cube, hypercube of as many dimensions as the space considered), however large, which contains all of its points. The disk of a circle is bounded, but a straight line indefinitely extended is not. The second concept, closedness, may be illustrated before it is defined. In two-dimensional space the set of points inside or on a circle is closed, but the set of points inside a circle is open. The set of all points to one designated side of a straight line is open, but its union with that line is closed. A line segment is closed only if its endpoints are regarded as included. To express sharply the distinction suggested by these examples, call a point x a *boundary*

---

[1] The reader should perhaps be cautioned that the three terms "boundedness," "boundary," and "bounding plane," while derived from the same etymological root, have quite different mathematical meanings, as their definitions given in the next few pages show.

point of a set A if, within any specified positive distance[1] d from x, however small, one can find a point of A as well as a point not of A. This definition does not require x itself to be a point of A. However, a *closed set* is defined as a set which contains all its boundary points.[2] Although it is hard to think of a situation where the presence or absence of a boundary point in a set of production possibilities is a meaningful empirical question, the distinction is needed because of the mathematical tools it makes available.

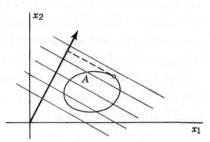

FIGURE 1.7. Maximization of a linear function on a compact set A.

Finally, a set is called *compact* if it is both bounded and closed. The union, the intersection, and the sum of a finite number of sets, each of which is bounded, or compact, are themselves bounded, or compact, as the case may be. The union and the intersection of a finite number of closed sets are also closed, but the sum of two (unbounded) closed sets need not be closed. With these preparations, we can formulate another useful theorem (illustrated by the set A in Figure 1.7).

THEOREM II. On a compact set, a linear function[3] reaches its maximum in a point of the boundary.[4]

It follows that if individual production possibilities are represented by compact sets, profit maximization is possible, individually and in the aggregate, for any system of prices. Since closedness is not a practical

---

[1] A wide class of definitions of "distance" is acceptable here. Interesting alternatives to Euclidean distance $d_1(x,y) = \left[\sum_k (x_k - y_k)^2 \right]^{\frac{1}{2}}$ are $d_2(x,y) = \sum_k |x_k - y_k|$ and $d_3(x,y) = \underset{k}{\text{Max}} |x_k - y_k|$. Again, it does not matter that all of these definitions depend on the arbitrary units of measurement in which amounts of commodities are expressed.

[2] A set A is called *open* if the set of all points not in A is closed. The entire space and the empty set are both open and closed.

[3] A continuous function, not necessarily linear, will also reach a maximum on a compact set (although not necessarily in a boundary point). This can be looked upon as a key result of the introduction of irrational numbers.

[4] The same maximum value may possibly be attained in more than one point of the boundary. However, if we exclude the trivial case where the function is a constant, the maximum cannot be attained in a point which is not a boundary point.

issue, the boundedness of production sets is the controlling consideration for the applicability of this theorem. It would seem that boundedness is a suitable assumption in what the economist is used to calling "short-run problems." While this designation suggests a time limitation, the common analytical characteristic of problems covered by this term appears to be the presence of certain fixed factors of production, not subject to change, or in any case not subject to increase, within the range of alternatives admitted in the problem. In all cases where these fixed factors place bounds on the achievable inputs and outputs of all other commodities, it would seem appropriate to postulate compact production sets.

If unbounded production sets are admitted, the question as to whether, and for what prices, profit maximization is possible has to be faced afresh. It will occupy us further in Sections 2.5 and 3.10 of this essay.

1.4 SEPARATION OF SUPPLY AND CONSUMPTION DECISIONS

The decentralization of decisions we have just considered spreads production decisions over a group of entrepreneurs or managers, all of whom are on the producing side of the "market" for consumers' goods. In Section 2, we shall encounter an application of the same theorem to the decentralization of consumption decisions among consumers, all of whom are on the other side of that market. But before proceeding to this, we must explore the possibilities of placing production decisions and consumption decisions in different hands by means of a price system. Concepts and theorems that assist this exploration will now be considered.

Any straight line in a two-dimensional space divides that space into three subsets: points on the line, those to one side, and those to the other side. Algebraically, the subdivision can be made by a linear function with coefficients so selected that the function has a constant value on the line, larger values on one side, and smaller values on the other. In n-dimensional space, a similar subdivision is made by any linear $(n\text{-}1)$-dimensional hyperplane. In general, we shall often call such a $(n\text{-}1)$-dimensional dividing hyperplane a *plane*, no matter whether it actually is a plane or a hyperplane. We shall call a (closed) *halfspace* the set of all points in such a plane or to one designated side of it. Then each plane defines two halfspaces, which have that plane as their intersection. A plane is called a *bounding plane* of a given point set A, if all points of A are contained in only one of the halfspaces associated with that plane. (See Figure 1.8a. We add for later reference that, in particular, a bounding plane of a point set A is called a *supporting plane* of A if it contains a point of the boundary of A). A plane is called a *separating plane* of two given point sets A and B (see Figure 1.8b) if it is a bounding plane to both, with the points of A in one of the halfspaces it defines, those of B in the other. (In particular, if two sets A and B have a common boundary

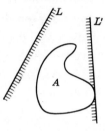
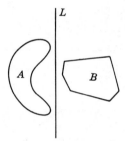

FIGURE 1.8a. Two bounding lines L, L' of a set A. L' is also a supporting line.

FIGURE 1.8b. A separating line L of two sets A and B.

point, any separating plane they may have must be a supporting plane to both A and B).

To illustrate the use of these concepts, we return to the classical and time-honored example of a man by whom production and consumption decisions are made in combination: Robinson Crusoe. In order to stay within the two dimensions of the printed page, let us consider only two commodities, the labor Robinson applies and the food he produces with it. As an input to production, labor "net output" is represented as an essentially nonpositive quantity. On the other hand, food net output is essentially nonnegative. Hence all sets we shall consider are subsets of the (closed) "second quadrant" (Figure 1.9a) cut out of the two-dimensional plane by the axes of a Cartesian coordinate system.

Since Robinson is in sole control of the resources of his island, his decisions as a production manager can be further subdivided into determining how much of these natural resources (land, irrigation water, etc.) to use in production, and choosing the methods by which these resources are combined with Robinson's labor in food production. A corresponding separation of resource use decisions from production decisions proper is therefore possible, and a separation of this kind will be studied in Section 2. To make such a separation appear realistic in the present example we would have to introduce a third dimension for at least one primary commodity—land, say—which we have already decided to avoid. We shall therefore represent Robinson's merged production-and-resource-use decisions, to be called briefly *supply decisions*, as the choice of a point w from a *supply set* W in the commodity space for labor and food only. It is then understood that the shape of the set re-

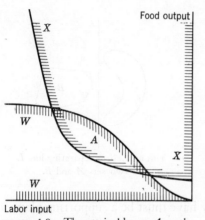

FIGURE 1.9a. The attainable set A as the intersection of the supply set W and the consumption set X.

flects the availabilities of land and other resources for production as well as Robinson's production technology. However, the supply set is defined without regard to the question whether Robinson as a worker and consumer is capable of supplying the labor input indicated by the abscissa of some point w of W on the basis of the food consumption indicated by its ordinate. The latter consideration is expressed by a *consumption set* X, containing all points x representing combinations of food supply and labor requirements with which Robinson can manage to survive. In Robinson's interest we must assume that the intersection of the supply set and the consumption set, to be called the *attainable set* A (Figure 1.9a), is not empty.

Let us postulate further that, as a consumer (and worker), Robinson is guided in his choices by a *complete preference ordering* of all points of the consumption set. This is a consistent rule which indicates, for any two points x and x' in that set, whether Robinson, if given the choice, prefers x, or x', or is indifferent between the two. In the latter case, we shall call x and x' *equivalent* (that is, in Robinson's preference structure), or x *equivalent to* x'. The rule is called consistent if it meets the *transivity requirement* that, whenever x is preferred or equivalent to x', and x' is preferred or equivalent to x'', then x is preferred or equivalent to[1] x''.

[1] It follows from this definition of transivity that x is actually preferred to x'' only if either x is preferred to x' or x' is preferred to x'' (or both).

The ordering is applied by postulating that, from any subset of points of the consumption set attainable to him, Robinson will whenever possible select a point that is preferred or equivalent to all other points in the attainable set.

It is often thought that every complete ordering can be represented by an ordinal utility function $f(x)$, in the sense that x is preferred to x' if and only if $f(x) > f(x')$, and equivalent if and only if $f(x) = f(x')$.

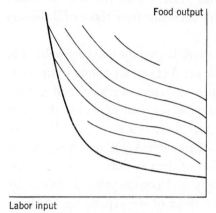

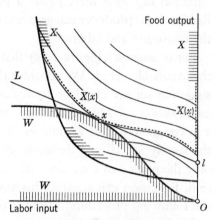

FIGURE 1.9b. Indifference curves representing a preference ordering on the
consumption set.

FIGURE 1.9c. Line L separating the supply set
W from the no-worse-than-x set $X(x)$.

However, several authors including Herman Wold and Gerard Debreu have realized that this needs proof,[1] and have successively and with increasing generality formulated conditions, essentially of continuity, under which they prove that a complete ordering permits expression by a continuous utility function.[2] We shall call such a preference ordering (*continuously*) *representable*, and draw our diagrams on the assumption that Robinson's preferences are of this type, even though our present reasoning does not depend on it. Figure 1.9b illustrates the preference

[1] A simple counter example given by Debreu is the so-called *lexicographic* ordering in a space of two commodities. In this ordering, the consumer would always prefer the bundle with the larger amount of the first commodity, and only among bundles for which that amount is the same would he prefer the larger amount of the second commodity.

[2] H. Wold, "A Synthesis of Pure Demand Analysis, part II," *Skandinavisk Aktuaritidskrift*, vol. 26, 1943, pp. 220–263. G. Debreu, "Representation of a Preference Ordering by a Numerical Function," in R. M. Thrall, C. H. Coombs, and R. L. Davis (eds.), *Decision Processes*, Wiley, New York, 1954, chap. XI (pp. 159–165).

ordering by a set of indifference curves, each of which consists of a set of mutually equivalent points.[1]

If, as indicated in Figure 1.9c, there is a *best* point x in the attainable set,[2] that is, a point preferred or equivalent to all others of that set, any Robinson worth his salt will be able to reach a satisfactory approximation to such a point unaided by prices on labor and food. But since our interest is in tools and concepts, not in Robinson, we will discuss a situation in which there exists a price system with the help of which Robinson the producer can separate his decisions from those of Robinson the consumer and laborer.

Let us assume (Figure 1.9c) that there is exactly one best point x in the attainable set A. We consider the set $X(x)$ of all points in the consumption set preferred or equivalent to x, which we shall call the *no-worse-than-x set*. This set and the attainable set then have only the point x in common. Let us assume finally that there is a separating line L of the supply set W and the no-worse-than-x set $X(x)$, which again has only the point x in common with either of the two sets. In such a situation, Robinson can separate his supply and consumption decisions by the following procedure. He uses the slope of the separating line L to define two prices, not both zero, one of labor (the wage rate) and one of food. As a production manager he chooses that point in the production set (the point x) which maximizes his revenue (Figure 1.9d). The amount of this revenue can be read off Figure 1.9d as the intercept Ol of L on the food axis multiplied by the price of food. He assigns this revenue to Robinson the consumer-worker as non-labor income. The latter, starting from this income, can now reach an (enlarged) opportunity set of labor-food bundles by trading his labor for food at the given prices. The set he can reach is that part of the second quadrant (Figure 1.9e) that lies "below" or on the line L. Since choice of a best point from this set leads him again to the point x, the separation of decision-making functions has given rise to compatible decisions by the two Robinsons.

We are not interested at this stage in the question whether or how, by

---

[1] To be precise, the preference ordering is defined not by these curves alone, but by a complete ordering of them, which is usually regarded as suggested by considerations of continuity and nonsaturation.

[2] This is necessarily the case if the attainable set is compact and the preference ordering representable (see footnote 3 on page 15).

some process of trial and error, Robinson can obtain knowledge of a price ratio that will do this trick. We are even less interested in the question whether a single person who operates simultaneously as supplier and as consumer should ever want to resort to implicit prices for decentralized decision making. The principal point to be derived from our discussion is that if a line of separation exists it defines a price system that makes such decentralization possible. This conclusion, seemingly artificial when related to a single decision maker, is part of the logical and mathematical basis for an understanding of the operation of

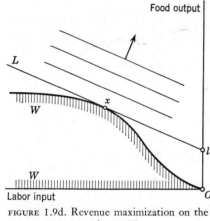

FIGURE 1.9d. Revenue maximization on the supply set W.

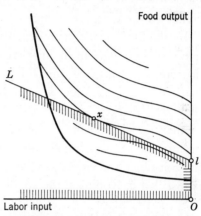

FIGURE 1.9e. Maximization of the utility function within the given budget.

competitive markets. It also suggests means of coordinating the decisions of many individuals in a single organization pursuing economic goals. For this reason, we record the result of our analysis in a formulation which is not limited to two dimensions.

PROPOSITION 2. If there is a single best point x in the attainable set A (the intersection of the supply set W and the consumption set X), and if there exists a plane L separating W from the set $X(x)$ of those points of the consumption set preferred or equivalent to x, in such a way that L has only the point x in common with W as well as with $X(x)$, then the point x will be independently selected by a profit-maximizing supplier faced with prices of which the ratios are defined by the slope of L, and by a consumer-worker choosing a best point obtainable at these prices from a basic income that just enables him to reach a point of L.

1.5 DECENTRALIZATION, INCENTIVES, AND ECONOMY OF INFORMATION[1]

We have now examined two examples of decentralization in economic decision making, one (Proposition 1) concerned with independent profit maximization by production managers, and the other (Proposition 2) with a separation of supply and consumption decisions. The highly elementary and mathematically trivial character of the reasoning employed in the discussion of these cases should not conceal their central importance to economic theory. In both cases, the decentralization achieved combines three aspects which deserve further comment.

In the first place, the decentralization *utilizes incentives* that are naturally operative in the market system. If in our first case, instead of department heads, we think of independent entrepreneurs operating in markets where all prices are given, the profit maximization with which they are "charged" corresponds to a motivation found strongly present in many real-life entrepreneurs. Likewise, in our second case, the preferences of the original undivided Robinson remain those of Robinson the consumer and worker, while a "natural" entrepreneurial motivation is instilled in Robinson the supplier.

Secondly, there is an *economy of information* associated with the decentralization in both cases. The independent entrepreneurs of Proposition 1 need to know only the given prices and their own production sets in order to take a correct action. Similarly, Robinson the supplier needs to know only his own supply set and the prices. As illustrated in Figure 1.9d, he can blot out from his consciousness all knowledge of preferences, which knowledge is adequately summarized for his purposes by the prices. Finally, as illustrated by Figure 1.9e, as consumer, Robinson needs to know only his own preferences and the income and price data that summarize supply possibilities for him.

The informational economy achieved in the allocation of resources through a price system has often been stressed by economists.[2] Because

---

[1] In the preparation of this section, I have greatly benefited from conversations with Professor Leonid Hurwicz and from the reading of as yet unpublished manuscripts of his authorship.

[2] See, for instance, F. A. Hayek, "The Use of Knowledge in Society," *American Economic Review*, vol. 35, September 1945, pp. 519–553. There is a striking similarity between the summarization of supply and preference data through prices and the notions of sufficient and efficient statistical estimation procedures, proposed by R. A. Fisher as devices for the

the collection and processing of information has a cost in time, effort, and other resources (which so far has rarely been introduced explicitly into the models of economics) it would often be worth a sacrifice in physical outputs to achieve informational economies of the type described. However—and this is the third aspect that the two examples of decentralization before us have in common—in these two cases *the economies of information handling are secured free of charge.* No loss in total profit in the first case, or in satisfaction level attained in the second case, results from the decentralization. It is therefore an important question of economic analysis to discern and characterize the situations, as regards both the technology of production and the structure of preferences, in which this costless economy of information handling is possible. The concept of a *convex point set* and the elementary properties of such sets enable us to specify an important class of cases in which the informational economies afforded by a price system are indeed obtained free. We therefore now turn to a brief discussion of this class of point sets.

1.6   CONVEX SETS AND THE PRICE IMPLICATIONS OF OPTIMALITY

A point set C is called *convex* if, whenever a and b are two different points of C, any point c of the straight line segment $\overline{ab}$ connecting a and

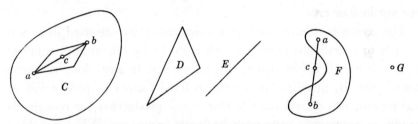

FIGURE 1.10. Convex sets C, D, E, G and a nonconvex set F.

b also belongs to C. In Figure 1.10 each of the sets C, D, E is convex. However, the set F is not convex, because the point c on the segment ab is outside F, while both a and b belong to F. The set G consisting of a

---

"reduction of data" and widely adopted and further developed by statisticians. The basic idea there is to find a set of numbers which adequately summarizes a much more detailed body of information for the purposes of a certain class of decisions. The idea of decentralization of decisions among agents with different motivations is apparently peculiar to economics.

single point and the empty set containing no point are both convex by default: they do not contain two different points. It is easily seen from the definition of convexity that both the intersection and the sum[1] of two or more convex sets are again convex.

A slightly more restrictive concept is that of *strict convexity*. To define it, let us call an *interior point* of a set C any point of C which is not a boundary point. Reference to the definition of a boundary point will show that an interior point c of C is the center of a circle (sphere, hypersphere) of positive radius (however small) which is entirely contained in C. A set C is now called strictly convex if, whenever a and b are two different points of C, every point of the straight line segment $\overline{ab}$ other than a and b is an interior point of C. In two-dimensional space an equivalent formulation is that with any two different points a and b a strictly convex set C must contain an entire quadrangle (however thin) of which all angles are larger than 0° and smaller than 180°, and of which ab forms a diagonal. In Figure 1.10 C and G are the only strictly convex sets.

In some cases, one is interested in strict convexity not of an entire set, but for some part of its boundary. We shall say that a convex set A is *strictly convex in a boundary point*, a say, if whenever b is another point of A or of its boundary all points of the line segment $\overline{ab}$ other than a and b are in the interior of A. The set A in Figure 1.11 is strictly convex in a but not in b or c.

The concepts of convexity and strict convexity are used in various models to specify assumptions with regard to production possibilities and with regard to the nature of preferences. In any "long-run problems," that is, problems in which no fixed factors of production are recognized, one would require that every production set contain the origin, representing a state without inputs or outputs. Whenever this is the case convexity of a production set excludes increasing returns to scale and strict convexity definitely implies decreasing returns to scale. For, by the definition of convexity, if both the origin and a point a represent possible net output bundles (Figure 1.12) all points (such as b) of the line segment joining a to the origin are possible. These points

---

[1] With respect to the sum, a simple analytic proof can be based on the fact that each point c of a line segment ab can be represented by $c = \lambda a + (1 - \lambda)b$, where λ is a real number (a "scalar") such that $0 \leqq \lambda \leqq 1$.

achieve the same ratios of outputs to inputs as the point a, at a lower level of each output. The implication is that the productivity of mass production methods does not exceed that of production on any lower scale. Moreover, even if the point a represents (in a sense to be made more precise in Section 3.6) the best that can be done with the given inputs then, in the case of strict convexity of the production set, one can still do slightly better (proportionally) with half of the inputs (as illustrated by the point c in Figure 1.12).

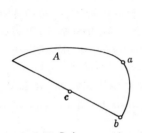

FIGURE 1.11. Strict convexity of
a set A in a point a.

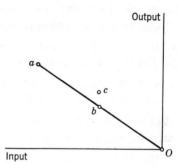

FIGURE 1.12. Constant (b) and decreasing
(c) returns to scale.

Such assumptions can lay no general claim to realism. They cannot be used when we want to express the production advantages that experience has shown to be achievable by putting resources in the form of large indivisible and coordinated pieces of capital equipment. Convexity can be used with some degree of approximation only in problems where the granularity arising from indivisibility of resources is unimportant. The case for strict convexity of production sets is in general very weak indeed. But in any case the principal reason for making a convexity assumption lies not in its degree of realism but in the present state of our knowledge. In our examination of the theory of resource allocation and competitive markets, we have found and shall find some propositions that do not depend, and other propositions that depend essentially, on convexity assumptions with regard to both production possibilities and preference structures (about which more below). The convexity concept therefore enables us to state minimum assumptions for the validity of important parts of existing economic theory, thus helping to reduce this part of our knowledge to its logical and mathematical essentials. An economy of thinking is thereby achieved which shortens the statement of what we currently know and which may also enable us to perceive more clearly, and perhaps approach with better equipment, the harder problems yet unsolved. This about sums up the case for the use of the convexity assumption on the production side.

On the consumption side the situation is not greatly different, although one may feel that once the rather sweeping implications of an individual preference ordering have been accepted the added restriction implied in a convexity assumption is by comparison a minor one. To formulate such assumptions, let us speak of a *convex preference ordering* if (1) the set of alternatives to which the ordering applies is represented by a convex point set, (2) whenever a is preferred to b, every point c of the line segment $\overline{ab}$, other than b itself, is preferred to b, and (3) if a is equivalent to b, every such point c is preferred or equivalent to b. Let us also speak of a *strictly convex preference ordering* if, besides (1) and (2) but instead of (3), we have the stronger statement (3') that whenever a and b are equivalent, all points of $\overline{ab}$ other than a and b are preferred to b.

The first implication of the assumption of a convex (or strictly convex) preference ordering is to preclude indivisible commodities. As soon as a commodity can be consumed in two different amounts, convexity of the consumption set implies that it can also be consumed in any intermediate amount.[1]

In order to perceive further implications, we note that[2] if a preference ordering is convex, then the set of all points that are preferred to any given point, and the set of all points preferred or equivalent to a given point, are both convex. If the preference ordering is also representable, then the latter set is closed as well.[3] If in addition the preference ordering is strictly convex, we have the case described by Hicks and Allen as the principle of the diminishing marginal rate of substitution,[4] differently but equivalently expressed. Instead of specifying a particular type of

---

[1] The only remaining possibility, that of a commodity which both has to and can only be consumed in one unit, does not seem a realistic one.

[2] See also Kenneth J. Arrow, "An Extension of the Basic Theorems of Welfare Economics," *Proceedings of the Second Berkeley Symposium on Mathematical Statistics and Probability*, University of California Press, Berkeley, Calif., pp. 507–532. See Lemma 1, p. 512. This article will be quoted hereafter as "An Extension. . . ."

[3] Provided the consumption set on which the preference ordering is defined is itself closed.

[4] J. R. Hicks and R. G. D. Allen, "A Reconsideration of the Theory of Value," *Economica*, vol. I, 1934, pp. 52–76 and 196–219; and J. R. Hicks, *Value and Capital*, 2d ed., Claremont Press, Oxford, 1946, chap. I. Hicks's statement (*Value and Capital*, p. 20) of this concept

curvature of the indifference surfaces, it is specified that, as successive additions and subtractions are made in any given fixed proportions to the flows of consumption of the various goods, the desirability of the resulting bundle can first increase (from a to b in Figure 1.13a) and can

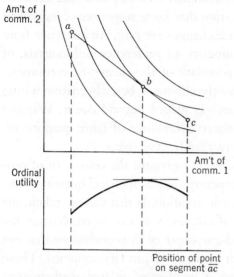

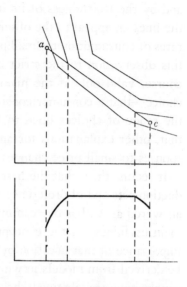

FIGURE 1.13a. Variation of the utility on a line segment in a strictly convex preference ordering.

FIGURE 1.13b. Variation of the utility on a line segment in a convex but not strictly convex preference ordering.

subsequently decrease (from b to c), but it cannot increase after it has once decreased. Neither can it, in the case of strict convexity, remain constant under two successive proportional net additions to flows, but

---

for the two-commodity case says that "the indifference curves must be convex to the axes." Perhaps this is a suitable point at which to caution the reader that the word "convex" has been used in somewhat different meanings in different contexts. The economist has used the word convex with reference to curves (rather than to point sets) in the same meaning in which the mathematician uses the expression "strictly convex function," i.e., a function such that linear interpolation between any two points always gives values higher than those of the function itself. While this defines convexity with respect to only one coordinate axis (that for the argument of the function), presumably an indifference curve "convex to the axes" is required to be representable by a strictly convex function no matter which of the two variables is chosen as the argument of the function. However, the notion of a convex or strictly convex preference ordering defined on page 26 above is preferable for two reasons. It takes into account not only the shape of the indifference curves but also the direction in which one goes from a given curve to a preferred one (see footnote 1 on page 20). It also remains applicable if oversaturation occurs in some part of the commodity space.

the latter stipulation is not made in the case of convexity only (as illustrated in Figure 1.13b).

Professor Hicks is entirely candid in justifying the principle of diminishing marginal rate of substitution first of all by its simplicity and by the fruitfulness of its implications. One can also read between the lines an appeal to the observation that large responses of individual rates of consumption to small price changes are rare. An inference from this observation to the strict convexity of preference orderings is, of course, valid only if the main postulate of the theory of consumers' choice—that a consumer consistently chooses a best alternative within the range of choices open to him—is placed beyond doubt. Without that, other explanations for an observed absence of large quantity responses to small price changes are readily available.[1]

It seems, then, that the best view is to regard the convexity of production sets and of preference structures as an empirical question to be answered as well as one can in each situation. If this view is taken, the main usefulness of the concept of convexity is that it emphasizes the importance of that question by the strength of the conclusions that can be derived from models in which convexity is, in fact, assumed. These conclusions are obtained through a number of related mathematical theorems about convex sets known as *separation theorems*, to which we now turn.

[1] Arrow, on page 529 of "An Extension . . . " (see footnote 3 on page 26), quotes a further argument once contributed by me in an oral discussion of the convexity of consumers' preference orderings. This argument for convexity (rather than strict convexity) runs as follows:

If in the commodity space a point b is located on a straight line segment $\overline{ac}$ joining two points a and c, and if the commodities whose rates of consumption differ as between a and c are storable at no cost, then the bundle represented by b is preferred or equivalent to the least preferred of the bundles a and c. The quoted reason is that the commodities in flow b can be split up and in part temporarily stored so as to permit alternating flows of consumption represented by a and c, respectively, during suitable fractions of time computable from the position of b on $\overline{ac}$.

It should be admitted that this argument, whatever it is worth, makes its point by mixing categories that the theorist may prefer to keep separate. It incorporates a part of technology, namely storage, with consumption. It ignores also the capital cost of storage. If the preference ordering is thought of as applying to sustained flows of consumption, the argument also introduces variation of flows into a static model, while ignoring the possibility of a preference for variation in consumption as such. Finally, it does not apply to models with dated commodities designed to express consumers' attitudes to consumption flows that change over time.

THEOREM III.1. If x is a point outside a convex set A, then there is a bounding plane of A through x.

This theorem is illustrated in two dimensions by Figure 1.14. Since we have not specified that the set A is closed, one may think of it as containing all, part, or none of its boundary points. This means that Theorem III.1 also covers cases as illustrated by Figure 1.15, where x is

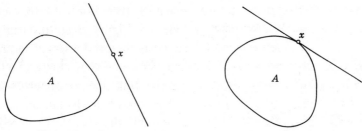

FIGURE 1.14. Illustration of Theorem III.1.   FIGURE 1.15. Illustration of Theorem III.2.

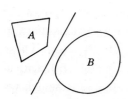 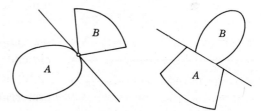

FIGURE 1.16a. Illustration of Theorem III.3 for closed sets.   FIGURE 1.16b. Two illustrations of Theorem III.3 for sets not both closed.

in the boundary of a convex set A, whenever x is not a point of A. However, the conclusion of Theorem III.1 does not really depend on x being excluded from A. The second theorem states this

THEOREM III.2. If x is a boundary point of a convex set A, then there is a supporting plane of A through x.

The third theorem concerns the separation of two convex sets.

THEOREM III.3. If A and B are two convex sets that have no point in common, then there is a plane separating A and B.

Figure 1.16a illustrates this theorem in a case where both A and B can be thought of as closed. Figure 1.16b shows two other cases to which Theorem III.3 can be applied if at least one of the sets is not closed. Again, it is possible to reformulate Theorem III.3 in such a way that common boundary points are allowed under certain safeguards,[1] but we shall not need to do so. One additional separation theorem, for convex cones, will be formulated in Section 3.9 at the point where it is needed. At this point we merely add that, if convexity is not assumed for the sets in question, the statements in Theorems III.1-3 are not generally true. For instance, another look at Figure 1.8b on page 17 suggests that, if the sets A and B are brought somewhat closer together, a separating line no longer exists.

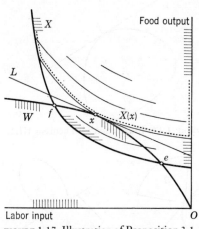

FIGURE 1.17. Illustration of Proposition 3.1.

We return to Robinson Crusoe to exhibit the service rendered by Theorem III.3 in a simple case.[2] We now disregard possible economies of scale in production by assuming the supply set W to be convex and closed (Figure 1.17). Symmetrically, we assume that Robinson's preference ordering is convex and representable by a continuous utility function, defined on a consumption set X which is convex and closed. In addition to these assumptions, we keep up Robinson's incentive by assuming that he nowhere in the attainable set reaches a point of saturation. That is, outside the attainable set A there are points preferred to all points of A. Finally, we assume that the attainable set is bounded but not empty. As an intersection of closed sets, W and X, it is closed. Since the utility function is continuous, there must be a best point[3] x in the attainable set A. As there is a better point x_o, say, outside A, the

---

[1] Safeguards are needed to rule out certain cases where both A and B are of smaller dimensionality than the space under consideration (such as two lines segments in two-dimensional space that intersect only in a common midpoint). For a proof of one such generalization of Theorem III.3, see Arrow, "An Extension . . . ," sec. 10. (Note that a more refined concept of interior point is employed by Arrow!)

[2] In the following discussion leading to Propositions 3.1–3.3 extensive use has been made of G. Debreu, "Valuation Equilibrium . . . ." See footnote 2 on page 9.

[3] See footnote 3 on page 15.

convexity of the preference ordering implies[1] that x must be in the boundary of the supply set W, as well as in the boundary of A.

Let us now consider the set of all points of the consumption set X that are preferred to x. We shall call this the *better-than-x set*, and denote it by $\mathring{X}(x)$. This set is convex because of the convexity of the preference ordering. It has no point in common with the attainable set A, because x itself is already a best point within that set. Neither does it have any point in common with the supply set W, because any point of W not in A is not in the consumption set X, and the better-than-x set $\mathring{X}(x)$ is defined as a subset of the consumption set. It follows that there is a line L separating the supply set W from the better-than-x set. Because of the convexity of the preference ordering and the fact that x is not a point of saturation, L runs through x, and through any point x' equivalent to x that may exist in the attainable set.[2] The following proposition formulates the economic meaning of this provisional result without limitation to only two dimensions.

PROPOSITION 3.1. If both the supply set and the consumption set are closed and convex, if their intersection (the attainable set) is bounded and not empty, and if the preference ordering is representable and convex, then there is a best point x in the attainable set. If the attainable set does not contain a point of saturation[3] then any best point of it lies in the boundary of the supply set. With any such point x can be associated a system of prices, not all zero, such that

(a) the maximum revenue attainable in the supply set is attained in x, and

---

[1] If x were in the interior of W, then the line segment $\overline{xx_0}$ (which is entirely in X because X is convex) would contain points of W, and hence of A, besides x. Because of the convexity of the preference ordering, such points would be preferred to x, and x would not be a best point of A, contrary to the premise.

[2] Since any such point x' is a point of W, and L a bounding line of W, x' can only be in L or on the "production side" of L. The latter alternative can be excluded. Using a point x_0 of $\mathring{X}(x)$ as in the footnote above, it would imply that $\overline{x'x_0}$ had points other than x' on the production side of L. However, the convexity of the preference ordering would cause such points to be preferred to x' and hence to x, contrary to the separation of W and $\mathring{X}(x)$ by L already established.

[3] If there is a point x of saturation in the attainable set, the statements (a) and (b) in the last sentence of the proposition remain trivially true provided all prices are equated to zero.

(*b*) the consumers' outlay necessary to secure any point preferred to x is not less than that needed to secure x.

If more than one best point exists in the attainable set, one single price system can be found such that statements (a) and (b) above apply to all such points.

These statements, valuable as they are, fall short of the mark in two respects. In the first place the statement labeled (b) does not preclude that a point preferred to x could be procured at the same outlay as that needed for x itself. If this were so one could not claim, as we wish to, that x is a best point among all those whose cost to the consumer does not exceed that of x. Secondly, if this difficulty were overcome we could still have a situation where either for Robinson the supplier or for Robinson the consumer (or for both) there is more than one point which, within the appropriate set, maximizes the revenue, or the satisfaction obtainable from the appropriate basic income (as the case may be). In such a situation no price system can by itself provide a complete decentralization of decisions. Communication in terms of quantities between the two Robinsons remains needed to avoid incompatible responses to the price system.

Of these two difficulties the second seems to be the less serious one. Even if we think ahead of a market with many producers, resource holders, and consumers there is likely to be quantitative communication between individuals on opposite sides of most markets. It is therefore already important if a price system can be found to exist which merely *sustains an optimum* once it has been established through quantitative communication, in the sense that no incentives to prefer other quantities exist. Meanwhile, it is worth expressing in a proposition that *both* the foregoing difficulties can be overcome at the same time if we are willing to make several assumptions of strict convexity.

PROPOSITION 3.2. If x is a best point in the attainable set and is not a point of saturation, if the supply set is strictly convex in x, if the consumption set either has x as an interior point or is strictly convex in x, and if the preference ordering is representable and strictly convex, then there exists a system of prices such that x is a unique point of maximum revenue in the supply set,[1] and such that x is a unique best point among all points of the consumption set whose cost to the consumer does not exceed that of x.[2]

In relation to our two-dimensional example, the premises of this proposition look reasonable. However, even in Robinson's case, the decreasing returns to scale implied in the strict convexity assumption made about the supply set must be motivated by the fact that the limited resources of his island were not explicitly introduced into the analysis as additional coordinates of the space in which the supply set is defined. Further difficulties would arise if we were to recognize Robinson's ability to make and use in food production tools which cannot be directly consumed, and if we should wish to determine a price of tools that would enable him to separate his tool-making decisions from those of food production. The commodity space would then have to be given three dimensions, of which the consumption set would become a subset extending only in the two dimensions of food and labor. The consumption set would then not possess any interior points relative to that three-dimensional space, and a fortiori no boundary points where it can at all be strictly convex.

It is conceivable that these difficulties could be overcome by further refinement of the concept of strict convexity[3] as applied to the consumption set, permitting us to state conditions that ensure decentralization through unique and compatible responses to incentives defined or circumscribed by suitable prices. Present appearances are, however, that if this is at all possible it would require technicalities of reasoning transcending the expository purpose of the present essay. For this reason we shall from here on abandon the idea of unique optimizing re-

---

[1] Suppose x' were another point of W at which the revenue equals that of x. Then the midpoint x'' of $\overline{xx'}$ is an interior point of W, and points x''' with a revenue exceeding that of x could be found in W in a neighborhood of x'', contradicting Proposition 3.1, statement (a).

[2] Suppose x' were another point of X, preferred or equivalent to x, of which the cost to the consumer does not exceed that of x. Then, whether x is interior to X or a boundary point where X is strictly convex, in either case the midpoint x'' of $\overline{xx'}$ is interior to X, preferred to x, and no more costly than x. But then, because of the continuity of the utility function, points x''' of X could be found in a neighborhood of x'', which are preferred to x and actually less costly than x, contradicting Proposition 3.2, statement (b).

[3] The concept that suggests itself is strict convexity relative to the smallest-dimensional linear subspace containing the set in question.

sponses, but continue to interest ourselves in conditions under which an optimum once established can be sustained by a price system.

The question then arises whether the first and more serious difficulty noted above, the insufficiency of statement (b) of Proposition 3.1 for our purposes, can be overcome without making assumptions of strict convexity. The reasoning leading to Proposition 3.2 shows already that this is so for any optimum x in the interior of the consumption set. It is not so for any optimum in the boundary. There is an exception, first

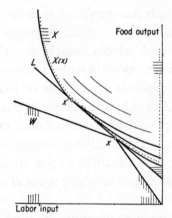

FIGURE 1.18. The exceptional case at the minimum for subsistence.

noted by Arrow,[1] which is one of those special cases of limited interest in themselves, and having an air of unreality about them, that sometimes need to be examined and allowed for—as the price of rigorous analysis—because they are contained in otherwise reasonable and simple assumptions that would have to be greatly complicated if one wished to exclude the odd case a priori. An example of the exception is illustrated by Figure 1.18. The unique optimum is in the point x.

The boundary of the consumption set contains a segment $\overline{xx'}$ of a line L which is tangent to the indifference curve consisting of points equivalent to x. However, all points of $\overline{xx'}$ other than x are preferred to x. In this situation, L is the only available line of separation, but it contains points preferred to x.

As pointed out by Debreu[2] in following up Arrow's observations, this case cannot arise if there is a point in the consumption set which, evaluated at prices associated with some suitable separating line, costs the consumer less than the optimum point x does.[3] This is of course

[1] "An Extension . . . ," theorem 4 and sec. 8, comment to fig. 3. Arrow uses the closed positive orthant as the consumption set.

[2] "Valuation Equilibrium . . . ," "Remark," p. 591.

[3] If x'' is such a point, and if x' were a point of L preferred to x, then $\overline{x''x'}$ would be, but for the point x', on the side of L where outlay is less than on L. However, because of the continuity of the utility function, there would then be points on $\overline{x''x'}$ sufficiently close to x' to be preferred to x, contradicting Proposition 3.1 statement (b).

bound to be true if a best point in the attainable set is an interior point of the consumption set. It can fail to be true only if the consumer's income is the minimum needed, at the decentralizing prices, for his survival.

The following proposition plugs the gap.

> PROPOSITION 3.3. If, under the premises of Proposition 3.1, one can associate with a best point x of the attainable set a price system satisfying statements (a) and (b) of that proposition, such that in addition there exists a point in the consumption set which at those prices has a value smaller than that of x, then (c) the consumer's outlay necessary to secure any point preferred to x is more than that needed to secure x.

1.7. THE ROLE OF CONVEXITY ASSUMPTIONS IN THE ANALYSIS

A few more words may be said here in elaboration of our remarks in Section 1.1 concerning the mathematical tools used and their relation to the problems for which they are used. The convexity assumptions made about supply or production possibilities and about preferences are in some sense minimum assumptions ensuring the existence of a price system that permits or sustains compatible and efficient decentralized decision making. Any assumptions as to the differentiability of either the utility function or the production function[1] are irrelevant to this question. More important, the statements derived include without any change in formulation cases where Robinson is by his own incentives led to a point x on the boundary of the consumption set. Robinson may be so energetic that he prefers to work up to the very limit of his strength (Figure 1.19a). Or he may be so lazy as to prefer hovering on his subsistence level (Figure 1.19b). In neither case will a decentralizing price system be lacking as long as the premises of Proposition 3.3 are satisfied. However, even if production and utility functions are differentiable the traditional equality of marginal rates of substitution of leisure for food, in production and in consumption, does not follow in either of these cases.[2] The decentralizing price ratio will have to coincide with

---

[1] That is, a function used to represent the efficient boundary of the production set. For further discussion of this function, see Section 3.10 below.

[2] The reader may feel that the assumption of indifference curves that end up in the boundary of the consumption set is unrealistic on physiological or psychological grounds. Such an objection does not apply to similar "corner optima" we shall meet with in subsequent

the marginal rate of substitution in production if the production function is differentiable. The corresponding marginal rate of substitution in consumption (defined only if the utility function is differentiable) can

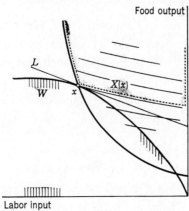

FIGURE 1.19a. The energetic Robinson.

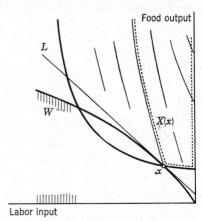

FIGURE 1.19b. The lazy Robinson.

be less than the price ratio in the case of the energetic Robinson, and higher in that of the lazy Robinson. Finally, no *unique* price ratio is obtained, even if the point x lies in the interior of the consumption set X, if it also happens to fall simultaneously in a kink of both the production function and the utility function (Figure 1.20). If x is an interior point of X, differentiability of even only one of these two functions at the point x will, of course, ensure uniqueness of the decentralizing system of relative prices.

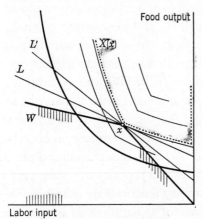

FIGURE 1.20. Case where the price ratio is not uniquely determined.

One other aspect of the mathematical tools here exhibited, mentioned already in Section 1.1, may again be emphasized. When Proposition 3.1 states about a point that it maximizes profits in the production set, or when Proposition 3.3 states that it is a best point within a given budget

sections, such as arise when a commodity is not consumed or when a factor of production or a method of production is not used. Hence, if we are stretching or distorting Robinson's psychology, it is done for a good expository purpose.

restraint, then these statements mean just that. They mean not merely that the point can stand comparison with all points in a small neighborhood that meet the same restraint, but actually that the point is as good as any point, *near or far*, meeting the same restraint. The convexity concept serves to isolate a class of cases in which the outcome of comparisons "in the large" can be inferred from more localized comparisons. For instance, while the point x in any of the Figures 1.17–1.20 was selected only so as to be best within the attainable set, we were able to conclude to the existence of prices such that the same point was bound to be most profitable in the entire production set. Likewise (barring one exception) the same point was found to be best among all consumption-wise possible points within the budget restraint. In cases where the convexity assumptions apply, therefore, there is no need to insert the qualification often omitted but always needed when sole reliance is placed on calculus or marginal equalities for the characterization of optima: that a local optimum is not necessarily an absolute optimum.[1]

1.8 VARIOUS MODELS OF RESOURCE ALLOCATION THROUGH PRICE SYSTEMS

The two sets of theorems which have been illustrated can be used in combination to construct models where supply and consumption decisions are first separated with the help of separation Theorem III.3, and subsequently further decentralized on both sides of the market over a number of consumers, producers, and resource holders with the help of the summation Theorem I. Several such models with quite diverse uses have been developed in recent years. Only some of these have placed allocative efficiency in the center of interest. Others have been concerned primarily with the mathematical description of competitive

---

[1] In the case of a twice differentiable utility function, the assumption of convexity (strict convexity) is equivalent to the requirement that the second variation of the utility function be nonpositive (negative) in all directions in which the first variation vanishes. This property has in turn been represented in the strict convexity case by its necessary and sufficient conditions in terms of alternating signs of principal minors of a determinant whose elements are the second derivatives of the utility function bordered by a row and column of first derivatives (see J. R. Hicks, *Value and Capital*, Appendix to chap. I). It would seem that the simple requirement of convexity is both intuitively clearer in its implications and more directly suitable for the comparisons "in the large" which the economist wishes to make when discussing equilibrium theory. However, the bordered matrix of second derivatives comes into its own in the quantitative study of responses of a consumer to given small income or price changes from an initial position in which every commodity entering into the utility function is actually being consumed (see J. R. Hicks, *Value and Capital*, Appendix to chaps. II and III).

equilibrium. Because of the mathematical affinity of all these models we shall here list a number of them, with some mention of what was each author's chief emphasis.

The outstanding classical studies in the field are a model of competitive equilibrium by Abraham Wald,[1] and a model of proportional growth of a competitive economy by von Neumann.[2] While these studies attracted little attention at the time of their publication, they have been at the basis of all subsequent developments, even if these at times took the form of rediscovery of ideas. The emphasis in both studies was on the mathematical existence of an equilibrium state or growth process within the postulates of the model. Moreover, at the end of von Neumann's article optimal properties of the growth process studied are also noted.

Another source of ideas has been the theoretically much simpler model of input-output analysis, developed over a long period of time by Leontief[3] with the main emphasis on empirical application to the production side of the economy.

Preoccupation with production and programming, this time with an emphasis on efficient allocation, also characterizes the work on linear programming by Dantzig,[4] and on linear activity analysis by the present author,[5] stimulated by related work of Samuelson.[6] This in turn stimu-

[1] A. Wald, "Über einige Gleichungssysteme der mathematischen Ökonomie," *Zeitschrift für Nationalökonomie*, vol. 7, 1936, pp. 637–670, translated as "On Some Systems of Equations in Mathematical Economics," *Econometrica*, vol. 19, October 1951, pp. 368–403. Earlier contributions from the same author are quoted in this article.

[2] John von Neumann, "Über ein Ökonomisches Gleichungssystem und eine Verallgemeinerung des Brouwerschen Fixpunktsatzes," in Karl Menger (ed.), *Ergebnisse eines Mathematischen Kolloquiums*, no. 8, 1935–36. Translated as "A Model of General Equilibrium," *Review of Economic Studies*, vol. 13, no. 1, 1945–46, pp. 1–9. Hereafter quoted as "A Model . . . ."

[3] Wassily Leontief, *The Structure of American Economy, 1919–1939*, Oxford University Press, New York, 1941. 2d ed. (enlarged) 1951. Both editions are based in part on earlier articles by the same author.

[4] George B. Dantzig, "The Programming of Interdependent Activities," and "Maximization of a Linear Function of Variables Subject to Linear Inequalities," chap. II (pp. 19–32) and chap. XXI (pp. 339–347) of T. C. Koopmans (ed.), *Activity Analysis of Production and Allocation*, Cowles Commission Monograph 13, Wiley, New York, 1951; this volume will hereafter be quoted as *Activity Analysis* . . . .

[5] Tjalling C. Koopmans, "Analysis of Production as an Efficient Combination of Activities," chap. III (pp. 33–97) of *Activity Analysis* . . . ; "Efficient Allocation of Resources," *Econometrica*, vol. 19, October 1951, pp. 455–465.

[6] Paul A. Samuelson, "Market Mechanisms and Maximization, I, II, III," Hectographed memoranda, the RAND Corporation, 1949.

lated two currents of research. One is a reformulation of welfare economics[1] by Arrow[2] and by Debreu,[3] extended to problems of allocation over time by Malinvaud.[4] The other current is concerned with models of international trade, and takes off from the work of Frank D. Graham,[5] conceived independently from, but strongly related in its ideas to, activity analysis. Originally expressed through numerical examples, Graham's model was analyzed in mathematical form by McKenzie and by Whitin, in studies concerned in part with model formulation,[6] in part with allocative efficiency,[7] in part with the existence of an equilibrium.[8]

The latter study is part of a renewed interest in conditions that ensure the existence of a competitive equilibrium. Besides McKenzie's study, there were an earlier study by Debreu,[9] a subsequent joint study by Arrow and Debreu,[10] a further paper by McKenzie,[11] and one by Gale,[12]

[1] For references to earlier work in welfare economics see footnotes on page 42.

[2] Kenneth J. Arrow, "An Extension . . . ," (see footnote 3 on page 26).

[3] Gerard Debreu, "The Coefficient of Resource Utilization," *Econometrica*, July 1951, pp. 273–292, especially section 6. Hereafter quoted as "The Coefficient . . . ." "Valuation Equilibrium and Pareto Optimum," *Proceedings of the National Academy of Sciences*, vol. 40, July 1954, pp. 588–592, hereafter quoted as "Valuation Equilibrium . . . ."

[4] Edmond Malinvaud, "Capital Accumulation and Efficient Allocation of Resources," *Econometrica*, vol. 21, April 1953, pp. 233–268, hereafter quoted as "Capital Accumulation . . . ."

[5] Frank D. Graham, *The Theory of International Values*, Princeton University Press, Princeton, N.J., 1948.

[6] Thomson M. Whitin, "Classical Theory, Graham's Theory, and Linear Programming in International Trade," *Quarterly Journal of Economics*, vol. 67, March 1953, pp. 520–544.

[7] Lionel W. McKenzie, "Specialization and Efficiency in World Production," *Review of Economic Studies*, vol. 21, June 1954, pp. 165–180; "Equality of Factor Prices in World Trade," *Econometrica*, vol. 23, July 1955; pp. 239–257; "Specialization in Production and the Production Possibility Locus, *Review of Economic Studies*, vol. 20 (I), 1955–56, pp. 56–64.

[8] Lionel W. McKenzie, "On Equilibrium in Graham's Model of World Trade and Other Competitive Systems," *Econometrica*, vol. 22, April 1954, pp. 147–161.

[9] Gerard Debreu, "A Social Equilibrium Existence Theorem," *Proceedings of the National Academy of Sciences*, vol. 38, October 1952, pp. 886–893, hereafter quoted as "Social Equilibrium . . . ."

[10] Kenneth J. Arrow and Gerard Debreu, "Existence of an Equilibrium for a Competitive Economy," *Econometrica*, vol. 22, July 1954, pp. 265–290. Hereafter quoted as "Existence . . . ."

[11] Lionel W. McKenzie, "Competitive Equilibrium with Dependent Consumer Preferences," *Second Symposium on Linear Programming*, National Bureau of Standards, 1955, pp. 277–293.

[12] David Gale, "The Law of Supply and Demand," *Mathematica Scandinavica*, 3 (1955), pp. 155–169

which among them constitute the present state of development of the ideas on this problem originated by Wald and von Neumann.

Finally, von Neumann's ideas about efficient allocation over time were generalized in a study by Georgescu-Roegen,[1] in the study by Malinvaud already mentioned, and in a recent study by Samuelson and Solow.[2]

The models of competitive equilibrium and of linear activity analysis will be discussed in some detail in Sections 2 and 3, respectively. Of these two models that of competitive equilibrium is *in a mathematical sense* the more general one. In fact, we shall be able to derive the main results of activity analysis by a specialization of the model of competitive equilibrium (and a slight sharpening of the separation theorem used in it). This procedure will serve to bring out the underlying mathematical unity of the two models, as well as to supply one particular application of the somewhat abstract model of competitive equilibrium in which its mathematical constructs can be more easily visualized geometrically.

For these reasons we have placed the discussion of competitive equilibrium before that of activity analysis. *In an economic sense*, however, one may claim in one important aspect a higher degree of generality for the model of activity analysis. It constructs a theory of valuation of resources that assumes nothing more, on the consumption side of the market, than a state of nonsaturation with respect to each commodity classified as desired for consumption. The only information about consumers' preferences required by the model therefore is a specification of those commodities that have utility to some consumer—a requirement independent of assumptions of consistent and non-interacting preferences on the part of consumers. Therefore, if the sequence of subject matter in our presentation had been chosen so as to reflect increasing definiteness and hence restrictiveness of assumptions, rather than decreasing mathematical generality, we would have placed the activity analysis model before the model of competitive equilibrium.

---

[1] N. Georgescu-Roegen, "The Aggregate Linear Production Function and Its Application to von Neumann's Economic Model," chap. IV (pp. 98–115) of *Activity Analysis* . . . ; see footnote 4 on page 38.

[2] Chaps. XI and XII of R. Dorfman, P. A. Samuelson, and R. Solow, *Linear Programming and Economic Analysis*, McGraw-Hill, New York, forthcoming.

2. COMPETITIVE EQUILIBRIUM AND PARETO OPTIMALITY

2.1 INTRODUCTORY REMARKS

The idea that perfect competition in some sense achieves efficiency in the maximization of individual satisfactions runs through the whole of classical and neoclassical economic literature. At the time when utility was thought of as both measurable and comparable between different individuals this idea was expressed by attributing to perfect competition the property of maximizing the sum of the utilities of all consumers. This view could not be maintained after interpersonal utility comparisons were questioned. However, Pareto[1] introduced a conceptual refinement that saved the proposition. He suggested that competition brought about a state in comparison to which no consumer's satisfaction can be made higher, within the limitations of available resources and technological know-how, without at the same time lowering at least one other consumer's satisfaction level.

It was also realized at an early stage, and emphasized particularly by Marshall[2] and by Pigou,[3] that the proposition is valid only if all effects of one man's choice on another man's well-being are transmitted through purchase and sale of commodities. This precludes strict physical interaction between production processes. It also requires that the satisfaction of each consumer is affected only by his own consumption and work, and not in addition by other people's consumption or by any production processes except through the fact that he contributes labor.

Finally, it was perceived that a competitive equilibrium, whether efficient or not, could not persist in just any technological environment. In particular, in industries where returns to scale continue to increase even at levels of output comparable to the size of the market, competition will over time "destroy itself."

Pareto also gave the impetus to a converse train of reasoning,[4] which has since been greatly developed by other authors into what has become

---

[1] Vilfredo Pareto, *Manuel d'économie politique* 2d ed., M. Giard, Paris, 1927, chap. VI, pars. 32–51.

[2] Alfred Marshall, *Principles of Economics* 8th ed., Macmillan, London, 1920, Book IV, chap. XIII and Book V, chap. XIII.

[3] A. C. Pigou, *The Economics of Welfare* 4th ed., Macmillan, London, 1932, chaps. IX, X, XI.

[4] *Manuel* . . . , chap. VI, pars. 52–64.

known as the "new welfare economics." This reasoning starts by postulating a "Pareto optimum," that is, a state in which no one's satisfaction can be raised without lowering someone else's. Conditions characterizing such a state were formulated and discussed by Allais,[1] Barone,[2] Bergson,[3] Hicks,[4] Hotelling,[5] Kaldor,[6] Lange,[7] and Lerner,[8] and were found to be such as are satisfied by a competitive equilibrium. This is in no way a trivial turning around of the earlier argument. It is more fundamental in that it does not take as given such institutional facts as production by firms and exchange through markets, but starts from a formulation of the purposes—the satisfactions of consumers—to be served by these or any other proposed arrangements. At the same time, as we have already seen in our discussion of the splitting up of Robinson Crusoe's decisions, the converse reasoning requires somewhat deeper mathematical theorems and also depends on somewhat more restrictive assumptions with regard to production possibilities and consumers' preferences.

In the present discussion of the relations between competitive equilibrium and Pareto optimality, we shall broadly but not in all details follow the studies of Arrow[9] and Debreu,[10] the latter more closely on those points where their reasoning or their models differ from each other.[11] We follow these studies because with the help of the tools dis-

[1] M. Allais, *A la Recherche d'une discipline économique*, Ateliers Industria, Paris, 1943, tome I, chap. IV, sec. E; "Économie pure et rendement social," Paris, 1945.

[2] E. Barone, "The Ministry of Production in the Collectivist State," translated from the Italian original of 1908 in F. A. von Hayek, (ed.), *Collectivist Economic Planning*, Routledge, London, 1935, pp. 245–290.

[3] A. Bergson, "A Reformulation of Certain Aspects of Welfare Economics," *Quarterly Journal of Economics*, vol. 52, February 1938, pp. 310–334.

[4] J. R. Hicks, "The Foundations of Welfare Economics," *Economic Journal*, vol. 49, December 1939, pp. 696–712.

[5] H. Hotelling, "The General Welfare in Relation to Problems of Taxation and of Railway and Utility Rates," *Econometrica*, vol. 6, July 1938, pp. 242–269.

[6] N. Kaldor, "Welfare Propositions of Economics and Interpersonal Comparisons of Utility," *Economic Journal*, vol. 49, September 1939, pp. 549–552.

[7] O. Lange, "The Foundations of Welfare Economics," *Econometrica*, 1942; pp. 215–228; O. Lange and F. M. Taylor, *On the Economic Theory of Socialism*, University of Minnesota Press, Minneapolis, 1938.

[8] A. P. Lerner, *The Economics of Control*, Macmillan, New York, 1946.

[9] "An Extension . . . ," (see footnote 3 on page 26).

[10] "The Coefficient . . . ," sec. 6, and "Valuation Equilibrium . . . ," (see footnote 3 on page 39).

[11] Arrow treats all production as a choice from one aggregate production set, without the decentralization over producers considered by Debreu. The latter admits an infinite number

cussed in the preceding section they overcome some of the defects of earlier formulations of the propositions in question.

The problem of specifying conditions under which a competitive equilibrium is possible has been the subject of several recent studies, which have been quoted[1] in Section 1.7. We shall in the present discussion only summarize and briefly comment on the results reached with regard to this highly important problem.

2.2 POSTULATES AND DEFINITIONS

It may facilitate reference if we set out the basic assumptions of the model to be discussed in a number of postulates. This may be looked upon as a device for separating the reasoning within the model from the discussion of its relation to reality. The postulates set up a universe of logical discourse in which the only criterion of validity is that of implication by the postulates. Outside of and separate from this process of deduction, there is the evaluation of the model with regard to the range of phenomena which it may be used to represent in one interpretation or another, with regard to the degree of approximation attained in this representation, and with regard to the relevance of the conclusions in the light of the value judgments that ultimately motivate economic analysis.[2]

---

of commodities, and in that case makes for one proposition an assumption of free disposal (at least of small amounts) of each commodity. In the case of a finite number of commodities, both authors include cases where production forces unwanted commodities on consumers. Arrow includes states of complete saturation (bliss) in his formulations, which are not covered by Debreu.

Arrow's paper contains a general discussion of his model in the perspective of earlier literature, and reflects a concern with exposition also in its more technical parts. However, many readers may find that they perceive the essence of the arguments more readily if on first reading they disregard the clauses in the theorems designed to cover points of bliss. Debreu's articles are in the form of concise statements of the logical and mathematical essentials of the theories in question, addressed to the technical reader. They have been extremely valuable in the preparation of Sections 2.3 and 2.4.

Debreu states that recognition of the possibility of an infinite number of commodities has helped to clarify rather than complicate the proof. A more detailed statement of the relevant properties of a linear function of infinitely many variables would help in the further exploration of these possibilities.

[1] See footnotes 8–12 on page 39.

[2] Further discussion of the postulational method in economic theory will be found in the second essay of this volume, especially in Sections 5–7.

POSTULATE 1, on *decision makers*. There is a given number of decision makers, which can be subdivided into l consumers, m producers, and p resource holders. There is a finite number n of commodities, subdivided into types of labor and other commodities. Each decision maker makes one decision which consists in the choice of an amount of each commodity, that is, of a point in the commodity space.

POSTULATE 2, on *consumers*. The point x^i chosen by the ith consumer is constrained to a consumption set X^i, $i = 1, \ldots, l$, in which each point has a nonnegative coordinate for each commodity other than labor. On this set there is given a complete preference ordering for the ith consumer. The consumption set and the ordering on it are independent of the choices of other decision makers.

POSTULATE 3, on *producers*. The point y^j chosen by the jth producer is constrained to a production set Y^j, $j = 1, \ldots, m$, in which each point has a nonpositive coordinate for each type of labor. This set is independent of the choices of other decision makers.

POSTULATE 4, on *resource holders*. Each resource holder controls a nonnegative quantity of each commodity which is not a type of labor, and chooses to release of each such commodity a nonnegative amount at most equal to what he holds.

After our discussion in Section 1, these postulates do not require much comment. The restrictions on the signs of commodity amounts in Postulates 2, 3, and 4 are introduced for vividness of description, but are immaterial to the reasoning.[1] Likewise, the resource holders are separated from other decision makers not out of logical necessity, but because the function of control of resources is in principle distinct from those of production and consumption. It is therefore worthwhile to examine the efficient exercise of that function in isolation. Of course, in connecting the postulates with reality, some decision makers will be found merged in the same person. In particular, resource holders and

---

[1] One could also limit consumers to nonpositive amounts of labor by distinguishing as different commodities services directly consumed and the labor that provides them while treating the transformation of the latter into the former as production.

producers that are individuals (as distinct from organizations such as firms, authorities) are also consumers. The propositions of the model then apply to the extent that merged decision makers do indeed compartmentalize their decisions in the manner implied in the premises of these propositions.

In a model of a closed economy one wishes to exclude choices by the various decision makers that would imply disappearance of commodities into an outside world, or importation from outside. However, the intentional disposal of commodities for which disposal is possible can be recognized as a "productive" activity open to the appropriate producers (with or without cost in terms of required inputs of other commodities to disposal activities). Also, in a model that recognizes successive time periods, movements of storable commodities into or out of storage can be regarded as particular production possibilities. Finally, as said in Postulate 4, primary resources such as the services of land, or access to waterways or to mineral deposits available to the economy in question, can be released by each resource holder to the extent covered by his control or ownership. With these understandings, we can express the sealed-off character of our economy in a formal definition.

> DEFINITION 1. A bundle of choices[1] (one by each decision maker) is said to *balance* if for each commodity the net sum of all amounts chosen by producers and resource holders equals that of all amounts chosen by consumers.

We are now ready to define precisely the two main concepts between which connections are laid in the propositions below. In the first of these definitions and in subsequent discussion we shall, whenever a price system is given, use the term *value* of a choice to mean the sum of the amounts of commodities chosen, each multiplied by the appropriate price. For a producer the value of his choice then is his revenue or profit.

---

[1] It would be more in line with common usage of words here to speak of a *set* of choices. However, this would be a misuse of the term *set* in its mathematical sense of a collection of elements. In the present case each choice is not a nameless element of some set but is associated with a particular decision maker. In mathematical terms we have a function from the set of integers labeling the decision makers to the commodity space. In order to stay closer to traditional economic terminology, however, the term *bundle of choices* has been adopted by analogy with the well-established term commodity bundle. Similarly, we speak of a *price system* rather than a set of prices (one for each commodity), although price vector would correspond more closely to mathematical terminology.

For a resource holder it is his income from lease or sale of resources, and for a consumer his outlay on consumption less his wage income.

DEFINITION 2. A *competitive equilibrium* is a balancing bundle of choices satisfying Postulates 1–4, and a system of prices, one for each commodity, such that, if all "values" are computed at those prices,

(a) the choice of each consumer is preferred or equivalent to all other choices in his consumption set that are of equal or lesser value,

(b) the choice of each producer yields the maximum value attainable in his production set,

(c) the value of the commodities released by each resource holder is the maximum value attainable to him under Postulate 4.

For producers and consumers, these statements express achieved maximization of profit and of satisfaction, respectively. The statement for resource holders implies that every commodity with a positive price is released to the extent of its availability, and that nothing is released of any commodity with a negative price. The amount to be released of a commodity with a zero price is not specified in the definition.

DEFINITION 3. A *Pareto optimum* is a balancing bundle of choices satisfying Postulates 1–4, such that there exists no alternative balancing bundle of choices satisfying the same postulates, in which the choice of at least one consumer is preferred by him to his choice in the first bundle, while for no consumer the choice in the first bundle is preferred to that in the alternative bundle.

This definition expresses the idea of efficiency in the maximization of individual satisfactions.

2.3   THE PARETO OPTIMALITY OF COMPETITIVE EQUILIBRIUM

In order to avoid the complications of saturation, we shall consider only competitive equilibria which leave every consumer with something to be desired. In fact, if we are to prove our proposition, we shall need a somewhat stronger assumption. Thus far nothing has been said about divisibility or indivisibility of commodities. The postulates introduced are entirely compatible with a technology in which each commodity has a smallest indivisible unit. We now need to add a postulate which presupposes that at least some commodities are divisible to any desired degree. This postulate requires that whenever the satisfaction of a consumer is not complete, it is capable of being increased somewhat by arbitrarily small changes in his consumption.

> POSTULATE 5, *Local non-saturation.* Within any preassigned positive distance,[1] however small, from any point in the consumption set of any consumer which is not a point of complete saturation, there is another point of the consumption set preferred to it.

This implies that, with increasing well-being, saturation with respect to *all* divisible commodities cannot arise before complete saturation is reached (if the latter is possible). Such an assumption seems less objectionable indeed than some others that we have already made!

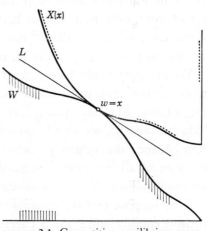

Equipped with these premises, we are within reach of the proof of our proposition. Suppose we are given a state of competitive equilibrium (in later comparisons to be called the original state) such that no consumer is completely saturated. We shall support the reasoning with the psychological, not logical, help of a diagrammatic representation (Figure 2.1) of this state in the space where each coordinate of a point x measures for

FIGURE 2.1. Competitive equilibrium represented by a separation of sum sets.

the corresponding commodity the algebraic sum of the (positive or negative) amounts chosen by all consumers. For a balancing bundle of choices this must coincide with the point w of which each coordinate is the sum of the amounts of the corresponding commodity chosen by producers and resource holders.

Let us call producers and resource holders together *suppliers*, and use the term *supply set* for any set to which the choice of any one of them is

[1] See footnote 1 on page 15 for the concepts of distance that may be used here.

confined in accordance with Postulates 3 or 4. The definition of competitive equilibrium then states that each supplier's original choice maximizes the value function in his supply set. By Theorem I.1 (page 12) the point w, the sum of all suppliers' choices, maximizes the value function on the sum of all supply sets, which we shall call the *aggregate supply set* W (see Figure 2.1). It consists of all points which can be decomposed (in at least one way) into possible individual suppliers' choices.

Before engaging in a similar construction on the consumption side, let us explore the implications of the definition of competitive equilibrium for the individual consumer a little further. It is given that the original choice x^i of the ith consumer is a best choice among those in his consumption set that are of equal or lesser value. It follows immediately that any choice preferred by him to x^i must have a greater value.[1] Postulate 5 permits us to supplement this with the statement that any choice equivalent to x^i cannot have a smaller value.[2] From these two statements, it follows that x^i minimizes the value function in the *no-worse-than-x^i set* $X(x^i)$ of the ith consumer.

We are now ready to construct the sum $X(x)$ of all individual no-worse-than-x^i sets, to be called the *no-worse-than-original set*. Although the notation $X(x)$ fails to express this it depends in general on all individual choices x^i, not merely on their sum x. Again according to Theorem I.1, the value function reaches its minimum on $X(x)$ in the point x, the sum of all consumers' original choices, which in turn equals the sum w of all suppliers' original choices (Figure 2.1).

Now suppose that the original state, which by assumption is a competitive equilibrium, is not a Pareto optimum. Then there is an alternative balancing bundle of choices x'^i in which the choice of one consumer, Mr. Jones, say, is preferred to his original choice, while every other consumer's choice is preferred or equivalent to his original choice. It

---

[1] From this fact we deduce in passing that if as we assume x^i is not a point of complete saturation the prices cannot all be zero, because in that case all values would be zero and no greater value could be reached.

[2] Provided x^i is not a point of saturation. To show this, assume that a point $\bar{x}^i$ is equivalent to x^i, and that its value falls short of that of x^i by some positive amount ϵ. Then, according to Postulate 5, we can find, within a distance from $\bar{x}^i$ small enough not to raise the value by more than $\frac{1}{2}\epsilon$, another point $\bar{\bar{x}}^i$, say, preferred to $\bar{x}^i$ and hence, through transitivity of preferences, to x^i. But since the value of $\bar{\bar{x}}^i$ is still at least $\frac{1}{2}\epsilon$ below that of x^i, this contradicts the premise that x^i is a best point among all points of equal or lesser value, thus confirming the conclusion in the text.

follows from what has been said that the value of the alternative choice is higher than that of his original choice for Jones, and lower for no other consumer. Hence the value of the sum x' of consumers' choices in the alternative state is higher than that (of x) in the original state. On the other hand, the value of the sum w of the suppliers' choices was already maximal in the original state, and therefore cannot be higher for the sum w' in the alternative state. But x' and w' cannot balance if their values are different. This contradiction proves that the original state is a Pareto optimum. The following proposition is thereby established.

PROPOSITION 4. If, besides Postulates 1–4, Postulate 5 of local nonsaturation is also satisfied, any competitive equilibrium (see Definition 2) in which no consumer has reached a state of complete saturation is a Pareto optimum (see Definition 3).

The foregoing argument reduces to its logical essentials the classical belief in the efficiency of competition as a mechanism for allocating resources in production and consumption. It establishes that, if there exists one common price system which when used in all profit and utility maximizations induces or permits compatible decisions (that is, a "balancing bundle of choices"), then its use in this way also guarantees the efficient utilization of resources for the satisfaction of consumers preferences, in the sense defined. The main mathematical basis for this classical result is the interchangeability of set summation and maximization of a linear function (Theorem I.1 on page 12). In addition, a rather weak continuity property of preferences, introduced through Postulate 5, is used. The reasoning does not depend on convexity of production sets or of preference orderings, or on differentiability of either production or utility functions. Neither could it be simplified if such assumptions were made.

2.4   PRICE IMPLICATIONS OF PARETO OPTIMALITY

A competitive equilibrium, even if it is also a Pareto optimum, may involve a more unequal distribution of income than is regarded as desirable from a social point of view. The concept of a Pareto optimum is insensitive to this consideration, and in that respect the term "optimum" a misnomer. A term like "allocative efficiency" would have been more accurately descriptive of the concept. We have retained the term "optimality" because it is rather strongly established, and followed precedent in attaching the name of Pareto in the double role of a qualifying adjective and a tribute to the author of the concept.

Terminology apart, new light is shed on the flexibility of the competitive market organization if we can prove that any given Pareto optimum, fair or foul, and however attained, can at least be imagined reenacted as a competitive equilibrium. Such a proposition cannot be true under conditions as general as those stipulated in Proposition 4.

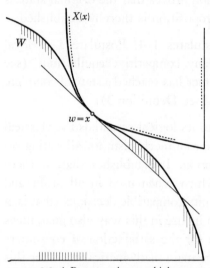

For instance, Figure 2.2 exhibits, in an economy of only one producer and one consumer, a Pareto optimum which is not a competitive equilibrium. In the situation pictured there is no price-ratio which holds the profit-maximizing producer in the optimum. The problem therefore arises of specifying circumstances of technology and preference under which one can be assured that every Pareto optimal state can be sustained by a suitable price system. The following proposition asserts that circumstances described by certain conditions of convexity hold

FIGURE 2.2. A Pareto optimum which cannot be sustained by a price system.

that assurance, if again we exclude the exceptional case involving a minimum income for subsistence, recognized in Section 1.5 above.

PROPOSITION 5. If in an economy satisfying Postulates 1–4 each producer is limited to a convex production set, and if each consumer is guided by a convex and representable preference ordering, one can associate with every Pareto optimum (see Definition 3) in which at least one consumer is not saturated a system of prices, not all zero, such that conditions (b) and (c) of Definition 2 of a competitive equilibrium are satisfied, and such that for each consumer any choice preferred or equivalent to his choice x^i in the Pareto optimum does not have a smaller value than the latter choice. If for each consumer there exists somewhere in his consumption set a choice of smaller value (at such prices), then the given Pareto optimum also satisfies condition (a) of Definition 2, and hence is a competitive equilibrium.

The premises of this proposition, of course, rule out indivisible commodities. Also, the premise of a convex preference ordering implies

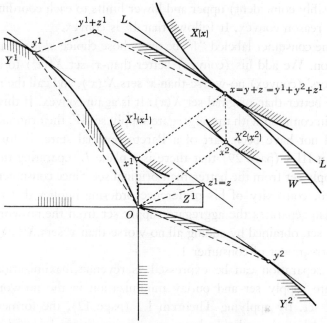

FIGURE 2.3. Illustration of Proposition 5.

Postulate 5 of local nonsaturation, and is, of course, more restrictive. There is therefore no need to reassert that postulate in Proposition 5.

The reasoning underlying Proposition 5 is similar to that which led us to Propositions 3.1 and 3.3 in Section 1 relating to a single producer and a single consumer. The main complication is that the reasoning is now applied to suitably constructed sums of sets on each side of the market. Figure 2.3 provides an illustration for two producers, one resource holder and two consumers. A literal interpretation of the diagram would imply that there are only two commodities which figure simultaneously as resources and as consumers' goods, and each of which is transformable into the other by one of the producers. One should however rather look on this diagram as suggestive of a more realistic situation involving more commodities and therefore requiring a larger number of dimensions for its accurate representation. In any case, the reasoning does not depend on the diagram.

Let W again denote the aggregate supply set, the sum of all production sets Y^j and all resource sets Z^h. The former are convex by assumption. The latter are by Postulate 4 rectangular blocks of points defined by (possibly coincident) upper and lower limits to each coordinate, and for that reason convex. It follows that W is convex.

Let the consumer labeled "1" be one whose choice x^1 is not a point of saturation. We add his (convex) better-than-x^1 set $\mathring{X}^1(x^1)$ to all other consumers' (convex) no-worse-than-x^i sets $X^i(x^i)$, and call the resulting sum the better-than-original set $\mathring{X}(x)$. It is again convex. If this set had a point in common with the aggregate supply set W, the original choices x^i could not have been part of a Pareto optimal state. It follows by Theorem III.3 (page 29) that there is a plane L separating the aggregate supply set from the better-than-original set. Since consumer 1 is not saturated, convexity of his preference ordering implies that the same plane also separates the aggregate supply set from the no-worse-than-original set, obtained by adding all no-worse-than-x^i sets $X^i(x^i)$ without special treatment of consumer 1.

This separation can be expressed as revenue maximization in the aggregate supply set and outlay minimization in the no-worse-than-original set. By applying Theorem I.2 (page 12), the former can be translated into the individual revenue maximizations by producers and resource holders that figure in Definition 2 of competitive equilibrium. Finally, by applying the reasoning of Proposition 3.3, page 35, to each consumer, one can show from the premise precluding a choice at the subsistence minimum that outlay minimization implies the maximization of satisfaction of each consumer within the appropriate budget restraint, thus meeting the remaining stipulation (b) in the definition of competitive equilibrium.

Proposition 5 is the central proposition of the "new welfare economics." Starting from the ideal of allocative efficiency expressed in the notion of Pareto optimality, it states more readily applicable price criteria which under certain itemized conditions imply the realization of this ideal. Its mathematical basis is, again, the interchangeability of set summation and maximization of a linear function, this time applied in reverse through Theorem I.2, and a separation theorem for convex sets. The use of the convexity concept overcomes two weaknesses of the treatment of the problem by calculus concepts. It allows comparison of the given Pareto optimal state with all relevant alternatives rather than those in a neighborhood only. It also avoids the necessity of supplementing the marginal equalities of rates of substitution that have figured so strongly in the literature by marginal inequalities to recognize the frequently occurring case where some commodities are not consumed by some consumers. The reasoning just given deals with both cases without needing to distinguish between them.

The application of the price criteria of Proposition 5 does not necessarily presuppose the existence of a competitive market organization. Discussions of pricing as a tool for planning and operating a socialist economy likewise derive from our proposition.[1] However, one can in particular interpret the proposition as a statement of conditions under which the simplicity of incentive structure and the economies of information handling characteristic of a competitive market organization can be secured without loss in efficiency of allocation. To wit: nonincreasing returns to scale for each producer, a convex and representable preference ordering for each consumer, absence of interaction between any two production processes, and independence of any man's preference structure from any production process and from any other man's choice.

This is a formidable bill of requirements, the limited realism of which has been fully brought out in the literature.[2] Even so, the informational simplifications offered by the market organization are sufficiently impressive to make the conditions under which they can be attained worth knowing. The price system carries to each producer, resource holder, or consumer a summary of information about the production possibilities, resource availabilities and preferences of all other decision makers. Under the conditions postulated, this summary is all that is needed to keep all decision makers reconciled with a Pareto optimal state once it has been established. Understanding these particular conditions is a

---

[1] See the references to publications of E. Barone, O. Lange, and A. P. Lerner in footnotes 2, 7, 8 on page 42.

[2] With regard to interaction between choices and preferences, see for instance J. S. Duesenberry, *Income, Saving and the Theory of Consumer Behavior*, Harvard University Press, Cambridge. Mass., 1949.

suitable first step in preparation for the more difficult problems of evaluating the services rendered by the market system under somewhat different and more realistic conditions.

Another qualification needs to be made. As explained at the beginning of this Section 2.4, Proposition 5 applies to any Pareto optimal state that can somehow be attained or imagined possible within technological, resource, and preference data. However, in assessing the meaning of the statement that such a state can be reproduced as a competitive equilibrium, we must keep in mind that Definition 1 of such an equilibrium specifies no rules by which the total income of each consumer is determined. It only gives information about how his decisions with respect to labor rendered affect the amount he can spend for consumption. To duplicate any imagined Pareto optimum through a competitive equilibrium will therefore require some particular distribution of rights to the income from ownership of resources and from profitable production—or some redistribution of such income flowing from given ownership and participation arrangements—through quite possibly discriminating head taxes and subsidies. The practical difficulties of bringing about such a redistribution without thereby affecting the principles of choice stipulated in the definition of competitive equilibrium somewhat diminish the distributional flexibility of the competitive market organization, referred to earlier. These observations, which have found full expression in the literature of welfare economics, do not detract from the logical validity of the statements made in Proposition 5, but point to important further problems of balancing distributional objectives against allocative efficiency.

One further remark may be made on the possibility of negative prices. If a commodity having a negative price in a competitive equilibrium enters into consumption, its price is a subsidy paid to the consumers in question for putting up with the nuisance the "consumption" of the commodity causes. A negative price of any commodity is possible only if its disposal requires positively priced inputs, since a negative price on any commodity subject to free disposal is incompatible with competitive equilibrium. Free disposal means that in at least one of the production sets Y^j the presence of any point y^j implies the presence of all other points in which only the coordinate of the commodity in question is different, and is smaller. If such a commodity had a negative price the producer in question could increase his revenue by "buying" a larger amount of that commodity and disposing of it.

2.5   EXISTENCE OF A COMPETITIVE EQUILIBRIUM WITH RULES OF INCOME FORMATION SPECIFIED

When spinning theories to the effect that a state satisfying one definition (such as that of competitive equilibrium) also satisfies another definition (such as that of a Pareto optimum) and conversely, one must always be on guard against spinning a vacuous theory. Suppose there is some hidden contradiction in either definition, so that no specimen of either type of state exists even as a mathematical entity? It is not an answer to this question to argue that situations approximately having the appearance of a competitive equilibrium are observed in real life. The test of mathematical existence of an object of analysis postulated in a model is in the first instance a check on the absence of contradictions among the assumptions made. If we assume that not all members of a body of contradictory statements can have empirical relevance, this logical test has to be passed before any question about the relation of a model to some aspect of reality can seriously be raised.[1]

It is possible to specify reasonable assumptions under which the definition of a Pareto optimum is not vacuous. One must, of course, stipulate that the attainable set, that is, the intersection of the sum of all supply sets with the sum of all consumption sets is not empty. Otherwise, not all consumers could survive, a situation not contemplated in the definition of a Pareto optimum we are using.[2] One would hardly object, in a first exploration, to specifying that all consumption and production sets are closed, and that all preference orderings are continuously representable. If one were to specify in addition that all production and consumption sets are bounded, a suitable reasoning would be readily at hand to establish the existence of at least one Pareto optimum.[3] However, these specifications would be somewhat unnatural. In the case of production, in particular, one would thereby deny the unlimited reproducibility of production processes discussed further in Section 3.4 below. A case could perhaps be made for specifying a limited capacity to consume even in the presence of unlimited resources, if by consumption one means

---

[1] Passages in smaller type such as that following here can, if desired, be passed by without losing the main threads of the reasoning.

[2] See however, the further discussion of survival in Section 2.7 below.

[3] Such a reasoning can be based on the theorem stated in footnote 3 on page 15. Of course, "in general" there will exist infinitely many Pareto optima.

physical consumption. However, is there any compelling bound on waste in consumption?

Fortunately, a closer study of the geometrical configuration of the production and consumption sets makes it unnecessary to speculate about such questions. This is brought out in a study by Debreu (as yet unpublished in 1957), which in turn extends an earlier discussion by the present author of a similar but simpler problem concerning productive efficiency alone. The latter discussion is retraced in Section 3.10 below. Its extension to the present problem involves somewhat more technical reasoning,[1] which can with the permission of its author be summarized roughly as follows. In addition to the assumptions already stated, it is specified that no consumer can consume (in the narrow sense) a negative amount of any consumption good or service, whereas labor services of any kind rendered (treated as negative consumption!) cannot exceed a given absolute bound for every consumer-worker. Each production set is assumed to be convex and to contain the origin, a state with no inputs or outputs. In addition, two specifications are made about the configuration of the production sets rather than about the individual sets. The first, to be discussed more fully in Section 3.5 below (see Postulate 11), says that production of a positive amount of any one or more commodities can only be achieved by producers' choices that together imply using up a positive amount of at least one other commodity. The second, an assumption of *irreversibility* of production, says that if given positive outputs of some commodities can be produced from certain inputs of other commodities, there exists no combination of producers' choices that reverses the outcome by producing the same inputs (in the same amounts) from those given outputs. The fundamental traits of the technology of production and consumption expressed by these specifications turn out to be sufficient to ensure the existence of a Pareto optimum. The reason is that, in the configuration described, the requirement that aggregate supply equals aggregate consumption permits the use of only a bounded subset of each production and consumption set, even though individually each of these sets may be unbounded.

These considerations suffice to establish the nonvacuous character of our discussion so far. If in a given model a Pareto optimum exists, then Proposition 5 indicates conditions under which this is also a competitive equilibrium, in which case a competitive equilibrium as we have defined it also exists. However, that result still falls short of what economists look for in a descriptive theory of competitive equilibrium. It has been

---

[1] The underlying idea is already present in Arrow and Debreu, "Existence . . . ," secs. 3.3.0–3.3.2.

said already that Propositions 4 and 5 are silent on the question how consumers' incomes are determined. The interpretation of Proposition 4, for example, is therefore something like this: If Postulates 1–5 are supplemented by one or more postulates specifying how the income of each consumer is determined, and if Definition 2 of competitive equilibrium is modified in its clause (b) to say that each consumer chooses a best point from among those that can be purchased from his income, and finally *if such a competitive equilibrium exists* in that model, then it is a Pareto optimum.

Actually, the rules governing income formation have a greater degree of simplicity, obviousness, and approximation to reality than the postulates about maximization of satisfaction or even of profit. Proposition 4 is therefore of limited usefulness until it is established that simple and reasonably realistic rules of income formation are compatible with the more subtle postulates and conditions of competitive equilibrium already introduced.

It turns out that this objection raises questions of great mathematical depth, requiring for their treatment tools quite different from those so far discussed, and of a more advanced character. The appropriate concepts and theorems are found in the relatively young mathematical field of *topology*—crudely put, the study of ways in which a set can "hang together." The class of theorems crucial in this connection are known as fixed-point theorems.

A simple prototype of this class of theorems says, roughly, that if one is given a continuous mapping (however distorting) of the points of a circular disk into points of another circular disk of the same radius, and if thereafter the second disk is placed in any position on top of the first, then there will be at least one point which is found directly under (coincides with) its image. Later versions allow greater generality in the shape and dimensionality of the set of points considered, and allow each point of the first set to be mapped not merely into a single point, but into some subset of the points of the (identically shaped) second set, with appropriate generalization of the concept of continuity. The statement then becomes that, upon putting the two sets together, at least one point of the first set coincides with some point of its image subset in the second set. In the application to competitive equilibrium, the mapping projects the bundle of the choices made by the various market participants, now to be regarded as one single point, into a certain set of choice bundles. This set contains for each participant all those choices that maximize his goal (profit, satisfaction), in comparison with all the choices that remain available to him, given the way in which the choices made by other participants affect his budget restraint. If each participant finds that his choice maximizes his particular goal within the subset of choices remaining available to him, then he has no incentive to change his choice, and a competitive equilibrium therefore exists.

In view of the technical character of the problem, it is not surprising that the important contributions have come from mathematicians and from economists with the highest mathematical powers.[1] It is, however, surprising that the fundamental importance of the problem to the entire edifice of the theory of competitive markets does not seem to have been commented on or even recognized by economists generally, other than the small group of European economists writing in German whose penetrating observations and searching questions originally started Abraham Wald off on his investigations.[2] It is true that there is ample precedent in physics for the bypassing of questions of the mathematical existence of analytical constructs by investigators anxious to explore the useful properties these constructs can be shown to have provided they exist at all. But the fruits of such studies are like predated checks until the noncontradictory character of their premises has been established.

We shall not attempt here to give a full report of the studies quoted above, but merely summarize the results reached by Arrow and Debreu in the second, the more difficult and more realistic one, of the two cases they study.[3] In addition to assumptions similar to our Postulates[4] 1–4 and the premises of Proposition 5, the authors make all the assumptions about the individual production and consumption sets and their configuration

---

[1] See footnotes 1–2, on page 38, and footnotes 8–12 on page 39.

[2] H. Neisser, "Lohnhöhe, Beschäftigungsgrad im Marktgleichgewicht," *Weltwirtschafliches Archiv*, 1932, pp. 415–455, especially pp. 424–425.

F. Zeuthen, "Das Prinzip der Knappheit, Technische Kombination, und Ökonomische Qualität," *Zeitschrift für Nationalökonomie*, vol. 4, 1933, pp. 1–24, especially pp. 2–3, 6.

H. von Stackelberg, "Zwei Kritische Bemerkungen zur Preistheorie Gustav Cassels," *Zeitschrift für Nationalökonomie*, vol. 4, 1933, pp. 456–472.

K. Schlesinger, "Über die Produktionsgleichungen der Ökonomischen Wertlehre," in Karl Menger (ed.), *Ergebnisse eines Mathematischen Kolloquiums*, no. 6 (1933–34), pp. 10–11.

[3] Existence . . . ," see footnote 10 on page 39.

[4] The more recent study of McKenzie, see footnote 11, on page 39, achieves a weakening of Postulate 2 that permits dependence of each consumer's preferences on the prices and on other consumers' and producers' choices.

that we have already enumerated when discussing the question of the existence of a Pareto optimum. They further limit each consumer's outlay to at most the amount of his income. With each consumer acting as a resource holder and holding title to given fixed proportions of the profits made by the various producers, his income is defined as the sum of the value of the resources he makes available, of the profit shares distributed to him, and of the wages earned by his labor. It is also assumed that no saturation can be reached by any consumer within the limitations imposed by total available resources, by technological possibilities, and by provision for the survival of all others.

The hardest part in the specification of the model is to make sure that each consumer can both survive and participate in the market, without anticipating in the postulates what specific prices will prevail in an equilibrium. To achieve this the authors assume first of all that the aggregate supply set contains a point which supplies just a little more of every commodity than is necessary, as indicated by some point in the aggregate consumption set, for every consumer to survive. Secondly, they assume that each consumer can, if necessary, survive on the basis of the resources he holds and the direct use of his own labor, without engaging in exchange, and still have something to spare of some type of labor which is sure to meet with a positive price in any equilibrium. The latter assurance is obtained by assuming that each of the types of labor in question, in any situation that can conceivably be reached within the limitations of resources, technology, and survival of all consumers, has a positive marginal productivity with regard to at least one out of a certain class of commodities, each of which, again in any situation reachable within the same limitations, can still add to the satisfaction of every consumer. From these assumptions, the authors prove the existence of a competitive equilibrium.

These important results illustrate vividly the great difficulties to be overcome, and the extent of rethinking of supposedly familiar problems needed, if even only the more classical portions of economic theory are to be rebuilt on a rigorous basis. In particular, most authors have ignored the analytical difficulty of formulating a model that ensures the possibility of survival, blithely admitting any nonnegative rates of consumption as sustainable. Arrow and Debreu face this issue, and find it to be a complicated one. Since their results need to be examined in relation to the treatment of time in the interpretation of the model, we shall postpone further comment on this complex of questions until Section 2.7, after a more general discussion of the various interpretations of the model of competitive equilibrium in Section 2.6.

Before turning to this discussion it is worth pointing out that in this particular study our authors have abandoned demand and supply functions as tools of analysis, even as applied to individuals. The emphasis is entirely on the existence of some set of compatible optimizing choices. This question can be answered without making assumptions that cause unique choices to be associated with any prevailing prices, a precondition for the definition of single-valued demand and supply functions. The problem is no longer conceived as that of proving that a certain set of equations has a solution. It has been reformulated as one of proving that a number of maximizations of individual goals under interdependent restraints can be simultaneously carried out.

2.6 INTERPRETATIONS OF THE MODEL

The model of competitive equilibrium that we have described, if looked at just as a system of postulates and conclusions derived therefrom, is amazingly rich in interpretations. Some of these go well beyond the class of phenomena in relation to which the model was originally conceived. In the present section, we shall comment only on interpretations where the "consumers" are meant to correspond to real-life consumers, and where the "producers" correspond to firms or to definite identifiable productive establishments. We shall reserve other interpretations that concentrate on the production side of the economy to the next Section 3.

As indicated already, a first choice in interpretation arises with regard to the treatment of time. The simplest interpretation in this regard is that of a stationary state, in which all choices are made once and for all, in terms of rates of flow that are to remain constant for an indefinite period of time. In a way this interpretation raises the least difficulties, because its abstract character is obvious to all and thus serves to silence detailed objections on grounds of realism. The great value of this interpretation lies in its combination of simplicity with relevance to the more fundamental problems of the economic organization of society that have been and will be with us for a long time.

An alternative interpretation is that in which time is broken up into successive periods, and commodities are characterized not only qualitatively but also by the period in which they are available.[1] In this case a choice by a consumer is in fact a plan for future consumption extending over all periods considered.[2] His preference ordering is thought of as an ordering of all such plans. Likewise, each producer chooses a production plan, while the production set now has a time structure which may require inputs to be available in periods preceding those in which the outputs they help produce can be obtained.[3]

Some of the more obvious shortcomings of the model in this interpretation must be looked upon as the price to be paid for as yet avoiding the complications attending any attempt to introduce uncertainty into the model. Consumers choose a plan for their lifetime, in full present knowledge of their future preferences, of the time of their death, and of the place occupied in their preference structure by the resources handed on at death to their heirs. Choices for production or consumption units not yet in existence at the beginning of the period must be made by proxy. Producers are fully informed about the nature and timing of future improvements in technology relevant to their operations. Markets exist in which prices are quoted for all future periods considered. Finally, resources at the end of the entire period covered by the model must either be allowed to be depleted, or else be incorporated in the preference structure of consumers.[4]

A beginning has been made with an interpretation in which uncertainty is explicitly incorporated in the model.[5] In this interpretation, a commodity is identified by three labels, its qualitative description, the time of its (conditional) availability, and the future eventuality (or "state of nature") on which its availability is dependent. Market prices

[1] A similar locational differentiation of commodities will be considered in Section 9 of the second essay of this book.

[2] See Gerhard Tintner, "The Maximization of Utility over Time," *Econometrica*, vol. 6, 1938, pp. 154–158.

[3] See also J. R. Hicks, *Value and Capital*, 2d ed., Clarendon Press, Oxford, 1946, especially chaps. IX, XV, XVIII.

[4] For further comment on this point, see Section 4.2 of this essay.

[5] K. J. Arrow, "Le Rôle des valeurs boursières pour la repartition la meilleure des risques," *International Colloquium on Econometrics, 1952*, Centre National de la Recherche Scientifique, Paris, 1953; "The Allocation of Risk Bearing," paper presented at the Detroit meeting of the Econometric Society, Christmas 1954, abstract in *Econometrica;* Gerard Debreu, "Une Economie de l'incertain," unpublished manuscript.

of these "three-dimensional" commodities reflect (quite possibly different) individual subjective probabilities associated with the various states of nature that may occur in the future. As Arrow observes, in this interpretation the convexity of individual preference orderings implies that each consumer is averse from or, in a limiting case, just neutral toward, risk bearing. We shall postpone comment on this interpretation until Section 11 of the second essay.

2.7   SURVIVAL OF CONSUMERS IN A COMPETITIVE EQUILIBRIUM

We now return briefly to the question of the survival of consumers in the Arrow-Debreu model of competitive equilibrium in which uncertainty is not recognized. If, contrary to the authors' indications, their model were given a stationary state interpretation, it would be found best suited for describing a society of self-sufficient farmers who do a little trading on the side. In modern society few of us can indeed survive without engaging in exchange. Because of the simplicity of the stationary state model and its usefulness for some purposes, there is considerable challenge to further research on the survival problem in that context. Such research could go in several alternative directions to serve different purposes. One "hard-boiled" alternative would be to assume instantaneous elimination by starvation of those whose resources prove insufficient for survival, and to look for conditions ensuring existence of an "equilibrium" involving survival of some consumers. An alternative more realistic for highly industrialized private enterprise societies would be to recognize the existence of income transfers through taxation and social insurance, and to look for conditions, including tax and benefit schedules, ensuring general survival in an equilibrium. Finally, either as a further alternative or in addition to the foregoing, one might find it possible to specify lower limits on the productivity of the various types of labor, expressed in terms of quantities of commodities rather than values, and to specify upper limits on quantitatively defined minima for subsistence, so as to ensure the possibility of survival of all consumers through the sale of their labor whenever other resources are insufficient.

It has been pointed out to me orally by Debreu that the treatment of time adopted by Arrow and Debreu in which each choice is a plan extending over a sequence of future periods permits a more subtle version of what was called above the "hard-boiled" interpretation of the model in regard to the survival problem. The plan formed by each consumer in response to the price system includes a specification of the length of life compatible with his present resources, his ability to do remunerative work or shift for himself, and other aspects of his life plan. All that is to be assured by the postulates is survival of every consumer at least into the first period. The amount and initial distribution of resources and skills in the population determine the pace and extent, if any, of starvation.

Granted the inadequacies of any model unable to recognize the element of uncertainty in individual survival, this interpretation has an appeal of descriptive accuracy with regard to societies or phases of development in which income transfers are quantitatively unimportant. It neatly clarifies a group of questions in regard to which the liberalist and Marxist schools of economic thought have never quite achieved communication.

2.8 DESCRIPTIVE AND NORMATIVE APPLICATIONS

Within each of the various interpretations of the model of competitive equilibrium discussed, one can make a further distinction which concerns the *application* rather than the interpretation of the model. In one application, which might be called the *descriptive* one, markets believed to be competitive are observed and the model assures us that such markets achieve efficient allocation, if not necessarily a most desirable distribution, of resources. In this application, the main emphasis is on Proposition 4, while Proposition 5 states one set of conditions under which Proposition 4 can be operative. In another application, let us say the *normative* one, allocative efficiency is embraced as part of a given norm, and competitive markets, or administrative prices responded to as if they were market prices, are recommended as a means of achieving this norm. The most clear-cut case of this application is in the recommendations by Barone, Lange, Lerner, and others for the operation of a socialist economy through price-guided allocation.[1] In this application

[1] For references see footnotes 2, 7, 8 on page 42. The studies referred to go further than the model here considered in that they allow situations arising from indivisibilities where some Pareto-optimal states can be sustained only if some producers accept, or are induced to accept, choices that maximize revenue merely in comparison with slightly different choices; but not in comparison with distant alternatives such as abstention from production. The

the main emphasis is on Proposition 5, or any generalization of it that may be found to apply in other technological circumstances. Intermediate cases have also been considered. For instance, Lerner's *Economics of Control* envisages a mixed economy with genuine competitive markets where technological conditions so permit and a controlled form of price-guided allocation elsewhere.

The variety of these applications shows that the distinction between descriptive and normative applications is extraneous to the model. Whether a statement derived from the postulates of the model is used descriptively or normatively depends not on the logical content of the statement but on the extent to which the choices with which the model deals are regarded as subject to the influence of the user of the analysis.

Since the firm at least in principle controls its own internal production decisions, the application of our model to the coordination of such decisions can also be regarded as a normative one. In this application Proposition 5 suggests the idea of extending a given external price system to intermediate commodities and to primary resources that are not actually traded with outside parties. We shall return to this application in Section 3 below.

2.9 FREE ENTRY

There is a difficulty associated with Postulate 1 if the model is used as descriptive of a competitive market economy. We have reserved discussion of this difficulty to the last because it forms a suitable transition to Section 3 which follows. It arises from the specification in that postulate of a given number of decision makers. With respect to consumers, there is perhaps only a mild objection to this. In the stationary interpretation one can certainly look upon the consumers as a given number of claimants for sustenance, found to be in existence. In the interpretation of an economy looking forward over time, one could with some distortion of reality treat decisions creating new consumption units as being given in advance, or at least as arrived at independently by noneconomic motivations. Similarly, initial holdings of resources may be

---

same is true for Hotelling's proposal of marginal-cost pricing by public utilities in "The General Welfare in Relation to Problems of Taxation and of Railway and Utility Rates," *Econometrica*, vol. VI, 1938, pp. 242–269.

regarded as historically given. However, the creation or dissolution of a productive unit is by its very nature an economic act. In particular, free entry into any line of production has always been specified as implied in the concept of perfect competition. This aspect has so far not been incorporated into the model under discussion.

This difficulty is related to the question whether the production sets incorporate decreasing or constant returns to scale. It is suggested by the analysis of Section 3 that production sets exhibiting decreasing returns to scale correspond to situations where production depends not only on the inputs recognized by the model but also on some limited and indivisible resources not explicitly recognized. Examples are favorable locations or unique managerial abilities. Anticipating this conclusion in the present reasoning, let us consider a production set containing the origin and a different and strictly convex point x in its efficient boundary.

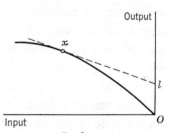

FIGURE 2.4. Profits under decreasing returns to scale.

Then, as Figure 2.4 suggests, any prices compatible with production at x in what we have thus far called a competitive equilibrium leave a positive profit (Ol in the figure). The availability of additional production sets of precisely the same shape to any individual or group wishing to set themselves up as entrepreneurs (possibly hiring among other things their own labor as managerial effort) would at such prices provoke further entry. It follows that a postulate assigning production sets with decreasing returns to scale to a number of producers given in advance is tantamount to prescribing and freezing the assignment to various production processes of a certain number of indivisible commodities. Since these commodities are not introduced explicitly, but only implicitly through their influence on the shapes of the production sets, such a model cannot be used to explore possible gains in efficiency through reshuffling of these indivisible resources among producers. It is suitable, however, for tracing the effect of a given distribution of ownership or control of indivisible resources on the profits arising therefrom, which are perhaps more appropriately described as rents.

Similar remarks apply to the technological knowledge and experience incorporated in a production set. If the transfer of such knowledge between producers is impeded for an indefinite period by preservation of production secrets, or if the use of such knowledge is preserved for its originators or sponsors during a limited period by patents, then an abridgment of perfect competition and of efficient utilization of resources with the help of knowledge available to anyone exists. The point is not to condemn such arrangements, which may well be justified by the incentive for inventive activity inherent in them.[1] The point is merely that a model that assigns specific production sets exhibiting decreasing returns to scale to a given number of producers is suited only for tracing the effects of a given distribution of nontransferable knowledge and of implied indivisible resources. It cannot serve for discussing the best utilization of all available knowledge and resources when there are no impediments to their diffusion or transfer of control (other than learning or transfer costs).

These remarks suggest the need for a further exploration of the production side of our model, which can best proceed in stages. The first stage would assume away all indivisibilities and all obstacles to the general availability of technological knowledge. We shall see in the next section that this leads to a model of production with constant returns to scale. The largely unsolved problems posed by indivisibilities will be commented on further in Section 9 of the second essay of this book.

3. PRODUCTIVE EFFICIENCY AND THE PRICE SYSTEM

3.1. CONNECTIONS BETWEEN THEORY AND PRACTICE

The problem area in economic theory to which the propositions reviewed in the preceding Section 2 belong is one of the oldest, and at the same time one of the most abstract, areas of economics. It is all the more remarkable and illuminating that the explicit use of the properties of convex point sets, which proved so helpful in this area, originated in a recent development in mathematical economics oriented toward highly practical problems. Known under the name of *linear programming*, this development appeared in its early phases to be primarily a computation method designed to deal with a certain class of maximization problems.

---

[1] See, for instance, Edith Penrose, *The Economics of the International Patent System*, Johns Hopkins Press, Baltimore, Md., 1951.

Representatives of this class seemed to arise in a great variety of circumstances.[1] The common mathematical feature of these problems was that they involved the maximization of a linear function of variables constrained by linear inequalities. The development received a strong impetus from the interest of the United States Air Force in the problems of programming its activities by mathematical methods,[2] and in particular from the work of Dantzig on model formulation and on computation procedures for these purposes.[3]

Thus the emphasis in linear programming was from the beginning on the computation of explicit solutions to complicated practical allocation problems for which numerical data are available. However, the connections between these methods and the much older idea of pricing, implicit or market, of scarce resources soon became apparent to the economists who took part in the development.[4] At the same time, they considered more general cases involving the simultaneous maximization of several linear functions in analogy to Pareto's idea of the simultaneous maximization of all consumers' satisfactions. The term *(linear) activity analysis*

[1] Relatively early examples of various types of these problems include, in chronological order:

F. L. Hitchcock, "The Distribution of a Product from several Sources of Numerous Localities," *Journal of Mathematics and Physics*, vol. 20, 1941, pp. 224–230;

George F. Stigler, "The Cost of Subsistence," *Journal of Farm Economics*, vol. 27, May 1945, pp. 304–314;

A. S. Cahn, "The Warehouse Problem" (abstract), *Bulletin of the American Mathematical Society*, vol. 54, October 1948, p. 1073;

Clifford Hildreth and Stanley Reiter, "On the Choice of a Crop Rotation Plan," in T. C. Koopmans (ed.), *Activity Analysis of Production and Allocation,* Wiley, New York, 1951, chap. XI, pp. 177–189. This book is quoted hereafter as *Activity Analysis . . . .*

[2] Marshall K. Wood and George B. Dantzig, "The Programming of Interdependent Activities: General Discussion," and Marshall K. Wood and Murray Geisler, "Development of Dynamic Models for Program Planning," chaps. I (pp. 15–18) and XII (pp. 189–215), respectively, of *Activity Analysis . . . .*

[3] George B. Dantzig, "The Programming of Interdependent Activities: Mathematical Model," and "Maximization of a Linear Function of Variables Subject to Linear Inequalities," chaps. II (pp. 19–32) and XXI (pp. 339–347) of *Activity Analysis . . . .*

[4] Tjalling C. Koopmans, "Optimum Utilization of the Transportation System," in *Proceedings of the International Statistical Conferences*, 1947, Washington, vol. 5 (reprinted as supplement to *Econometrica*, vol. 17, July 1949), pp. 136–146.

Paul A. Samuelson, "Market Mechanisms and Maximization," unpublished memorandum, the RAND Corporation, 1949.

Robert Dorfman, *Application of Linear Programming to the Theory of the Firm*, University of California Press, Berkeley, Calif., 1951.

came to be associated with this generalization.[1] Concurrently with these developments, mathematicians showed the importance of the concept of convexity for a good understanding of the connections between implicit prices and the given quantitative data.[2,3]

Research on the computational methods of linear programming continues unabated, and the application of these methods to practical problems of government and business has spread rapidly and widely. At the same time, the essential relatedness of linear programming and activity analysis to classical economic theory has become much clearer. As already explained,[4] it is therefore now possible, and perhaps convenient in an exposition addressed to economists, to present the propositions of linear activity analysis as special cases of those of the classical model of competitive equilibrium. It will likewise be convenient here to discuss activity analysis primarily in the terminology of the theory of production, although we have already seen that its mathematical structure permits a wider range of interpretation and application.

3.2   THE REPRESENTATION OF TECHNOLOGICAL POSSIBILITIES

In the preceding Section 2, we have described the production decisions open to one "producer," or "entrepreneur," as a choice from a given production set. This is a rather abstract concept, which needs

---

[1] Tjalling C. Koopmans, "Analysis of Production as an Efficient Combination of Activities," chap. III (pp. 33–97) of *Activity Analysis . . .* , and "Efficient Allocation of Resources," *Econometrica*, vol. 19, October 1951, pp. 455–465.

[2] See the contributions of David Gale, Murray Gerstenhaber, Harold W. Kuhn, and Albert W. Tucker to Part Three of *Activity Analysis . . .* (chaps. XVII, XVIII, XIX).

[3] Note added in proof: I have recently become aware that prior to most of the publications cited the basic ideas of linear programming and implicit pricing had been developed to a considerable degree by the Russian mathematician, L. V. Kantorovitch. See his publications: *Matematicheskie metody organizatii i planirovania proizvodstva (Mathematical Methods in the Organization and Planning of Production)*, Izdanie Leningradskogo Gosudarstvennogo Universiteta, Leningrad, 1939, 68 pp.; "On the Translocation of Masses" (in English), *Comptes Rendus (Doklady) de l'Académie des Sciences de l'URSS*, 1942, vol. XXXVII, nos. 7–8; (jointly with M. K. Gavurin) "Primenenie matematicheskikh metodov v voprosakh analyza grusopotokov (The Application of Mathematical Methods to Problems of Freight Flow Analysis)," in *Problemy povysheniia effektivnosty raboty transporta (Problems of Raising the Efficiency of Transportation)*, Izdatel'stvo Akademii Nauk SSSR, Moscow-Leningrad, 1949, ed. by V. V. Zvonkov. The paper published in 1949 is mentioned as in preparation at the end of the paper published in 1942. For references to related ideas in Scandinavian publications see footnote 3 on page 185.

[4] See Section 1.7.

to be examined further before we can assess its usefulness in analysis and in application. Traditionally economists have described production alternatives not by a set, but by the somewhat more special concept of a *production function*. The latter concept has been used in relation to a productive establishment, to a firm, or to an industry. It has even been applied to an entire economy, in which case the term *transformation function* has been used more often. We therefore also need to clarify the connection between production sets and production functions.

With reference to a firm or industry producing a single commodity, the production function is thought of as a function of the available quantities or flows of "productive agents," also called "factors of production," or "inputs." For any given input quantities (or flows as the case may be), the "dependent variable" represented by the function is usually defined as the maximum output quantity (or flow) that can be produced, in a given state of technological knowledge, from the specified inputs. In the case of joint production of several commodities, all outputs but one are placed side by side with the inputs as "independent variables" or "arguments" of the production function. The dependent variable is then defined as the maximum output of the singled-out commodity, attainable from the specified inputs along with the other specified outputs. This same concept applies to the transformation function of an entire economy.

The use of the production function for the representation of technological possibilities has produced a great deal of valuable insight in the market behavior of the profit-maximizing firm. Its responses to changes in prices or in conditions of demand for its products, of supply for its factors, have been studied intensively with this tool. There are, however, several reasons for taking one's starting point a little further back, in the concept of choice from a set of alternatives. One of these is that the notion of a production function is awkward for production processes in which the number of inputs and outputs is larger than the number of numerical parameters that are needed to distinguish the process from other available processes. Simple examples are those chemical processes that can absorb some or all of their inputs only in fixed ratios to each other.

A more important reason is that the definition of the production function itself already presupposes a "physical" maximization of output from given inputs. While in a market economy this physical maximization within the establishment can be looked upon as the first of several prerequisites for profit maximization, this first prerequisite is by no means a matter of course. The developments alluded to in the preceding Section 3.1 have arisen because it often is a highly complicated problem. The science of management should therefore start at the beginning of the problem, with a description of the range of alternatives open to the production manager, and use it in deriving prescriptions for achieving the physical maximization presupposed in the production function.

Economists have often regarded such management problems as outside the domain of economics and more properly entrusted to the production engineer or manager. While the recognition and formulation of problems is more important than their assignment to professions, it does appear that economics has suffered from looking on the production function as a boundary of its domain of competence. Without a more thorough analysis of the choices open to the productive establishment, the economist's prescriptions for profit maximization are nonoperational and his descriptive assumption of profit maximization is not subject to direct empirical test. Rare is the industrial firm that knows and charts its own production function as the economist defines it. The form in which knowledge of technological possibilities is kept and transmitted is normally quite different. It may be a statement of possible rates of output and required rates of input to each of the individual processes (often associated with particular pieces of equipment) that are combined in the productive establishment. Or the statement may record several alternative ways of using given equipment, which may also be capable of continuous interpolation.

The choice of the best modes of operation and of the best combination of such processes is indeed one particular manifestation of the general problem which forms the recurrent theme of economics: the best utilization of scarce means for given ends. The insights into this general problem that economics has gained primarily by the study of allocation through a price system and a market mechanism are relevant also to allocation problems arising within the productive establishment. Where exchange and pricing do not exist as market phenomena, they may still be useful as constructed conceptual aids to decision making.

Finally—and this is perhaps the most important consideration—even with regard to the allocation problems of an entire economy there are good reasons for starting with the construction of models of production possibilities before institutional assumptions are specified. In the modern world largely the same fund of technological knowledge and experience is utilized under an amazing variety of institutional arrangements, ranging all the way from American corporate and individual enterprise to Soviet communism. Within Western "capitalism," governmental and private enterprise operate side by side in different or even in the same industries. Within the private "sector," the problems of explaining how production tasks are distributed as between different firms, and of recommending how they could best be distributed, belong to one of the most challenging and least clarified areas of economics. There is therefore a need for the evaluation of institutional arrangements as well as for the prediction of production capabilities in any particular institutional setting. To make progress in these various directions, it may help to start from models that formalize nothing but the range of technological alternatives open to a producing organization, whether an individual, a plant, a firm, a governmental agency, or society as a whole. In this way the character and range of the possible decisions are clarified before the decision makers, their functions and their incentives enter upon the stage of the analysis.

3.3 LINEAR ACTIVITY ANALYSIS

The (linear) activity analysis model to be described in the present Section 3 can be looked upon as one step in that direction. It represents technological possibilities by a set of postulates that are perhaps as simple as they can be chosen and yet permit useful analysis, applicable rather well to some situations, only in rough approximation to a wider range of phenomena, and not at all to some other situations.

The fact that the model is devoid of "institutional" specifications contributes to its flexibility of interpretation. Thus, the activity analysis model can be used almost by itself alone for an abstract analysis of the price implications of efficient utilization of resources, and of the use of prices as a means of sustaining efficient utilization. In this use of the model the only supplementation needed to introduce the purpose of production is an assumption that no saturation has been reached in the demand for any of the finished goods that are being produced. Alternatively, the model can be "inserted" in the general model of competitive equilibrium discussed in the preceding Section 2, to give background to the assumptions about production possibilities of individual firms made in that model.

The activity analysis model can further be used for the numerical solution of practical problems of efficient or most profitable programming or allocation within a production establishment or other economic decision unit. Finally, one particularization of the model constitutes the theoretical framework of the technique of empirical economics known as input-output analysis.

We shall now review the basic postulates[1] of activity analysis in relation to general knowledge of production possibilities. Thereafter we shall show how the main propositions of activity analysis can be derived as particular cases of those of the preceding Section 2 relating to competitive equilibrium. Finally, we shall comment briefly on various applications of the (linear) activity analysis model. Further comment on the extent and limits of the applicability of this model will be reserved for the second essay, Sections 8–11.

3.4   THE BASIC POSTULATES

The postulates of linear activity analysis concern two original entities, *commodities* and *activities*, of which the relevant properties are specified by the first four postulates.

> POSTULATE 6, on *commodities*. There exists a finite number n of commodities, classified (exhaustively and without overlapping) into l desired, p primary and $n-p-l$ intermediate commodities. Each commodity can exist in any nonnegative amount in which it can be produced or withdrawn from nature. The joining and separating of amounts of the same commodity can be represented by addition and subtraction of the numbers that measure these amounts.

As is often the case in a system of postulates, the meaning of some of these specifications will become clear through later postulates.

---

[1] For two earlier statements of postulates, see G. B. Dantzig, "The Programming of Interdependent Activities: Mathematical Model," chap. II of *Activity Analysis . . .* , and T. C. Koopmans, "Analysis of Production as an Efficient Combination of Activities," chap. III of same.

"Desired" commodities represent goods and services whose consumption or availability is the recognized purpose of production. Primary commodities are withdrawn from nature. Intermediate commodities are those that merely pass from one stage of production to another, without either being wanted in themselves or being available in nature. Here "nature" is used as a general term designating any source of commodities outside the productive system studied.[1]

The specification about addition and subtraction of amounts of the same commodity implies that each commodity, unlike paintings or poems, is *homogeneous* in the sense that equal amounts are interchangeable in all their uses.

> POSTULATE 7, *existence of basic activities.* There exists a finite number *m* of basic activities. An activity is characterized by a net output number for each commodity.

These activities correspond to the basic methods of production that constitute technological knowledge and experience. As before, if an activity associates a positive net output number with a certain commodity, that commodity is produced by the method of production in the amount indicated. If the net output number is negative, that commodity is an input and the absolute magnitude of the net output number is the required amount of the input. If the net output number is zero, the commodity is not involved in the method.

The notion of constant rates of net output of various commodities as being characteristic of a method of production is useful only in relation to production processes that are *reproducible.* By this is meant that, given the availability of the required kinds of inputs, the same inputs will produce the same outputs if the method of production in question is duplicated at another time and/or place.

For methods of production in which all circumstances that appreciably affect the outcome are controlled, the presumption of reproducibility expresses a very basic fact of experience: constancy of the laws of nature as established by physics, chemistry, biology, and physiology.

---

[1] In order to maintain the nonoverlapping character of the commodity classification, some artificial commodity concepts may need to be introduced. For instance, if labor is a primary input but leisure a desired commodity, one may introduce "man-hours" as a primary commodity and have its use as labor in actual production compete with its use in a "process" which converts "man-hours" into an equal number of desired "leisure-hours."

While there is neither an a priori reason why such constancy should prevail, nor experimental evidence that it is absolute, the presumption is sufficiently borne out by experience to endow a model based on it with applicability in a variety of situations.[1] The position is different with regard to those processes of agricultural production which are strongly affected by weather fluctuations unpredictable with any degree of certainty, or with regard to prospecting for minerals under incomplete information about conditions in the crust of the earth. In such cases a model presupposing reproducible production processes would at best be a first approximation with some relevance to long-period averages of output rates, and at worst a very misleading tool of analysis.

A word should be said also with respect to the specification of finite numbers of commodities and of basic activities. Many commodities are subject to quality gradations which scientists have found it useful to describe by continuous variables. Examples are the composition of an alloy, and the place or time of availability of any commodity. Methods of production can also be controlled through continuously variable parameters such as temperature, pressure, or admixture of fertilizer or catalyst. However, it is reasonable to believe that in many situations a more appropriate model with an infinite basis can be approximated as closely as desired by a finite model.[2] Moreover, it is believed that with appropriate refinements of the postulates the more important results obtained from finite models can also be proved for infinite models.

The next two postulates are concerned with ways in which additional *derived activities* can be obtained from those in the basis.

> POSTULATE 8, on *additivity*. For any two activities, there exists a third activity in which the net output for any given commodity is the sum of the net outputs for that commodity in the two given activities.

The implication of this postulate is one of noninteraction between productive processes. Given the resources required for each of two

---

[1] Labor skills of different cultures or degrees of training, or the services even of identical soils under different climates, can always be treated as different commodities.

[2] For an exception to this statement, see the discussion in Section 4.9 (page 124) of a technology in which capital saturation is not possible.

methods of production, both can be engaged in simultaneously without either one of them affecting the outcome of the other.

Economic literature abounds with examples of interaction, such as water or air pollution, drawing on subsoil water or oil, effect of deforestation on water runoff, etc. These examples have drawn most attention when the interacting processes are administered by different profit- or utility-maximizing units, because, as we have already recognized, such cases constitute exceptions to the propositions about the efficiency of resource allocation through competitive markets.[1] It is likely that interactions between different operations of the same productive establishment are of even more frequent occurrence. However, in many cases, what appears to be interaction between processes, within or between firms, arises from joint use of indivisible inputs rather than from direct physical interaction. These cases are here ruled out by the next postulate we will consider. Where direct physical interaction is present, applicability of the present model can sometimes be usefully restored by lumping together the interacting activities into one single activity, which has as its net output for any commodity the sum of the net outputs for that commodity in its constituent activities as resulting from interaction.

In a diagrammatic representation in the commodity space, the additivity postulate implies that if any two points a and b represent possible activities, then their vector sum $s = a + b$ as illustrated in Figure 1.1, page 9, also represents a possible activity. An important implication of the additivity postulate is obtained by repeatedly adding an activity vector to itself. This leads to the inference that, if a point a is possible (Figure 3.1), then any point $2a, 3a, \ldots$, obtained by multiplying this point out of the origin by a positive integer is also possible.

Everything said so far is compatible with the existence of indivisible commodities, that is, commodities of which only amounts that are an integral multiple of some smallest possible unit can occur. In the present first exploration, we shall use a postulate that treats commodities as perfectly divisible. This limits the applicability of the model to cases

[1] See Section 2.1 and the literature cited in footnotes 2 and 3 on page 41.

where the granular character exhibited by most commodities can be ignored in first approximation.

> POSTULATE 9, on *proportionality*. If an activity $a = (a_1, a_2, \ldots, a_n)$ is possible, then every activity $\lambda a = (\lambda a_1, \lambda a_2, \ldots, \lambda a_n)$ of which the net outputs are proportional to those of a, with a non-negative proportionality factor λ, is also possible.

Geometrically, if a is possible, then the entire halfline out of the origin through a, henceforth to be denoted by (a), is also possible

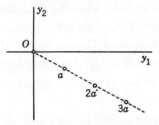
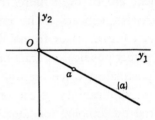

FIGURE 3.1. Repeated addition of a vector a to itself.

FIGURE 3.2. Illustration of the proportionality postulate.

(Figure 3.2). Since zero is a nonnegative number, this postulate implies in particular that the null activity (with no inputs or outputs) is possible. Generally, the postulate implies what is known as constant returns to the scale of production.

The various activities represented by all points λa, $0 \leq \lambda$, of the halfline (a) based on one activity a differ only with regard to the scale of operations. It is therefore useful to have a name for such a family of activities. We shall use the word *process* in general for any set of technologically related activities, and in particular, in the present context, for a set represented by a halfline ending in the origin.[1] The activity a

---

[1] In earlier publications on activity analysis, I have associated the word "activity" with a halfline rather than with a point. However, this leaves one without a word to correspond to a point, while the need for such a word will become stronger when attempts are made to drop the proportionality postulate. Since terminology in this area is still fluid, and since "activity" seems the more particular, "process" the more general term, the proposed rewording may prove useful. It also removes one objection to the term "activity analysis." This term was always thought of as a designation for the technique of representing production possibilities by mathematical models, not limited to those involving the proportionality postulate. Associating the term "activity" with the point in the commodity space underscores this interpretation.

will be called the *defining* or *unit activity* of the process (a), the scalar λ the *level* of the activity λa.

Once the proportionality postulate is adopted, it becomes an arbitrary matter which of the activities of a particular process is declared to be the unit activity and is used to represent the process in the technological basis set up by the existence postulate.[1] Anticipating the proportionality postulate, therefore, the existence postulate could instead have specified a finite number of processes. The present sequence of postulates has been preferred in order to proceed by gradations from the fundamental and highly plausible to the approximate and optional. Now that we have adopted the proportionality postulate, however, we may as well think of the (revised) basis of the technology as a finite number of basic processes. We shall therefore now freely use the term *basic activity* for any nonnull activity selected from a basic process. Moreover, we shall use the word *technology* as synonymous with the collection of all basic and derived activities.

Now that all commodities have been assumed perfectly divisible we can specify in a simple manner the extent to which a primary commodity can be withdrawn from nature.

> POSTULATE 10 on *resource availability*. Each primary commodity can be withdrawn from nature in any nonnegative amount not exceeding some given positive upper bound of availability.

3.5 "PRODUCERS," AND THE IMPOSSIBILITY OF OUTPUTS WITHOUT INPUTS

It has already been stated that in the present context we do not necessarily specify whether and how control over the activity levels in the various processes is exercised by individual decision makers or by a centralized agency. At the same time, we intend to develop the main propositions of activity analysis as mathematical specializations of those of the theory of competitive equilibrium.[2] Strictly and merely in order to make these specializations, therefore, it will help us to imagine "producers," "consumers," and "resource holders," who may be entirely fictitious characters. We shall assign choice sets to each of them, and a simple preference ordering to each "consumer." There will

---

[1] Except, of course, that the null activity cannot represent any but the null process.

[2] See Section 1.8 above.

be as many "producers" as there are basic processes in the technology. The production set assigned to any one of them is the halfline representing one of these processes, to be referred to as "his" process. His "choice" will be an activity of this process (a point of this halfline). We note for later use that every halfline is a convex set.

The *aggregate production set*, now for brevity to be called the *producible set*[1] and to be denoted by Y, then is the sum of all halflines that represent processes in the basis. In the simple case of two processes involving two commodities only, this set takes the form of the sides (a^1), (a^2) of an

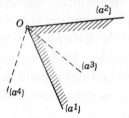

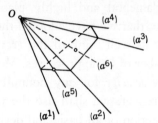

FIGURE 3.3. A convex polyhedral cone in two-dimensional space. (a^3) is redundant.

FIGURE 3.4. A convex polyhedral cone in three-dimensional space. (a^5) and (a^6) are redundant.

angle whose vertex is in the origin, plus the part of the plane between the sides,[2] as exhibited in Figure 3.3. Other processes added to the basis are redundant if their halflines such as (a^3) fall within the angle, and enlarge the angle in cases such as (a^4) where they fall outside.[3] Redundant processes are not particularly worth knowing under present assumptions, because they have nothing to offer that is not possible without using them. Any net output combinations they can realize can be exactly matched by a sum of suitable activities selected from other processes in the basis.

In three dimensions (Figure 3.4), a sum of halflines suitable as a basis is in general[4] a set in the shape of a bottomless pyramid having as

[1] In *Activity Analysis* . . . , chap. III, this has been called the possible point set.

[2] In the special case in which the two halflines are such that their union is a line their sum is also that line.

[3] Collections of halflines of which the sum is the entire commodity space will be ruled out as a basis by Postulate 12 below.

[4] In special cases the producible point set may contain an entire line or linear space of dimensionality less than n. While in *Activity Analysis* . . . , chap. III, simplification of proofs was obtained by an "irreversibility postulate" precluding these cases, this is not needed in the present context.

its edges all the nonredundant halflines in the basis. In a linear space of any number n of dimensions, the set obtained as the sum of a finite number of halflines is known to the mathematician as a convex polyhedral cone. It is called a cone because, along with every point a (other than the origin) contained in it, it also contains the halfline (a) through a. Its convexity follows from the fact that it is defined as a sum of convex sets, namely, halflines. It is called polyhedral because of the finiteness of its basis, which gives rise to "flat" sides or *facets* of all numbers of dimensions from 1 up to $(n - 1)$ inclusive.

Not all convex polyhedral cones make sense as representations of production possibilities. Two rather obvious postulates are needed to eliminate unsuitable cones. The first of these can now be given. The second (Postulate 12) will follow at the end of Section 3.6.

POSTULATE 11, on *the impossibility of outputs without inputs.* There is no possible activity (basic or derived) for which all net outputs are nonnegative and at least one is positive.

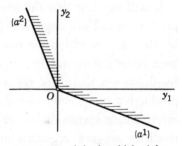

FIGURE 3.5. A basis which violates Postulate 11.

Geometrically this postulate says that, in order to be acceptable, a cone can have no point other than the origin in common with the nonnegative quadrant (in two dimensions, see Figure 3.4), octant (in three) or *orthant* (in n dimensions). Note that a cone may be unacceptable under Postulate 11 even though each of its basic activities is by itself acceptable. Such a situation is illustrated in two dimensions in Figure 3.5.

3.6 "RESOURCE HOLDERS," "CONSUMERS," AND THE POSSIBILITY OF PRODUCTION OF DESIRED COMMODITIES

We shall now introduce our other fictitious characters, always without prejudice to the flexibility of interpretation of our model with respect to the actual assignment of decision-making functions. We imagine a "resource holder" for each primary commodity, who selects the nonnegative amount withdrawn from nature within the bound of availability. "His" resource set therefore is a line segment defined by

$0 \leqq z_h \leqq d_h$, located on the nonnegative coordinate axis of the primary commodity identified by the subscript h. The aggregate resource set, hereafter to be called simply "the" resource set Z, is a sum of such intervals. In the case of two primary commodities this is a rectangle with one vertex in the origin. In the general case it is a higher-dimensional rectangular block in the subspace of primary commodities.

Finally, we associate with each desired commodity a fictitious and highly specialized "consumer" capable of absorbing any nonnegative amount of that commodity only. His consumption set is a particular halfline, namely, the nonnegative coordinate axis corresponding to the commodity in which he specializes. The sum of all individual consumption sets, to be called the *consumable set X*, then is the nonnegative orthant in the subspace of desired commodities only. To be precise, it is the set of all those points of which the coordinates for desired commodities are nonnegative and the coordinates for all other commodities are zero.

It will be clear that the special forms given to the choice sets in the present model are suggested not by any mathematical necessity, but by the uses to which the model may be put. Negative net outputs of both intermediate and desired commodities are made impossible because by definition there are no sources of these commodities outside the productive system considered. Positive net outputs of both primary and intermediate commodities are not allowed to arise because these commodities are not regarded as consumable. Strictly speaking, such a prohibition is of some importance only in situations where costs need to be incurred in order to prevent accumulating excesses of these commodities from obstructing production or being otherwise undesired. Rather than complicating our model with an extra (and overlapping) category of undesired commodities, we have required complete disposal of all excesses of nonconsumable commodities. The case of harmless waste materials can always be allowed for by including in the technology a free disposal process for each such commodity, which has it as the only input, and no outputs.

We will now translate in terms of the present model the concept of a balancing bundle of choices by all "agents," and illustrate it by Figures 3.6 and 3.7. According to Definition 1 (page 45), this is a bundle of choices by "consumers," "producers," and "resource holders" resulting in points x, y, z of the consumable set X, the producible set Y, and the resource set Z, respectively, such that

$$x = y + z, \qquad \text{or} \qquad y = x - z$$

Owing to the special forms of the sets X and Z and the nonoverlapping character of the commodity classification, the net output point y resulting from the basic activities chosen by "producers" uniquely determines the balancing choices by "consumers" and "resource holders."[1] For we must have, as a result of the stipulations made,

$y_k = x_k$ if k indicates a desired commodity
$y_k = 0$ if k indicates an intermediate commodity
$y_k = -z_k$ if k indicates a primary commodity

The idea of a balancing bundle of choices is therefore now expressible by the following concept of an attainable bundle of activities.

DEFINITION 4. A bundle of basic activities is called *attainable* if the resulting net outputs y_k are nonnegative for desired commodities, zero for intermediate commodities and nonpositive for primary commodities, and if the absolute amounts of the primary commodity inputs do not exceed the bounds of availability of these commodities given by Postulate 10.

Figure 3.6 illustrates this concept for a technology with a single process converting one primary commodity (labor, say, labeled $k = 2$) into one desired commodity (food, $k = 1$). The producible set Y is the halfline (y), the consumable set X is the nonnegative food axis, the resource set Z the line segment $\overline{Od}$. The net output point y resulting from a particular "producer's" choice determines uniquely both the point $x = (y_1,0)$ in the consumable set, representing the desired outcome of production, and the point $z = (0,-y_2)$ in the resource set, representing resource requirements. Attainable activities are all those resulting in net output points y of the line segment $\overline{Oe}$.

Figure 3.7 adds an intermediate commodity (tools, y_3) and shows two processes, one (a^1) for making tools out of labor, and one (a^2) for producing food from labor with the help of tools that wear out through

---

[1] In some technologies, however, it is possible for the same producible point y to result from more than one bundle of basic activities.

use. The producible set Y is now the angle spanned by the halflines (a^1) and (a^2). The consumable and resource sets are unchanged. However, in order to simplify the figure, the resource set has been represented by its negative $\overline{Of}$, the *resource input set* $-Z$, that is, the set of all vectors $-z$ of which the negative z is in Z.[1] Attainable bundles of

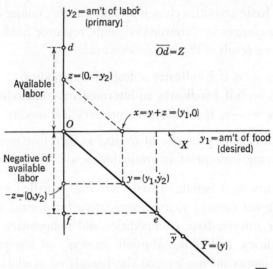

FIGURE 3.6. Illustration of the attainable set (the segment $\overline{Oe}$) for a technology with two commodities.

activities are all those resulting in net output points y on the line segment $\overline{Oe}$.

In order to be able to deal with problems of existence (of the yet to be defined equivalent of a Pareto optimum) as well as optimality, we must add one further postulate. This could simply specify the existence of an attainable bundle of activities of which the total net outputs are not all zero. However, if we did this we would be assuming more than needed to obtain the desired conclusion.

POSTULATE 12, on *the possibility of production.* There exists a producible point with nonnegative net outputs for all desired commodities, a positive output for at least one desired commodity and zero net outputs for intermediate commodities.

[1] This corresponds to the decomposition of y in the second form shown above, which can be thought of as $y = x + (-z)$.

Comparison with Definition 4 shows that the upper bounds on the availability of primary commodities have been ignored in this postulate. The reason why these restrictions need not be mentioned lies in the proportionality postulate. If some point $\bar{y}$ other than the origin (see Figure 3.6) that satisfies Postulate 12 should require larger inputs of primary commodities than are available, then by a sufficiently large

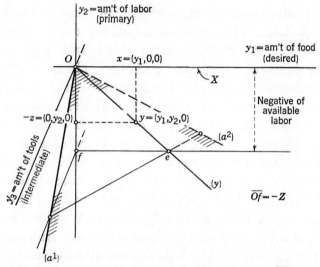

FIGURE 3.7. Illustration of the attainable set (the segment $\overline{Oe}$) for a technology with three commodities.

proportional reduction of the activity levels in all processes involved one can always reach another nontrivial producible point such as y in which the requirement for each of the finite number of primary commodities is brought within the (guaranteed positive) bound on its availability.

3.7 PRODUCTIVE EFFICIENCY

We must now introduce into the model some information about the purpose to be served by production. It is in the interest of wide applicability of the model to make the expression of this purpose as general as possible. A rather general formulation is obtained by specifying for each imaginary "consumer" the following (obviously convex) preference ordering: when confronted with a choice between two different nonnegative amounts of the commodity with which he is associated, our "consumer" always prefers the larger amount.

By this simple specification our model becomes applicable in all situations where, whatever the actual purpose of production, no saturation has yet been reached with respect to any of the desired commodities. Such an assumption seems an appropriate one in a study of productive efficiency. It takes as given the immediate purpose of production—to produce desired commodities—without getting involved in the details of further postulates of a theory of consumers' choice to explain for what purposes, up to what limit, and in what relative degrees the commodities in question are desired by consumers. The specification helps us perceive that the relations between prices and productive efficiency are independent of whatever particular postulates about consumers' choice one adopts. It turns out that an enumeration of the desired commodities which are scarce constitutes all the information about the purpose of production needed to establish these relations. Moreover, in cases where the particular theory of consumers' choice described in the preceding Section 2 is held to apply, our results will still be valid for a large class of utility functions, namely, all those in which with respect to each commodity at least one consumer is not saturated in any situation that can arise within the limitations of available resources.

With all our actors on the stage, their powers and preferences revealed, we are ready to derive the main propositions of (linear) activity analysis almost entirely by further translation of the concepts and propositions of the theory of competitive equilibrium. The present meaning of the concept of Pareto optimality is perhaps best expressed by the term *productive efficiency*. The following definition is a straightforward adaptation of Definition 3 (page 46) of a Pareto optimum to the specifications of the present model.

DEFINITION 5. An attainable bundle of basic activities is called an *efficient* bundle if there exists no attainable bundle which produces more of some desired commodity and no less of any other desired commodity.

The definition expresses that within the limitations of technology and resources no opportunity to increase the output of some desired commodity while holding the line on others has been overlooked or passed up.

It is easily seen that in both of our examples in Figures 3.6 and 3.7 there exists one single efficient bundle of activities, which results in a net output point denoted e in both cases. This is the point of maximum food production compatible with the given restrictions on labor (and tools). In models with more than one desired commodity, one will in general find that there exist infinitely many efficient bundles of activities, although degenerate cases with a single efficient bundle can still occur under Postulates 6–12.

3.8   EFFICIENCY OF PROFIT MAXIMIZATION AT SUITABLE GIVEN PRICES

Let us finally translate the concept of competitive equilibrium. Definition 2 on page 46 stipulates in clauses (a), (b), (c) the kind of choice to be made by each type of "agent" in response to some given system of prices. Clause (c) relating to "resource holders" is satisfied if we require that each positively priced primary commodity is withdrawn from nature up to its limit of availability, and that no negatively priced primary commodity is withdrawn at all. An even simpler statement is implied in clause (a) for "consumers." A reading of this clause shows that it is satisfied for a given "consumer" by any choice whatever from the consumption set allotted to him if the price of "his" commodity is positive, and cannot be satisfied by any choice if that price is negative or zero. Hence, clause (a) translates into the condition that all desired commodity prices are positive, and has no further implications with regard to the nonnegative amounts of these commodities produced.

Additional restrictions that connect prices and quantities arise from clause (b) concerning "producers'" choices. Figure 3.8 shows the three cases that can arise if a profit-maximizing "producer" is to select an activity from "his" process when faced with given prices on all commodities involved in the process. While the diagram is drawn for two commodities, the same three cases arise for any number of commodities. In the first case, every activity in the process brings a loss except the null activity. Hence the latter activity maximizes profit, a zero profit being the maximum attainable. In the second case, every activity in the process brings a zero profit, and profit maximization is compatible with the choice of any of the activities in the process. In the third case, every activity other than the null activity brings a positive profit, and there is no limit to the size of the profit obtainable, in view of the proportionality postulate. Hence, profit maximization is not possible in this case.

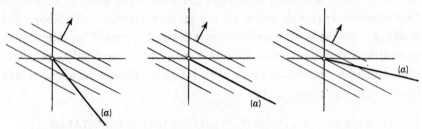

FIGURE 3.8. Three cases with regard to the profitability of a process (a).

Which of the three cases prevails for a given process and given prices $p_1, p_2, \ldots, p_n$, can be ascertained from the coefficients $a_1, a_2, \ldots, a_n$ of any activity that serves to define the process. The criterion is the sign of the expression

$$a_1 p_1 + a_2 p_2 + \ldots + a_n p_n, \qquad \text{also denoted} \quad \sum_{k=1}^{n} a_k p_k,$$

which represents the *profitability* of the defining activity. The three cases described are obtained when this expression is negative, zero, or positive, respectively. We shall refer to these cases as that of an *unprofitable process*, a *zero-profit process*, and a *profitable process*, it being understood that these distinctions depend on the given price situation. A zero-profit process can also be said to *break even*.

This highly elementary analysis shows that not every system of prices is compatible, under profit maximization, with a given technology. The point is important enough to be expressed by a formal definition.

DEFINITION 6. A system of prices will be called *compatible with a given technology* if

    (i) no process is profitable, and
    (ii) at least one process breaks even.

Clause (i) makes profit maximization possible, while clause (ii) ensures that it does not limit us to the trivial case in which no production takes place at all.

We are now ready to translate Proposition 4 of Section 2 (page 49), which asserts the Pareto optimality of a competitive equilibrium, into the terms of our present model of production. Comparison of the present postulates and definitions with those of the model of competitive equilibrium will convince the reader that the following proposition has now been established:

> PROPOSITION 6. If with respect to the model of linear activity analysis (as defined by Postulates 6–10) there is given a system of prices compatible with the technology, in which all prices of desired commodities are positive, then any attainable bundle of basic activities which is selected only from processes that break even, and which utilizes all positively priced primary commodities to the limit of their availability but does not draw on negatively priced primary commodities at all, is an efficient bundle of activities.

An important application of this proposition to economic theory relates to a productive system that is embedded in a market economy in a stationary state, and in which each process is engaged in independently by real-life profit-maximizing entrepreneurs sufficiently numerous to make them accept prices as given. The proposition then says that if the given prices are compatible with the technology—without that a nontrivial equilibrium is not possible—if the prices of desired commodities are positive, if processes that yield a negative profit are not used, and if processes that break even are employed at levels that together make up an attainable bundle of activities, then this bundle is also an efficient one. The proposition exhibits the logical and mathematical basis for the classical belief in the efficiency of a competitive organization of production in a technology with constant returns to scale in each method of production. It shows that this belief can be documented without specifying the purposes of production in any greater detail than the mere listing of desired commodities.

At the same time Proposition 6 sheds light on what one might call the geometrical relations between the price system and the technological data under efficient allocation. As suggested by Figure 3.9, if the price system is represented by a (hyper-)plane L through the origin, this plane contains all halflines representing basic processes in use—(a^1) and (a^2) in Figure 3.9—and either contains or has to the unprofitable side of it the halflines representing all processes in the technology—such as (a^3), (a^4), (a^5) in Figure 3.9. One can thus conceive of the price system of perfect competition as represented by a supporting plane (see page 17) of the producible set, where in the present model the latter has the form of a convex poly-hedral cone. In particular, the supporting plane and the cone have in common both the origin and the net output point y that results from an efficient bundle of activities. This geometrical image of the relations be-tween prices and technology is useful, for instance, in discussing the interaction of prices and technological progress, where the latter is represented by the addition of new halflines to the basis of the cone.[1]

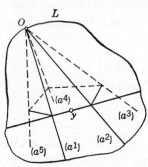

FIGURE 3.9. Relations between the price system and the technol-ogy under efficient allocation.

3.9   THE PRICE IMPLICATIONS OF EFFICIENCY

We now proceed to the translation of Proposition 5 of Section 2 (page 50). The following formulation includes a slight strengthening of the statement, to which we return below.

PROPOSITION 7. In the linear activity analysis model (defined by Postulates 6–10) there is associated with each efficient bundle of activities at least one system of prices compatible with the tech-nology, such that every activity in that bundle breaks even, such that desired commodity prices are positive and such that the price of a primary commodity is nonnegative, zero, or nonpositive, ac-cording as its available supply is fully used, partly used, or not used at all, respectively.

In this proposition, as in its prototype (Proposition 5), no prices are assumed given, nor is a market organization presupposed. The proposi-

[1] See, for instance, Herbert A. Simon, "Effect of Technological Change in a Linear Model," chap. XV (pp. 260–277) of *Activity Analysis* . . . .

tion merely states that any efficient bundle of activities, no matter how achieved or even if merely imagined, implies the possibility of a price system that bears the same relation to the technology and to the processes used as would exist in a competitive market organization, or in any other form of price-guided allocation based on Proposition 6. Hence Proposition 7 assures us that, under the technological conditions assumed, the method of price-guided allocation envisaged by Proposition 6 does not preclude any efficient modes of production. Efficiency implies prices, and any efficient state or program can be sustained by suitable prices. Where markets on which such prices can establish themselves are lacking, these prices can be determined by computation from the technological data characterizing processes in existence and processes in use. We shall discuss some applications of Propositions 6 and 7 along these lines in Section 3.12 below.

The slight strengthening referred to above consists in omitting a qualification which complicated Proposition 5. The exclusion of a state where some "consumer" is at the "minimum for subsistence" was dropped. This qualification is made unnecessary by the polyhedral character of the producible, consumable, and resource sets now under discussion. It may be worthwhile to indicate the reasoning that leads to this conclusion, because it gives the flavor of the type of reasoning specific to linear activity analysis. The reader who wishes to examine this argument will observe, however, that up to the point where a stronger separation theorem is invoked, the reasoning merely translates the general argument of Section 2 in terms of the present choices of production, consumption, and resource sets.

As suggested by Figure 3.9, one could determine the price system implied in an efficient bundle of activities from a (hyper-)plane through the origin which is a supporting plane to the cone representing the producible set.[1] However, we shall employ an equivalent construction which is more in keeping with the present derivation of the propositions of activity analysis as specializations of those of the theory of competitive equilibrium. We shall find the price system from another plane parallel to the one just mentioned which is a supporting plane to the (aggregate) supply set W, the sum of the producible set Y and the resource set Z. While our reasoning will be general, we shall illustrate it by the example of Figure 3.10, derived from that of Figure 3.6 by

---

[1] This procedure was followed in chap. III of *Activity Analysis* . . . .

adding to the technology another basic process (a^2) which is obviously inferior to the process (a^1) already there. The producible set Y is now the angle spanned by the halflines (a^1) and (a^2). The consumable and resource sets X and Z, respectively, are the same as before. The supply set $W = Y + Z$ is the shaded area indefinitely extended. Obviously, the efficient net output point e, and the fact that there is only one such point, is not affected by the addition of an inferior process (a^2). We therefore now let the producible point y in Figure 3.6 coincide with the point e.

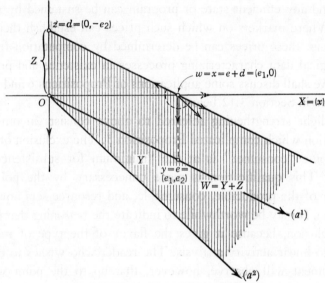

FIGURE 3.10. The price implications of efficiency.

Returning to the general reasoning, the efficiency of a given bundle of activities implies its attainability. This in turn implies that the producible point $y = e$ resulting from this bundle of activities is the difference $y = x - z$ of two points, one $x = e + d$ in the consumable set X and one $z = d$ in the resource set Z. Differently but equivalently expressed, the point w of the supply set W defined by $w = y + z$ coincides with a point x of the consumable set X. We take w as a starting point and enumerate all directions of travel along a straight line in the commodity space which lead from w to some other point $\overline{w}$ of the supply set (without regard to whether $\overline{w}$ is also consumable). We must include the directions of all halflines representing processes that are present in the given efficient bundle of activities—(a^1) in Figure 3.10—as well as the negatives of these directions, because the activity level of a process in use can be increased as well as decreased. We must further include the directions of all halflines of basic processes in the technology not present in the given bundle—(a^2) in Figure 3.10—but not their negatives, because the activity levels of such processes are zero to begin with and can therefore only be increased, not decreased. Of all primary commodities used to some extent —labor in Fig. 3.10—the amount used can be decreased, of all those not fully used—the case does not occur in Figure 3.10—the amount can be increased. This leads to the inclusion of the directions of the negative and/or positive coordinate axes corresponding to the primary commodities in each of these categories, as implied in the given point y. Now all of the directions of change enumerated can be used in combination, with any nonnegative weights. Hence all directions of travel out of w in which one does not immediately leave the supply set W fill a convex polyhedral cone spanned by the halflines enumerated, to be called the *differential supply cone in w*. (In Figure 3.10 this is the halfplane spanned by the halflines with w as common vertex that are designated by solid arrows.)

Remembering that w coincides with a point x of the consumable set, we next enumerate all directions of travel out of x that lead to points $\bar{x}$ of the better-than-x set. Obviously, these are the directions of all positive coordinate axes corresponding to desired commodities—the single food axis in Figure 3.7 designated by a dotted arrow—and all other halflines of the cone spanned thereby, to be called the *desired cone in x*.

The efficiency of the given bundle of activities now signifies that the better-than-x set and the differential supply cone in $w = x$ have no point in common. Looking at all points of these two sets with our eye placed at $w = x$, this can be translated into the equivalent statement that the differential supply cone in w and the desired cone in x, which have a common vertex[1] $w = x$, have no halfline in common.[2] The conclusion of Proposition 7 can now be obtained from the following separation theorem for convex polyhedral cones.

THEOREM III.4. *If of two convex polyhedral cones C and D which have a common vertex but no common halfline one (D) does not contain an*

---

[1] The above discussion is somewhat inaccurate in that terminology appropriate to cones with the vertex in the origin—such as a cone being "spanned" by certain halflines—is applied to cones with a different vertex. A mathematically correct discussion would therefore look on the differential supply cone and the desired cone as sets in a different space, obtained from that at hand by selecting a new origin in the point $w = x$.

[2] If these two cones had only one point besides the vertex in common, they would, as cones, have an entire halfline in common. These cones can therefore be looked upon as scanning devices that will register any opportunity for improvement, whether "near to" or "far from" the point of departure, by exhibiting a common halfline.

entire line, then there is a plane L separating C and D, such that L contains no point of D other than its vertex.[1]

This theorem is illustrated in two dimensions by Figure 3.11. In our application the cone D is the desired cone in x, spanned by halflines parallel to the positive coordinate axes for desired commodities. Since L intersects D in the point $w = x$ only, the price system defined by L can be chosen so as to exhibit a positive price on each desired commodity. By similar reasoning applied to the special form of the other cone C, in our case the differential supply cone in w, we find that L must contain all those halflines which are represented in the basis of C together with their negatives, and must either contain or have to the side other than that containing D all halflines present in the basis of C without their negatives. It follows that the price system in question is compatible with the technology, makes processes represented in the given bundle of activities break even,

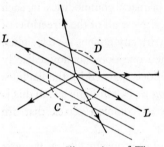

FIGURE 3.11. Illustration of Theorem III.4 in two dimensions.

and finally also satisfies the statements about primary commodity prices[2] made in Proposition 7, which is thereby established.

3.10 THE EXISTENCE OF AN EFFICIENT BUNDLE OF ACTIVITIES

The question as to the existence of at least one efficient bundle of activities in which some desired commodity is produced in a positive amount has been left aside until now. It can be answered on the basis of the two postulates so far unused, (11) of the impossibility of outputs without inputs and (12) of the possibility of production of at least one desired commodity. The reasoning may be briefly sketched.

Postulate 11 says that the producible cone Y has no halfline in common with the nonnegative orthant P, say, of the commodity space. It follows from

---

[1] A proof can be derived from Theorem 12, clauses (1e) and (2) and Theorems 13 and 1 of M. Gerstenhaber, "Theory of Convex Polyhedral Cones," chap. XVIII (pp. 298–316) of *Activity Analysis* . . . . In particular, if neither C nor D contains a line, the proof implies that L can be chosen as so to intersect either cone only in the origin. The statement of the theorem is also valid for closed nonpolyhedral cones.

[2] In *Activity Analysis* . . . , chap. III, a conclusion of nonnegativity of primary commodity prices was obtained from what amounts to a free disposal assumption for primary commodities, implied in the fact that (in equation 5.2, page 79) positive net outputs of these commodities were permitted. No such assumption was made in the present context.

Theorem III.4 that there exists a plane separating Y and P, which defines a system of positive prices for *all* commodities such that no process in the technology is profitable.[1] At those prices, the value of any producible point is nonpositive.

Consider next what happens if we add to Y the resource set Z to form the supply set $W = Y + Z$. Every point z of the resource set, other than the origin, has a positive value in the price system under consideration. It follows that the highest value attainable in Z is attained in the point in which the amount of each primary commodity equals the upper bound of its availability. Call this value v. Since no point of Y has a positive value, no point of the supply set $W = Y + Z$ has a value exceeding v.

Postulate 12 says that there is at least one point x_o (besides the origin) in the intersection of the supply set W with the consumable set X (the nonnegative orthant in the subspace of desired commodities only). Since every commodity has a positive price, the point x_o has a positive value. The intersection of W and X, i.e., the attainable set A, is bounded because the value of its points is bounded from above by v, whereas all prices underlying the valuation are positive, all quantities in X nonnegative. As an intersection of closed sets, it is also closed. Hence by Theorem II (page 15) it contains a point w of maximum value. Since the value of w is at least that of x_o, it is positive, hence w is not the origin. Any further increase in one desirable commodity coordinate of w within the attainable set A without a decrease in another would raise the value further, because all coordinates of primary and intermediate commodities are zero in A. Hence no such changes are possible within the attainable set, and therefore w is the result of an efficient bundle of activities.

3.11   THE EFFICIENT POINT SET, THE PRODUCTION FUNCTION, AND MARGINAL RATES OF SUBSTITUTION

The net output point y resulting from an efficient bundle of activities will be called an *efficient point*. In general, there will be more than one efficient point, and different efficient points may be associated with different systems of prices of desired commodities. If the technology is sufficiently rich in processes that offer substitution possibilities, one may be able, within a certain range, to specify all desired commodity outputs but one, and find an efficient point at the maximum output of the remaining one compatible with the already specified outputs and the resource limitations. If this maximum output is then in addition con-

---

[1] Since there may be no process that breaks even, this price system is not necessarily compatible with the technology.

sidered as a function of the available amounts of primary commodities, one has returned to the concept of a production function or transformation function described at the beginning of this Section 3. The linear activity analysis model thus is a means of deriving both the domain of definition and the form of the production function from more basic technological information. Because of the finiteness of the technological basis the graph of the production function is put together from "flat" linear pieces known as *facets*. Each facet is made up of efficient points obtainable from the same combination of processes, and differing from each other in the activity levels only. Substitution of inputs or outputs within one facet therefore takes the form of simultaneous changes in the activity levels of two or more processes, so coordinated as not to affect the net outputs of commodities not involved in the substitution. If a facet has the number $l + p - 1$ of dimensions required to make up a flat piece of the production function, constant rates of substitution (in efficient production) between all pairs of commodities (inputs, or outputs, or one of each) are uniquely determined by the facet, and are applicable to all substitutions possible within that facet. Each of these rates of substitution equals the price ratio, for the pair of commodities in question, associated by Proposition 7 with any point of the facet. However, points on the "edges" of a facet, which are points common to more than one facet, possess infinitely many associated price systems, including those specific to the facets they help join. Finally, if the net output of one commodity is being increased through a decrease in that of another commodity (all other net outputs being held constant), any change in the marginal rate of substitution can occur only at a point where two or more facets join, and then occurs discontinuously, the change being necessarily such as to raise the price of the commodity whose net output is being increased relative to that of the commodity whose net output is being decreased. This is a consequence of the convexity of the producible set, which in turn arises from the proportionality and additivity postulates of the technology.[1]

However, if the number of processes is too small, or if the set of processes is otherwise degenerate either through linear dependence or through inferiority of some processes under all conceivable price systems, the efficient point set may shrink to a configuration of facets of

[1] See *Activity Analysis* . . . , chap. III, secs. 4.5–4.10.

lesser dimensionality, or even to a single point. In this case there is no production function in the usual sense of the term, but the concept of the efficient point set considered as dependent on resource availabilities remains at hand to take its place.

If Postulate 8 is generalized to permit an infinite number of activities, one can define models that lead to the production functions with continuous derivatives throughout their domain that have been postulated in most economic literature.[1] In this case, the price ratios are uniquely determined in all points in the interior of that domain, and are equal to the marginal rates of substitution applicable to infinitesimally small changes in net outputs. Thus, the price system associated with an efficient point likewise represents the more general concept, which can serve to determine marginal rates of substitution whenever the latter are definable, but which remains available as an instrument of decentralization of decisions even if marginal rates of substitution do not exist, or depend on the directions of net output change considered.

3.12 THE DESCRIPTION OF PRODUCTION IN A MODEL OF GENERAL EQUILIBRIUM

We have obtained the propositions of linear activity analysis by specifying special types of "dummy" consumers, producers, and resource holders in the general model of competitive equilibrium of Section 2. We can now turn around and reinsert the model of activity analysis as a description of the supply side of the economy in a genuine model of competitive equilibrium. The simplest way to achieve this is, as our characters are reconverted from dummies to live actors, to leave the choice sets of producers and resource holders unchanged, and to change only the characterization of each consumer into a convex preference ordering on a consumption set in the space of desired commodities. In this case, all Pareto optima in which there exists for each desired commodity at least one consumer not saturated with it would be efficient points, located on the graph of the transformation function if there is one.

An increase in realism would be obtained if, on the one hand, the same process would be used by many producers and, on the other hand, in-

---

[1] Because of the proportionality postulate (10), these functions would still be homogeneous of degree one.

dividual producers were regarded as capable of operating several processes side by side. A further improvement would be obtained if the use of some processes were regarded as inseparable from the ownership of related entrepreneurial resources.

Within the premises of the model of competitive equilibrium, such rearrangements of the choice sets of the market personnel would have no effect on the character or the Pareto optimality of the equilibrium described. However, they would give a better starting point for the recognition of additional facts of economic life, such as indivisibilities of physical or entrepreneurial resources, incomplete information about the future, the effect of location, and other sources of imperfect competition.

In order that the term "activity analysis" not be precluded from the development of more realistic models of the structure of production, the adjective "linear" is used where needed for emphasis in referring to the model described in this Section 3.

3.13 LINEAR PROGRAMMING

The postulates specifying that the numbers of commodities and of processes are finite have hitherto seemed a somewhat arbitrary limitation of the model. They become a definite advantage, however, in those practical applications where one desires to compute efficient bundles of activities from numerically given basic processes and resource limitations. In a finite linear activity analysis model, one can in principle compute and describe the entire efficient point set (the production function if there is one) by enumeration of all the vertices of all the facets of which it is composed. However, only for models with small numbers of commodities and activities would such a computation be both feasible with existing equipment and of value to a user.

Somewhat larger models can be computed through if only a single desired commodity is present. In this case the problem of finding an efficient bundle of activities reduces to that of maximizing the output of that one commodity under given availability limits of primary inputs. Problems of this type are called *linear programming* problems.[1] The de-

---

[1] We recall that mathematically, a linear programming problem is defined as the maximization of a linear function of variables restrained by linear inequalities. In the case mentioned, the function to be maximized is the output of the desired commodity as a function of the activity levels selected for all processes in the technology. The restraints on these activity

termination of imputed prices[1] for intermediate and primary commodities associated with a solution of a linear programming problem is called (for geometrical reasons) its dual problem.[2]

One rarely finds applications of linear programming in which the one desired commodity is actually a physical commodity. However, there is an important class of applications to the firm which sells its outputs and possibly buys some of its inputs under conditions of perfect competition, that is, at prices that do not depend on the amounts of its sales or purchases. In such cases all traded commodities can be turned into intermediate commodities by introducing sale and purchase processes. The defining activity of a sale process has one unit of the commodity to be sold as its only input, money as its sole output, with the given price as the output coefficient. Purchase processes are defined correspondingly, with money as the sole input. In the so modified model the search for an efficient bundle of activities becomes the determination of a profit-maximizing production, purchase, and sales program subject to availability limitations on not traded and not readily expanded primary resources, such as the services of plant and equipment.

An extremely lucid exposition in diagrammatic terms of this problem has been given by Dorfman,[3] using as his example a firm producing both automobiles and trucks under four different capacity limitations. His exposition covers also the imputation of prices to the scarce primary resources (capacities) which are not traded. In this connection, a point may be raised which concerns the emphasis rather than the substance of his observations. Professor Dorfman places considerable emphasis on the following consequence of the mathematical symmetry between a linear programming problem and its dual: Just as a solution of a linear

---

levels are those expressing their nonnegativeness, the availability limits on primary commodities, and the zero-net-output requirement for intermediate commodities ("$y_k = 0$" can be written as "$y_k \geqq 0$ and $y_k \leqq 0$").

[1] Also known as shadow, accounting, implicit, intrinsic, or efficiency prices.

[2] For a mathematical discussion of the symmetry of a linear programming problem and its dual, see Gale, Kuhn, and Tucker, "Linear Programming and the Theory of Games," chap. XIX (pp. 317–329) of *Activity Analysis* . . . .

[3] Robert Dorfman, "Mathematical, or 'Linear,' Programming: A Nonmathematical Exposition," *American Economic Review*, vol. XLIII, December 1953, pp. 797–825. See also, by the same author, *Application of Linear Programming to the Theory of the Firm*, University of California Press, Berkeley, Calif., 1951, where nonlinear problems arising from imperfect competition are also considered.

programming problem indicates activity levels that maximize the output of the desired commodity under given availability restraints on primary commodities, so a solution of its dual problem indicates imputed prices that minimize the total imputed value of the available primary commodities (expressed in units of the one desired commodity) under the restraint that no process in the technology shall be profitable. This proposition is basic to the mathematical structure of linear programming (and *mutatis mutandis* of activity analysis). It is also important through the computational savings it may make possible even if all one wants to do is to solve the given linear programming problem.[1] However, it does not convey the full motivation for taking an interest in the imputed prices. Why should an entrepreneur attach any particular importance to minimizing the imputed value of his nontraded primary resources? And if for some reason he did, why should he accept the nonprofitability of every process as a restraint?

It would seem that the mathematical symmetry of the two problems does not carry over to the economic interpretation and motivation. The prime importance of the imputed prices associated with an efficient bundle of activities appears to reside in the two properties of lending zero profitability to all processes represented in that bundle and of not permitting positive profitability of any process in the technology. Through these two properties the imputed prices provide criteria for decisions as to what processes are to be used. These criteria can also tentatively be applied to processes not represented in the technology from which the imputed prices were computed. Processes unprofitable under these prices are unworthy claimants for the scarce capacities in question.[2] Processes that break even are acceptable alternatives in combination with or as substitutes for those already in use. Processes that are profitable call for recomputation of the original linear programming problem with a technology to which they have been added. Such a recomputation will lead to revision of the imputed prices and in general also to incorporation of the processes found profitable at the old prices

---

[1] See Dorfman, *op. cit.*, p. 818.

[2] Or, at best, no better claimants. They can be equally acceptable if the conditions from which the imputed prices are computed leave some degree of indeterminacy that was resolved by arbitrary choice.

in the new efficient bundle of activities.[1] In this way, the firm solves its internal allocation problems by computation procedures that imitate the action of a competitive market with regard to resources not actually traded. It is for reasons of this order that in Propositions 6 and 7 (pages 87 and 88) we have presented the basic results of activity analysis in a form in which the mathematical symmetry in the relations of quantities and prices is allowed to be somewhat obscured in order that the economic relevance of the propositions may stand out more clearly.

Returning now to our discussion of linear programming problems in general, it should be said that our identification of the maximand with a single desired commodity introduces only one class of applications of linear programming. Another mathematically equivalent class arises with the position of primary and desired commodities interchanged. In problems of this class a specified bundle of desired commodities is to be provided at minimum cost in terms of money or some other single controlling primary commodity. Stigler's problem of the minimum-cost diet, already referred to above,[2] is a prototype of this class. Required amounts of various nutrients are prescribed, and the money cost of a bundle of foods securing these nutrients is to be minimized. Stigler's somewhat whimsical study of human diets along these lines has been followed by several more practical studies of minimum-cost feed mixes for animals.[3] Another problem in this class is that of carrying out a given transportation program at a minimum total freight bill or a minimum commitment of transportation equipment,[4] which has found a large number of applications.[5] In these problems imputed prices, besides

---

[1] For further remarks along these lines see T. C. Koopmans, "Uses of Prices," in *Proceedings of the Conference on Production and Inventory Control*, Case Institute of Technology, Cleveland, Ohio, 1954.

[2] See footnote 1 on page 67.

[3] Frederick V. Waugh, "The Minimum Cost Dairy Feed," *Journal of Farm Economics*, August 1951, pp. 299–310.

W. D. Fisher and L. W. Schruben, "Linear Programming applied to Feed Mixing under Different Price Conditions," *Journal of Farm Economics*, November 1953, pp. 478–483.

[4] See the studies by Hitchcock, Kantorovitch, and Koopmans, cited in footnotes 1 and 4 on page 67 and footnote 3 on page 68; and Tjalling C. Koopmans and Stanley Reiter, "A Model of Transportation," chap. XIV (pp. 222–259) of *Activity Analysis* . . . .

[5] E.g., Merrill M. Flood, "Application of Transportation Theory to Scheduling a Military Tanker Fleet," *Journal of the Operations Research Society of America*, vol. 2, May 1954, pp. 150–162.

providing criteria for the use of processes, also (when determinate) serve to measure the resource cost of the unit of each of the transportation flows stipulated by the program. The imputed prices thus allow those who have set the program to reconsider and revise it in the light of the unit cost of each of its constituents, revealed by the computation.

There are many allocation problems involving multiple objectives for which no market valuations exist to establish comparability, while at the same time several scarce primary resources are required to serve these objectives. Problems of this kind arise particularly in connection with governmental tasks, such as resource development, municipal services, or national defense. Two devices, which in a sense are opposites, can be used singly or in combination to facilitate computational exploration of such problems by linear programming methods. One of these consists in arbitrarily establishing comparability of desired commodities by the adoption of tentative equivalence ratios based on judgment. This is tantamount to declaring at what relative prices the policy maker will trade one desired commodity (or purpose attainment) for another, no matter what net output bundle results from the trade, if only it frees some resources for a further increase in some output. The tentative equivalence ratios can then be revised by trial and error if they seem out of kilter with the particular net outputs resulting from an "efficient" bundle of activities computed on the basis of these ratios.

An opposite device consists in defining a single desired commodity, the unit of which is a tentatively specified bundle of the various commodities wanted. The latter commodities are thereby individually demoted to the category of intermediate commodities. This procedure is tantamount to declaring that the various commodities are wanted only in definite fixed proportions, irrespective of their individual imputed prices (resource costs). Again, the proportions specified can be revised in the light of the imputed prices obtained. It goes without saying that only explorations of the problems in question are achieved by these two devices.

The computation method most fully developed and used so far for linear programming problems is Dantzig's *simplex method*.[1] This method

---

[1] George B. Dantzig, "Maximization of a Linear Function of Variables Subject to Linear Inequalities," and "Application of the Simplex Method to a Transportation Problem," chaps. XXI and XXIII of "*Activity Analysis . . . .*" For a more recent improvement see

operates through continual revision of a tentative attainable bundle of activities selected from a set of processes, appropriate in number, called its *basis*. The method is closely related to the idea of imputed pricing of commodities. At every step tentative prices are computed from the requirement of zero profitability of processes in the basis. Thereupon another process profitable at those prices is added to the basis, one that breaks even is dropped, and new prices associated with the new basis are computed.[1] The method comes to a stop when at the prices associated with the basis then under examination no profitable process remains in the technology. By Proposition 6 an efficient bundle of activities, in the present context a point of maximum output of the single desired commodity, has then been reached.

3.14   INPUT-OUTPUT ANALYSIS

Another specialization of the model of activity analysis yields the model adopted by Professor Leontief,[2] long before the development of linear programming and activity analysis, as a framework of hypotheses for the empirical study of quantitative relationships between output levels in various industries. In the present context, we shall consider only the mathematical structure of this model in relation to other models here considered. In the last essay of this volume (Section 5 on page 187) we shall consider the model's suitability for predicting or describing the relations between industrial outputs. Our observations will in both cases be confined to the so-called *open* input-output model.

The desired commodities have the central position in this model. Each desired commodity (in empirical application identified with the output of one industry) can be produced by one process only, which has that commodity as its sole output, and other desired and possibly pri-

---

G. B. Dantzig and W. Orchard Hays, "The Product Form for the Inverse in the Simplex Method," *Mathematical Tables and Other Aids to Computation*, vol. 8, no. 46, April 1954, pp. 64–67.

[1] Actually Dantzig uses an algorithm in which the prices at each stage are not explicitly computed, but in which the profitabilities of processes not in the basis are obtained directly from the coefficients of the processes in the basis. The above description may better convey the essence of the method to the economist.

[2] Wassily W. Leontief, *The Structure of American Economy*, 1919–39, 2d ed., Oxford University Press, New York, 1951. Leontief and others, *Studies in the Structure of the American Economy*, Oxford University Press, New York, 1953.

mary commodities as its inputs. There are no intermediate commodities in our sense. The postulates of additivity and proportionality are adopted for all processes.

In applications to the problems of an underemployed economy with excess capacity and unemployed labor in all industries, limitations on the availability of primary commodities can be disregarded. Hence no such commodities need to be explicitly introduced in the model. In this case no optimization problem arises, and the main problem that has been considered is that of computing total output levels of each industry from specified net output requirements (often called the "bill of goods") for the product of each industry, on the basis of empirically estimated input-output coefficients. The computation involved consists in the solution of a system of linear equations of which the total industry output levels are the unknowns, the input-output coefficients form the square matrix of coefficients, and the given bill of goods supplies the right-hand members.

It is not a priori certain that any given bill of goods can be produced by such a model, even if one disregards primary commodity requirements. Obviously, by inserting sufficiently high input requirements per unit of output of each industry one can construct a model which does not permit any positive rates of net output. A condition similar to our Postulate 13 therefore needs to be imposed. Such a condition was made specific (in terms of determinants constructed from input-output coefficients) by Hawkins and Simon,[1] and further sharpened by Georgescu-Roegen.[2] These authors also proved that, if an input-output model is capable of producing some bill of goods with positive ratios between the net outputs of all desired goods, then it is capable of producing bills of goods with any positive ratios between the net outputs of these goods that one may specify. The underlying reason is suggested by Figure 3.12 for the case of two industries. Since only desired commodity coordinates are shown, the two processes are represented by halflines in the second and fourth quadrant, respectively. The cone spanned by

[1] David Hawkins and Herbert A. Simon, "Some Conditions of Macroeconomic Stability," *Econometrica*, vol. 17, July–October 1949, pp. 245–248.

[2] Nicholas Georgescu-Roegen, "Some Properties of a Generalized Leontief Model," chap. X (pp. 165–176) of *Activity Analysis* . . . . Also, "Leontief's System in the Light of Recent Results," *Review of Economics and Statistics*, vol. 32, 1950, pp. 214–222.

these two halflines either does not contain any point interior to the first (the positive) quadrant (cases A and B), or else it contains all such points (case C).

The geometrical configuration that leads to this result has other interesting consequences when one single primary commodity is introduced, for instance universal labor, which is required to some extent for every process in the technology. In this case a simple optimization is involved, which is achieved by requiring that all available labor be used.

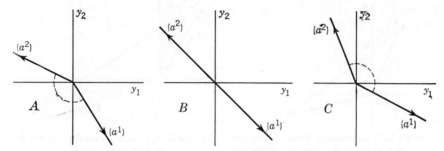

FIGURE 3.12. Possibility (C) and impossibility (A, B) of production in an input-output model for two industries.

The remaining quantitative problem is that of characterizing the efficient point set, in this case the set of all points in the space of desired commodities that represent nonnegative outputs producible by using all the available labor. For this problem it is convenient to define the unit activity of each process in such a way as to absorb the entire available amount of labor. Any bundle of activities that absorbs this same amount then is a weighted average of these unit activities. As Figure 3.13 suggests, the efficient point set is that part of one single (hyper-) plane that falls within the nonnegative orthant (the segment $\overline{bc}$ in Figure 3.13). Thus, all marginal rates of substitution between desired commodities and the one primary commodity are constant no matter what the bill of goods is. We have here a one-factor (for instance, a labor) theory of value. Relative prices reflect only the amounts of the universal primary factor absorbed in one unit of each commodity, and are therefore independent of the composition of demand.

A further proposition is suggested by Figure 3.14. If each industry commands several processes, each of which still has the desired commodity specific to that industry as its sole output, and if only one scarce primary commodity exists in the economy considered, then one can select one preferred process from among those available to each industry (e.g., a^1 and a^2 in Figure 3.14) in such a way that all efficient points can be reached by combining only preferred processes. This was first perceived independently by Samuelson[1] and by Georgescu-Roegen.[1]

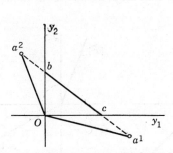

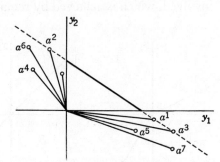

FIGURE 3.13. Input-output model for two industries with one scarce primary commodity.   FIGURE 3.14. Case of several processes for each of two industries.

Proofs using the set-theoretical tools that seem most appropriate to the problem were contributed by the latter, by Koopmans and by Arrow.[2] The implication of the proposition is that, if the output of each industry can be treated as a homogeneous commodity, and if labor (say) is the only scarce primary commodity, then perfect competition will enforce (or in any case permit[3]) uniformity in the technology of each industry provided no joint production processes are available to any industry.

This conclusion cannot be drawn when joint production processes are available, or when more than one scarce primary commodity exists.[4]

[1] Paul A. Samuelson, "Abstract of a Theorem Concerning Substitutability in Open Leontief Models," chap. VII (pp. 142–146) of *Activity Analysis* . . . , and Nicholas Georgescu-Roegen, see the references in footnote 2 on page 102.

[2] Tjalling C. Koopmans, "Alternative Proof of the Substitution Theorem for Leontief Models in the Case of Three Industries," and Kenneth J. Arrow, "Alternative Proof of the Substitution Theorem for Leontief Models in the General Case," chaps. VIII (pp. 147–154) and IX (pp. 155–164) of *Activity Analysis* . . . .

[3] It is possible for two different processes to coexist in an industry, but only if each of them is equally suitable as the representative of that industry. This possibility is illustrated by points a^1 and a^3 in Figure 3.14.

[4] See Tjalling C. Koopmans, "Maximization and Substitution in Linear Models of Production," in *Input-Output Relations, Proceedings of a Conference*, Stenfert-Kroese, Leiden, 1953.

4. PRODUCTION OVER TIME; CAPITAL AND INTEREST

4.1 THE TIME DIMENSION

We have already seen that the logical connections between competitive equilibrium and Pareto optimality discussed in Section 2 are equally valid for models relating to a finite number of successive future time periods, in which the same physical commodity available at different time periods is treated as that many different commodities.[1] The same observation applies of course to models concerned only with productive efficiency, such as those discussed in Section 3.

The most obvious limitation of this interpretation of our models arises from the assumption of complete information about future technology and, where relevant, about future preferences. It might therefore seem as if there is little point in a further discussion of this interpretation that is not directed at overcoming that obvious limitation. However, there are still a few points on which further clarification can be achieved before that big step is taken. One of these concerns the choice of the length of the horizon for which plans are assumed to be made. The second concerns the question how the concepts of capital and interest that have evolved in business practice with regard to allocation over time fit in with the concept of prices associated with efficient allocation that we have emphasized so far. Finally, the notion of a stationary state (with or without capital saturation), which has been discussed off and on in the literature, also receives further clarification in the light of our model.

Progress in these various directions has been made in a fundamental study by Edmond Malinvaud,[2] which we shall follow in broad outline, though not in precise detail. Malinvaud's study in turn rests on the developments reported in Sections 2 and 3 and on the extensive literature of capital theory quoted in his article.

4.2 THE END OF THE HORIZON

We begin our discussion of the first point with a remark about the commodities available at the beginning of the first period. These are

[1] See Section 2.6 (page 60) above.
[2] "Capital Accumulation and Efficient Allocation of Resources," *Econometrica*, April 1953, pp. 233–268, hereafter quoted as "Capital Accumulation. . . ."

likely to be commodities in various stages of completion, from primary resources through goods in process and capital equipment down to finished goods. However, the question whether this initial bundle of commodities was efficiently chosen is outside the scope of the theory. It is simply there. This is best expressed by treating all commodities available at the beginning of the first period as primary resources, irrespective of their technical state of completion.

More difficult problems arise out of the finiteness of the number of periods in the models so far considered. This limits the flexibility of the models in two respects. In the first place, one may wish for certain purposes to treat time as a continuous variable, expressed by a real number, rather than a discrete variable expressed by an integer. If this were proposed merely as a means of achieving greater realism of description, it would seem to be a point of pedantic purism. In most situations the use of periods of one minute's length could not truthfully be regarded as any less realistic than a continuous treatment of time. However, there is ample precedent in applied mathematics to suggest that often the use of continuous variables, even where the underlying phenomenon is itself measured by an integral multiple of a small unit, can greatly simplify the analysis of many problems.[1]

Malinvaud is not concerned with a continuous time concept, but with another limitation of the model inherent in a finite number of time periods, which is a matter of substance rather than form of analysis. It arises from the fact that there is no sharp point of demarcation in the future beyond which the availability of commodities is no longer of interest to the decision maker.

Let us call the *horizon* of a model the union of all time periods recognized in it. In a model with a horizon of finite length, one can represent the interests of consumers beyond the end of the horizon by attaching desirability to each commodity available at the end of the horizon, irrespective of its technical state of completion. This would form a natural counterpart to the treatment of all commodities at the beginning of the horizon as resources. However, if the model is designed to study joint maximization of satisfaction levels in all periods of the horizon

---

[1] For similar comments, see L. J. Savage, *Foundations of Statistics*, Wiley, New York, 1954, p. 77. Of course, in problems solved by numerical computation, one is likely to revert to a discrete treatment of time for computational purposes.

there is something unsatisfactory in end-of-horizon claimants for maximization that are not themselves satisfaction levels but mere amounts of commodities. The relative weight to be assigned to the maximization of each of the latter depends, whether we admit it or not, on the ability of the commodities involved to contribute to the satisfaction of consumers beyond the horizon. And even in a model that studies only joint maximization of outputs of desired commodities within the horizon, the "desirability" of commodities available at the end of the horizon depends on their convertibility into actually desired commodities beyond the horizon, which in turn depends on the technology available beyond the horizon.

There is therefore an inevitable arbitrariness in models that specify a horizon of a definite length. Malinvaud avoids this by studying models with an infinite horizon. This may be looked upon as a useful idealization in the same way in which differentiability of a production function —a concept involving the infinite in a different way—has proved a useful idealization in another context.

It often happens that by overcoming one objection arising from a concern with realism, another lack of realism is shown up more strongly. It may be felt that it is premature to take cognizance of the indefinite continuation of economic activity while maintaining the assumption that future technology (and possibly preferences) throughout the infinite horizon are known at its beginning. However, analytical difficulties must be taken one by one, and there is no reason to suppose that the recognition of uncertainty will provide an automatic cut-off point to the horizon. It is therefore worthwhile to make the first study of an indefinitely extended horizon on the simpler basis of a model that presupposes complete certainty about the future.

4.3 A MODEL WITH AN INFINITE HORIZON

We shall now describe that part of Malinvaud's study that analyzes productive efficiency over time in terms of quantities of commodities withdrawable for consumption, rather than the satisfaction levels thereby attained or attainable. In order to concentrate on the new difficulties to be considered, we shall also accept his simplifying specifications that all commodities be regarded as desired at all times, and that all commodities can occur in nature. The distinctions between primary, intermediate and desired commodities are thus removed from the analysis.

The model then specifies a convex production set Y^t for each future time period ($t = 1, 2, \ldots$ ad inf.), representing the range of production possibilities that will exist at that time. This is an aggregate production set in the sense that it represents the production possibilities of the entire economy in one period. It is a disaggregated set in the sense that it refers to only one out of infinitely many future periods. This particular decomposition of the "all-over" aggregate production set,

$Y = \sum_{t=1}^{\infty} Y^t$, in the infinite-dimensional commodity space is adopted because we are interested primarily in the time structure of allocation and pricing problems. For a more realistic discussion of decentralization of decisions through the market, one would wish to recognize production sets that correspond to small parts of the technology but may extend over a number of successive periods.

Each production set Y^t is a set of ordered pairs $(-a^t, b^{t+1})$ of commodity bundles.[1] Here a^t represents inputs to, and b^{t+1} outputs of, the production possibility described by the pair. Among the inputs a^t are commodities produced but not consumed in earlier periods (capital in the narrow sense of the term) to be available at the beginning of the tth period for use in production. The remaining inputs are labor services and flows of natural resources, both of which may be regarded as flowing into production at an even rate during the tth period. The outputs b^{t+1} consist of commodities that will become available at the end of the tth [the beginning of the $(t + 1)$st] period, for use in either production or consumption in subsequent periods. This notion of a production set Y^t implies that the technology to be available in the tth period is fully known, but not necessarily available, in the first period.

The bundle b^1 of resources available at the beginning of the first period is regarded as given in advance. It can be thought of as including exhaustible natural resources, such as mineral deposits. Likewise the bundle z^t of self-renewing natural resources, such as water power or the

---

[1] More precisely, Y^t is a subset of the subspace of the commodity space relating to the periods t and $t + 1$ only. The minus sign in $-a^t$ reconciles our rule to express inputs by negative numbers with Malinvaud's notation a^t for the vector of absolute amounts of inputs.

services of land, to be available in each future period, are assumed known in advance. In fact, it will be convenient to treat the available resources b^1, z^t as not merely available but actually flowing into production. This is done by regarding continued underground storage of exhaustible resources, as well as nonuse of self-renewing resources, as possible forms of "production" allowed for in the production sets Y^t. On this basis, the bundle x^t available for "consumption" in the tth period is obtained from

$$x^t = b^t + z^t - a^t$$

by adding the bundle b^t handed down from production in the preceding period to the resources bundle z^t of the tth period and subtracting the bundle a^t of inputs to production (other than labor) during that period. Labor services are then represented by negative components of the bundle x^t.

4.4 RELATIONS BETWEEN EFFICIENT PROGRAMS AND ASSOCIATED PRICES

Let us call an *attainable* (production and consumption) *program* a statement of pairs of input and output bundles $(-a^t, b^{t+1})$ for all periods of the horizon, each within the appropriate production set Y^t, and a statement of all consumption bundles x^t obtained therefrom by the above formula,[1] given the resources bundles z^t and the initial availability bundle b^1. Let us call an attainable program *efficient* if there exists no attainable program (i.e., utilizing the same initial resources and the same resource flows in all periods of the horizon) which allows at least as much consumption of each commodity in each period and a larger consumption of some commodity in some period—the performance of labor being regarded as negative consumption.

If these definitions were applied to a finite horizon of T periods, say, one would have to include with the "consumption" x^T of the last period

---

[1] Malinvaud places no sign restrictions on the components of x^t. If desired the nonpositive character of the components corresponding to labor inputs can be imposed indirectly through a suitable form of the production sets. A restriction expressing the nonnegative character of consumption of commodities other than labor can be added without difficulty. Alternatively the model can be interpreted as representing an open economy which can "import" commodities from an outside world.

In the absence of additional sign restrictions on the points of Y^t, in spite of appearances to the contrary, Malinvaud's model does not incorporate the observation that in all production inputs must precede outputs. The reason is that what is here called an "input" becomes actually an output through mere change of sign, and conversely.

also the commodity bundle b^{T+1} available at the end of that period. In this case, the present model would be a special case of the model of Section 2, designed to study efficient production over time.[1] In the case of an infinite horizon, additional mathematical investigation is needed to explore the extension to this case of the propositions obtained for finite models.

Without examining the particular method of proof used by Malinvaud,[2] we shall summarize some of his results in two propositions.

PROPOSITION 8. Under the assumptions of the present model, one can associate with each efficient program $(-a^t, b^{t+1})$ a system of nonnegative prices, p_k^t, one for each commodity $k = 1, \ldots, n$, in each period $t = 1, 2, \ldots$ ad inf., such that

(a) the "profit"

$$\sum_{k=1}^{n} p_k^{t+1} b_k^{t+1} - \sum_{k=1}^{n} p_k^t a_k^t$$

computed for the production of each period is the maximum attainable at those prices in the production set Y^t of that period, and

(b) the cost of the inputs (other than labor),

$$\sum_{k=1}^{n} p_k^t a_k^t$$

for each period t is the smallest cost attainable by any input bundle for that period that permits the consumption levels $x_k^{t'}$, $t' \geq t$, of the given efficient program to be reached or exceeded for all commodities in that period and in all subsequent periods.[3]

---

[1] If the production sets Y^t are further specified to be suitable convex polyhedral cones, the model would also be a special case of that of Section 3.

[2] The principle of analysis used is that of first comparing an efficient program with those other attainable programs that differ from it only within the first T periods, and thereafter considering a limiting process whereby T is made indefinitely large. An alternative method would be to work from postulates defining a suitable infinite-dimensional linear space. The latter method is followed by Debreu in "Valuation Equilibrium . . . ." (see footnote 3 on page 39). Debreu's results do not apply without further extension to the present case, because he considers a finite number of producers. His results do apply, however, to a continuous treatment of time, or to a decentralization of decisions over a finite number of decision makers some of whom are planning for an infinite horizon.

[3] "Capital Accumulation . . . ," Theorem I (p. 245), as amplified on p. 247, lines 3–20.

Conversely, we have:

> PROPOSITION 9. If under the assumptions of the present model one can associate with a given attainable program a system of positive prices such that statements (a) and (b) of Propositions 8 are valid, then this program is efficient.[1]

These propositions extend the relationships between efficient modes of production and corresponding price systems to production programs of indefinite duration. It is again found that efficiency implies valuation through an associated system of prices, and that a program sustained by a suitable response to such prices is efficient. A few more remarks may be made as to what a "suitable response" means in the present context.

By giving sufficiently free rein to our imagination we can still visualize condition (a) of Proposition 9 (i.e., statement (a) of Proposition 8) as being satisfied through a decentralization of decisions among an infinite number of producers, each in charge of that part of the program relating to one future period. A further decentralization among many contemporaneous producers within each period can also be visualized.[2] But even at this level of abstraction, it is difficult to see how the task of meeting condition (b) could be pinned down on any particular decision maker. This is a new condition, to which there is no counterpart in the finite models considered in previous sections. The need for it in the present model can be illustrated by a simple example.

Let there be a forever nonperishable and always desired commodity which is storable at no cost, and let there be an efficient program with an associated price system in which the price of this commodity is the same in all future periods. Consider another attainable program which differs from the first one only in that a certain amount of this commodity is withheld from consumption in the first period and is instead put in storage forever. Then, as far as future consumption is concerned, the stored amount could as well have been left in the consumption of the first period. It follows that the program that stores it forever is not efficient. Nevertheless, the price system associated with the efficient program will meet condition (a) equally well in association with the

---

[1] *Ibid.*, Lemma 3, p. 246. As suggested by a comparison with Proposition 4 on page 49, the assertions of this proposition can be proved from weaker assumptions than the convexity of the production sets. It will further be noted that Proposition 9 requires positive prices, while Proposition 8 concludes only to the existence of nonnegative prices. As observed by Malinvaud (page 246, footnote 18), this gap could be closed by limiting the model to polyhedral production sets.

[2] "Capital Accumulation . . . ," Lemmas 4 and 5.

second, inefficient, program. Decentralization of decisions among an infinite sequence of decision makers does not avoid this type of inefficiency, because the responsibility for providing for the use of the stored commodity is always pushed off on the next man in the row! An explicit condition (b) is needed in Proposition 9 to preclude such never ending buck-passing. This loophole in the action of the price system as an allocator of resources arises from the infinite number of decision makers rather than from the infinite horizon. It would not arise if, as suggested by Debreu,[1] planning for an infinite horizon were regarded as carried out by a finite number of decision makers. Since conceptual difficulties arise in both interpretations, it may be well to remind ourselves at this point of the artificiality of studying one aspect of time—its indefinite duration—without another equally essential aspect—incomplete information about the future. It may be conjectured, for instance, that the introduction into the model of a combination of uncertainty about future technology and risk aversion on the part of producers would promptly close off the loophole.

4.5 MARGINAL RATES OF SUBSTITUTION BETWEEN PRESENT AND FUTURE COMMODITIES

The remarks made in section 3.11 about the connections between efficiency prices and marginal rates of substitution remain applicable in the present context. Thus, if the production sets are polyhedral cones of sufficient dimensionality (or more in general if their boundaries can be represented by piece-wise differentiable functions), the ratio p_l^t/p_k^1 of a future price of commodity l to the present price of commodity k whenever uniquely determined indicates a technological rate of exchange between future and present production of the respective commodities. In particular, if the price of gold in the first period is positive, we can adopt one ounce of gold in the first period as the *unit of value* for all periods. This is done by choosing the arbitrary multiplicative factor in all prices p_k^t so as to make

$$p_{\text{gold}}^1 = 1.$$

The prices p_k^t can then be regarded as present values of the unit of each commodity $k = 1, 2, \ldots, n$, available in each period $t = 1, 2, \ldots$, again in the sense of technologically possible marginal rates of substitution.

By forming other ratios of these prices or of linear combinations

[1] See footnote 2 on page 110.

thereof, one can in the same way obtain exchange rates between different commodities in different periods; between specified bundles of commodities in different periods;[1] or between bundles of commodities each of which straddles several periods in a specified manner. On the basis of these rates of exchange alone, one can analyze both the efficiency and the net output effects of any decision—such as an investment or inventory decision—that modifies future consumption within the range of applicability of the exchange rates.

Offhand such a procedure seems most suited for a somewhat paternalistically planned economy in which the relative value to consumers of production-wise equivalent quantities of different goods available at different periods is determined on the basis of planners' judgments. However, there is nothing logically incongruous about a competitive market organization of the economy in which each producer, in the light of information about quantities likely to be produced in the absence of action on his part, estimates such relative values to consumers, for the commodities involved in the processes he contemplates, and for the time periods relevant to his decision. On the basis of such estimates, he could then increase the rate of operation of those processes that by this calculation leave a profit, and abstain from processes that promise losses. The fact of the matter is, nevertheless, that business practice of the "capitalist" economy has developed the seemingly different concepts of capital and interest to deal with calculations of this kind. The question naturally arises where these concepts come in, how they are defined, and what purpose they serve.

More in particular, the economist has distilled from his analysis of this business practice a property, the equality of the marginal productivity of capital to the interest rate, which is regarded both as an implication of profit maximization in competitive markets, and as a criterion of efficient allocation of resources. The relation of this idea to the foregoing analysis demands clarification.

4.6 THE DEFINITION OF INTEREST RATES

The irrelevance-in-principle of the concept of interest to the problem of efficient allocation over time is clearly implied, if not explicitly

---

[1] An example of this case is worked out in Section 4.6 below.

stated, in Lindahl's penetrating exposition of capital theory.[1] That the point has not been generally realized[2] is perhaps due to the difficulty of dissociating a problem from the means of its solution worked out by a monetary economic organization.

Before an interest rate can be defined, it is necessary to define what constitutes repayment of the principal of a loan. This requires defining a separate monetary unit for each future period $t = 1, 2, \ldots$, as distinct from the unit of value already defined for all periods simultaneously. For instance, one may define one ounce of gold available in any future period as the monetary unit specific to that period. (In this case, the monetary unit for the first period would coincide with the already defined unit of value for all periods.) Having made this choice, the money rate of interest, expressed in so much per cent for the duration of one period, but applicable to a time span from the beginning of period 1 to that of period t, say, can be defined as a number[3]

$$r_{\text{gold}}^{1,t}$$

such that,[4]

$$p_{\text{gold}}^1 = (1 + r_{\text{gold}}^{1,t})^{t-1} \, p_{\text{gold}}^t.$$

Supplementing this definition, one can further define, besides the present values p_k^t which from here on we shall call *real prices* (for future delivery), future *money prices* p_k^{*t} by the formula

$$p_k^{*t} = \frac{p_k^t}{p_{\text{gold}}^t},$$

which makes the "money price" of an ounce of gold equal to unity in all

---

[1] Erik R. Lindahl, *Studies in the Theory of Money and Capital*," G. Allen, London, 1939. See in particular Part Three, "The place of capital in the theory of price" (Swedish original published in 1929), chap. III, sects. 2 and 3, especially pp. 327–328, 336, of the 1950 printing.

[2] See also a comment to that effect in P. A. Samuelson, "Foundations . . . ," p. 233, ftn. 30.

[3] This is the rate of a "pure" loan for which at the end of each period interest due is added to the principal, both principal and accumulated compound interest being repaid at the end of the time span of the loan. If the interest rates applicable to the individual periods that make up the time span of the loan are denoted $r^{1,2}, r^{2,3}, \ldots, r^{t-1,t}$, then $(1 + r^{1,t})$ is the geometric average of the quantities $(1 + r^{1,2}), \ldots$ If the quantities $r^{1,2}, \ldots$, differ from each other, $r^{1,t}$ will be slightly different from the rate on the more conventional type of loan on which interest is paid at the end of each period and principal repaid when the loan terminates.

[4] The notation $(x)^{t-1}$ is used to denote x raised to the power $t - 1$ (as distinct from the use of t as a direct superscript to designate a period).

periods. The conventional rules of financial accounting and discounting then apply to the money prices and interest rates so defined.

Let it be said again that, for the analysis of productive efficiency over time, such a superstructure of monetary concepts is not needed, and may indeed introduce misunderstanding. It is only when loans between economic agents are introduced into the analysis that a monetary unit for each future time period needs to be defined. At the same time an element of arbitrary convention is introduced into the analysis. If instead of an ounce of gold one employs a bushel of hard winter wheat No. 2 to define the monetary unit of each period, one will in general obtain a different system of interest rates.[1] One would obtain the same interest rates only in the highly special case in which the real prices of gold and of wheat happened to vary proportionally in all future periods.

4.7   THE MARGINAL PRODUCTIVITY OF CAPITAL

It can now be seen that the equality of the marginal productivity of capital to the rate of interest, which economic analysis has associated with an efficient program, is in no way affected by the arbitrariness of the definition of monetary units for future periods. The reason is that this equality, in its two uses mentioned at the end of Section 4.5, expresses our Propositions 8 and 9 in a monetary disguise.

To be more precise—and hence slightly more technical—let us consider an efficient program $(-a_k^t, b_k^{t+1})$ involving a consumption program

$$x_k^t = b_k^t + z_k^t - a_k^t,$$

and a system of real prices p_k^t associated with this program in accordance with Proposition 8. Consider a second technologically possible program $(-\bar{a}_k^t, \bar{b}_k^{t+1})$ which uses the same initial and current resources, and is such that the corresponding consumption program

$$\bar{x}_k^t = \bar{b}_k^t + z_k^t - \bar{a}_k^t$$

differs from that of the first program only in that in the first period $(t = 1)$ some consumption flows are less than, in the period $t = t'$ some flows are higher than, but in all other periods all flows are equal to, the corresponding flows for the first program. Subtraction of

[1] Lindahl, *op. cit.*, p. 328; Irving Fisher, *The Theory of Interest*, Macmillan, New York, 1930, p. 42; Malinvaud, "Capital Accumulation . . . ," p. 252.

the first above equality from the second gives us, for all commodities and periods,

$$\bar{x}_k^t - x_k^t = (\bar{b}_k^t - b_k^t) - (\bar{a}_k^t - a_k^t).$$

We evaluate all input, output, and consumption bundles of either program in each period by the real prices p_k^t associated with the first program, writing

$$\bar{A}^t = \sum_{k=1}^{n} p_k^t \bar{a}_k^t, \qquad A^t = \sum_{k=1}^{n} p_k^t a_k^t, \text{ etc.,}$$

for the present values so obtained. It then follows that, for each period t, the discrepancy between the two programs in the so defined value of consumption is

$$\bar{X}^t - X^t = (\bar{B}^t - B^t) - (\bar{A}^t - A^t).$$

By assumption the differences in quantities, and hence in value, between the consumption flows in the two programs vanish in all but the two periods $t = 1$ and $t = t'$. Nevertheless, we add up the differences in value for all periods $t = 1, 2, \ldots , t'$ to obtain

$$(\bar{X}^1 - X^1) + (\bar{X}^{t'} - X^{t'}) = \sum_{t=1}^{t'} (\bar{B}^t - B^t) - \sum_{t=1}^{t'} (\bar{A}^t - A^t),$$

and we arrange the terms in the right-hand member in a form more suited to the application of Proposition 8,

$$(\bar{B}^1 - B^1) + \sum_{t=1}^{t'-1} [(\bar{B}^{t+1} - \bar{A}^t) - (B^{t+1} - A^t)] - (\bar{A}^{t'} - A^{t'}).$$

The first term vanishes because the two programs utilize the same initial resources ($\bar{b}_k^1 = b_k^1$). The second term is nonpositive by Proposition 8, clause (a), and the third term is nonpositive by clause (b)—thus confirming the relevance of that clause. It follows that[1]

$$\bar{X}^{t'} - X^{t'} \leq X^1 - \bar{X}^1.$$

In words: the present value of the increase in consumption in period t' made possible by a decrease in period 1 does not exceed the present value of the latter decrease. If the production sets Y^t are polyhedral and if the second program is likewise efficient and located on the same facet as the first in each period, then a common price system is associated with both programs; and the same argument applied in the opposite

[1] The above reasoning consists, of course, in a repeated application of Theorem I.1 on page 12.

direction establishes the reverse inequality, hence the equality of the present values of the future increase and the present decrease in consumption. Likewise, if the production sets Y^t, $t = 1, \ldots, t' - 1$, have differentiable boundaries at the points indicated by the first program, the ratio

$$(\overline{X}^{t'} - X^{t'})/(X^1 - \overline{X}^1)$$

of these present values can be brought arbitrarily close to unity by choosing the decreases in first period consumption flows sufficiently small.

No mention has yet been made of capital and interest. Let us now in each period define one unit of the commodity $k = 1$ as the monetary unit. The per-period rate of interest r (previously denoted $r_1^{1,t'}$) on a loan contracted at the beginning of period 1 and to be repaid with compound interest at the beginning of period t', associated with the first program, is then given by

$$\frac{p_1^1}{p_1^{t'}} = (1 + r)^{t'-1}$$

Let us further regard the money value

$$\frac{1}{p_1^1} (X^1 - \overline{X}^1)$$

of the decrease in consumption (including increase in labor, if any) in the first period as a capital investment, the money value

$$\frac{1}{p_1^{t'}} (\overline{X}^{t'} - X^{t'})$$

of the increase in consumption (and/or decrease in labor) in period t' as its return. The marginal productivity[1] ρ of the investment can then be defined by

$$\frac{1}{p_1^{t'}} (\overline{X}^{t'} - X^{t'}) = \frac{1}{p_1^1} (X^1 - \overline{X}^1) \cdot (1 + \rho)^{t'-1}.$$

Then obviously, as a direct implication of these definitions, equality

$$\overline{X}^{t'} - X^{t'} = X^1 - \overline{X}^1$$

---

[1] For a discussion of alternative definitions of the marginal productivity of capital which do not entail equality to the interest rate under efficient allocation, see "Capital Accumulation . . . ," pp. 260–261.

of the present (real) values of the investment and of the return is the same thing as equality of the marginal productivity of the investment and the rate of interest, $\rho = r$. The more generally valid inequality which says that the present value of the return does not exceed that of the capital investment similarly translates into the equivalent inequality $\rho \leqq r$. Conditions that imply the former inequality also imply the latter (which translates Proposition 8) and conditions implied in the former are also implied in the latter (which translates Proposition 9).

For purposes of exposition we have here considered only the case of an investment concentrated in one single period, of which the return is concentrated in one other period. Similar conclusions apply, of course, to investments and returns that extend over several periods, possibly infinitely many. Again for simplicity, we formulate the translated propositions explicitly only for the elementary production processes of Malinvaud's model that connect two immediately succeeding periods.

PROPOSITION 10. Under the assumptions of the present model, given any efficient program $(-a^t, b^{t+1}), t = 1,2, \ldots$, such that the associated (real) price system of Proposition 8 permits the choice of a positively priced monetary unit for each period, one can specify a system of nonnegative money prices $p_k^{*t}, t = 1,2, \ldots$, and a system of one-period interest rates $r^{t,t+1}, t = 1,2, \ldots$, each not less than -1, such that, for each period t,

(a.1) if $(-\bar{a}^t, \bar{b}^{t+1})$ is another point of the production set Y^t which in comparison with $(-a^t, b^{t+1})$ represents a positive investment (an increase in the value of input)

$$\sum_{k=1}^{n} p_k^{*t}(\bar{a}_k^t - a_k^t)$$

then the marginal productivity

$$\frac{\sum_{k=1}^{n} p_k^{*t+1}(\bar{b}_k^{t+1} - b_k^{t+1}) - \sum_{k=1}^{n} p_k^{*t}(\bar{a}_k^t - a_k^t)}{\sum_{k=1}^{n} p_k^{*t}(\bar{a}_k^t - a_k^t)}$$

of the investment is at most equal to the interest rate $r^{t,t+1}$, (a.2) if $(-\bar{\bar{a}}^t, \bar{\bar{b}}^{t+1})$ is another point of the production set Y^t which in comparison with $(-a^t, b^{t+1})$ represents a positive disinvestment (a decrease in the value of input)

$$\sum_{k=1}^{n} p_k^{*t}(a_k^t - \bar{\bar{a}}_k^t)$$

then the marginal productivity loss

$$\frac{\sum_{k=1}^{n} p_k^{*t+1}(b_k^{t+1} - \bar{\bar{b}}_k^{t+1}) - \sum_{k=1}^{n} p_k^{*t}(a_k^t - \bar{\bar{a}}_k^t)}{\sum_{k=1}^{n} p_k^{*t}(a_k^t - \bar{\bar{a}}_k^t)}$$

associated with the disinvestment is at least equal to the interest rate $r^{t,t+1}$,

(b) condition (b) of Proposition 8 is satisfied.

Conversely, we have:

PROPOSITION 11. If under the assumptions of the present model and with a given choice of the monetary unit for each period one can associate with a given possible program a system of positive money prices p_k^t and of interest rates $r^{t,t+1}$, each exceeding -1, such that statements (a.1), (a.2) and (b) of Proposition 10 are valid, then this program is efficient.

The conditions (a.1), (a.2) of Proposition 10 are derived from the equivalent condition (a) of Proposition 8 *and conversely* by simple algebraic operations which the reader can easily reconstruct. The single condition (a) of Propositions 8 and 9 has been split up into two conditions (a.1), (a.2) in Propositions 10 and 11 in order to show that the interest rate is actually hemmed in (and in the case of a differentiable production function uniquely determined) by the inequalities[1] imposed on it. The requirement in Proposition 10 that the monetary unit shall in each period possess a positive real price under Proposition 8 is needed to preclude infinite or indeterminate values of the interest rate.

---

[1] Contradictory inequalities are, of course, precluded by the efficiency of $(-a^t, b^{t+1})$ and the convexity of Y^t. This is precisely what Proposition 10 says.

It is for the institutional economist or the economic historian to explain why the conditions (a.1), (a.2) of Proposition 10 correspond more closely to business practice than the logically equivalent condition (a) of Proposition 8. One is led to think of reasons similar to those adduced to explain the introduction of a single monetary unit in timeless situations, such as the greater simplicity of a system of money prices, one for each good, as compared with a system of mutually consistent barter ratios, one for each pair of goods. When time is introduced, the specification of a separate monetary unit for each time period similarly makes available a common measuring rod for the marginal productivity of investments, the system of interest rates. It is true that the marginal productivity figure for any particular investment is affected by the arbitrary choice of monetary units. As we have now seen, however, the redeeming feature of the system of interest rates is that efficiency comparisons between alternative investments are not affected by the choice of monetary units.

Undoubtedly, economic calculation by means of interest rates has been further favored by the development of a market for capital loans which permitted a separation of the ownership of capital from its application in production. On the other hand, there seems to be no reason why the same type of calculation should not be useful as well in the planning procedures of a socialist economy. Whether interest gives rise to an income to private owners of capital or is merely a calculating device to help make consistent investment decisions is highly important for the social structure, the income distribution, and the operation of incentives for saving and enterprise. However, this question is extraneous to our present topic of efficiency in the allocation of resources. Any institutional arrangement that succeeds in administering either the criteria of Proposition 8, or the equivalent criteria of Proposition 10, is—as far as allocative efficiency is concerned—appropriate to a technology with the properties we have assumed. The reasons that have favored the use of interest rates in accord with Proposition 10 appear to be operative as well in the framework of a socialist economy.

To illustrate this point further, it is interesting to speculate as to what form economic calculation would take in a world of fantasy in which all commodities were continually changing their physical and hedonistic characteristics, but in a completely predictable manner.

Propositions 8 and 9 would continue to state valid implications of, and criteria for, efficient production over time in such a world.[1] However, lacking the physical basis for an automatic and unpremeditated extension of the idea of a monetary unit to future periods, such a world might never develop the concept of an interest rate as an aid to economic or business calculation, even though that concept could have been made formally just as valid through any arbitrary definition of such units.

This consideration suggests that the concepts of interest and capital derive their usefulness, for business calculation as well as for government economic planning, from the approximate physical constancy of at least some commodities in the real world, and from the fact that changes in preferences and in technology are likewise gradual. Because of these circumstances, it makes sense to estimate the present value of a future commodity in two steps. The first step is an estimate of the future money price of the commodity in question, expressed in some appropriate monetary unit. This estimate depends primarily on anticipations regarding preferences and technology in relation to that particular commodity, and possibly also in relation to the monetary commodity. The second step is an estimate of the present value of the future money unit, as determined primarily by the marginal productivity of capital in general.

It may be added that it is only on the basis of the physical constancy of many commodities that one could implement Irving Fisher's highly important idea of defining and determining a *real rate of interest* by means of an index number.[2]

4.8 STATIONARY STATES

There is one case, of greater analytical than practical interest, in which such an index number problem does not arise. This is the case of a stationary state in which it is assumed that technology and available resources do not change at all over time. That is, the physical characteristics of commodities, the production sets Y^t and the resource bundles z^t do not actually depend on t. Attention is further concentrated on *stationary programs*, that is, programs in which the same input and output

---

[1] There is nothing in the proofs of these propositions that requires commodities available at different times but bearing the same commodity subscript to be physically identical.

[2] *The Theory of Interest*, Macmillan, New York, 1930, p. 42.

bundles, hence also the same consumption flows, are repeated in all periods. However, the definition of an efficient program considers as wide a range of alternatives as before, even if it is applied to a stationary program: it is required that from the same constant technology and resource flows, it shall not be possible to realize any other consumption program, constant or not, which is larger for some commodity in some period, smaller for none in any period. It can then be proved[1] that, in association with an efficient stationary program, one can meet the conditions of Proposition 8 by a system of money prices p_k^{*t} which is the same for all time periods $(p_k^{*t} = p_k)$. The choice of any one commodity (k, say) as the monetary unit for all periods then also entails a system of identical interest rates $(r_k^{t,t'})$ for all initial (t) and terminal ($t' > t$) periods of the loan. In addition, this universally applicable rate is independent of the choice (k) of the monetary commodity $(r_k^{t,t'} = r)$. It is for this reason that, in an analysis confined to stationary programs, one might easily overlook the arbitrary element in the definition of an interest rate, which is much more apparent in nonstationary circumstances.

4.9   IS CAPITAL SATURATION POSSIBLE?

Comparison of alternative stationary states with the same technology and current resource availabilities but different initial resource bundles throws some light on the question whether a state of *capital saturation* is possible. This may for purposes of this discussion be defined as a stationary program based on an initial resources bundle b^1 such that no further increases in some or all components of b^1 permit a permanent improvement in consumption. That is, no additional amount of initial resources permits an alternative stationary program which allows a higher consumption of some, and no lower consumption of any, commodity in *all* future periods. If this situation does not exist, we speak of *capital scarcity*.

A few simple examples will show that the possibility of capital saturation is an empirical question, which cannot be answered without further information about the technology studied. Let us consider an economy with only one primary commodity, labor, flowing in at the

---

[1] "Capital Accumulation . . . ," p. 259.

fixed rate of one unit in each period and having no disutility attached to its supply. Let us further assume only one desired commodity, steel, available initially in one unit. Let the technology provide a range of alternative processes of steel production, all defined so that the unit activity absorbs one unit of labor. Let the unit activity also require a beginning-of-period input of steel which depends on the process, but is in all cases recovered undiminished at the end of the period, in addition to the new steel produced by the process. Let, finally, the technology include a method for costless disposal of steel.

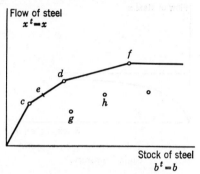

FIGURE 4.1. Case of capital saturation (at f).

Figures 4.1–4.3 exhibit a number of hypothetical cases involving only convex production sets. Since the coordinate for labor is -1 in all cases considered, the labor axis is not shown in the diagrams. If the technology comprises only a finite number of basic processes, from which additional activities can be derived in the manner described by the additivity and proportionality postulates of Section 3 (pages 74 and 76), we obtain a production set $Y^t = Y$ as pictured in Figure 4.1. The interest rate associated with the efficient stationary program represented by the point e is given by the slope of the line segment $\overline{cd}$, the increment in the flow of steel made possible by one unit increment in the stock of steel. At the efficient program f, any further increase in the stock of steel is incapable of bringing about a permanent increase in the flow of steel. This program is therefore one of capital saturation. It is compatible with a zero rate of interest.

This example suggests that in a technology derived from a finite basis, a state of capital saturation is always possible, and a zero rate of interest can be associated with it. Additional possibilities arise if an infinite collection of basic processes is given, provided there is no technological bound on the amount of capital that can be usefully combined with one unit of labor. In Figures 4.2 and 4.3[1] (Case A) any

[1] Drawn from the curves $x = 1 - \dfrac{1}{b+1}$ and $x = \log(b+1)$, respectively.

increment to the stock of capital has a positive productivity $\frac{dx}{db}$, but as the capital intensity of production is increased indefinitely, the marginal productivity of capital gets arbitrarily close to zero. The main difference between the two cases is that in the technology of Figure 4.2, there is an unsurpassable bound on steel flow which is proportional to labor input, while in the technology of Figure 4.3 (Case A), any flow of steel however large can be produced from only one unit of labor flow in

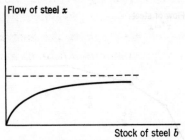

FIGURE 4.2. First case of asymptotic capital saturation.

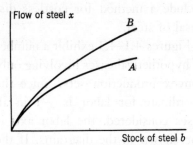

FIGURE 4.3. Second case of asymptotic capital saturation (A) and a case where capital saturation is not possible (B).

combination with a sufficiently high amount of capital. Finally, Figure 4.3 (Case B) shows a case[1] where the marginal productivity of capital and hence the rate of interest never fall below some given positive number (here .05) no matter how high the capital stock already in use.

These examples reveal possibilities that cannot be perceived from a model of technology derived from a finite basis. There is however an air of unreality about a discussion of the possibility of capital saturation that does not take technological progress into account. As larger and larger amounts of capital are combined with one unit of labor, this capital is likely to take the form of qualitatively different commodities. From the point of view of technological experience accumulated in response to a range of interest rates from 3 to 10 per cent, say, it is hard to say whether the exploration of methods of production appropriate to a 1 per cent rate constitutes technological innovation or a different application of given technological knowledge. This difficulty is, of course, inherent in the very idea of a stationary state, since any application of technological knowledge contains a necessary and produc-

[1] Drawn from the curve $x = .05b + \log(b + 1)$.

tive element of learning from experience. In a nonstationary model such learning can be treated as a—at least in part—foreseeable change in technological know-how.

We would have to go beyond the premises of the present discussion, however, if we wished to recognize the possibility of influencing the pace of technological advance by investment in research. The assumption of a convex production set is inappropriate for this purpose. Even apart from the obvious difficulty that there is uncertainty about the outcome of a given research effort, it is clear that the economic value of the results of a piece of research or of an invention depend on the scale of the production processes in which these results are applied. Our models therefore have no bearing on the problem of allocation of resources to research.

4.10   CONSUMERS' PREFERENCES OVER TIME

So far our discussion has been held almost entirely in terms of the price implications of productive efficiency, without regard to further problems of efficiency in the use of outputs to satisfy consumers' preferences. It will be clear, however, that one can, in analogy to our discussion in Section 2, introduce each consumer's preferences through a convex preference ordering on a suitable consumption set in which consumable commodities for all future periods within the anticipated life span of that consumer are represented. A Pareto-optimal program in which a positive interest rate is associated with a loan that bridges two periods then represents a situation in which consumers prefer to have the monetary commodity (or the bundle defining the monetary unit) available in the first period rather than have an equal amount of that commodity or bundle assured to them in the second period. Thus, capital scarcity and preference for present goods can be looked upon as necessarily connected characteristics of a Pareto-optimal program, one relating to the production side, the other to the consumption side of the economy.

There are, of course, conceptual difficulties in the notion of preference for present goods if it is applied to periods further apart than the life expectation of the economic individual. To explore these further would lead us beyond the scope of this already lengthy essay.

4.11   RIGOR VERSUS REALISM?

At the end of this essay, a question may be raised which has been with us since the beginning of economic science, but which may have arisen with renewed insistence in the mind of the reader of these pages. As we strive for greater rigor and precision in the formulation of postulates and propositions, the inadequacies and lack of realism of the postulates are thereby made to stand out in stronger relief. As we succeed in recognizing and incorporating one aspect of the real world in our models, our failure to incorporate other aspects becomes more apparent. Should we conclude from this consideration that rigor is the enemy of realism, and that some compromise between the two should be sought in economic analysis? The next essay is in part addressed to this question.

II

THE CONSTRUCTION
OF ECONOMIC KNOWLEDGE

In human conduct one condition does not control another, but altogether they mutually determine one another. To grasp at one view this manifold mutual action is a task that few can achieve. None can do it save those who have trained habits of scientific thought; and work with the aid of a special organon. [ALFRED MARSHALL, *The Present Position of Economics*, MACMILLAN, LONDON, 1885, P. 31]

II

THE CONSTRUCTION

OF ECONOMIC KNOWLEDGE

1. THE BAD REPUTE OF METHODOLOGY

If methods of scaling are ever applied to measure the relative prestige of various topics in economic research, methodological discussion will undoubtedly be found to rank near the low end of the scale. "I find it necessary in self-defense to start with a few words on the distasteful subject of methodology," announces Dennis H. Robertson in near-despair at the beginning of his exchange with the Keynesian theory of interest.[1] R. F. Harrod in his well-known methodological essay[2] can-

[1] "Mr. Keynes and the Rate of Interest," *Essays in Monetary Theory*, King, London, 1940.
[2] "The Scope and Method of Economics," presidential address before Section F of the British Association in 1938, *Economic Journal*, vol. 48, September 1938, pp. 383–412.

didly characterizes the risk incurred and the odium suffered by the economist who addresses his professional colleagues on methodological questions.

> Exposed as a bore, the methodologist cannot take refuge behind a cloak of modesty. On the contrary, he stands forward ready by his own claim to give advice to all and sundry, to criticise the work of others, which, whether valuable or not, at least attempts to be constructive; he sets himself up as the final interpreter of the past and dictator of future efforts.

In spite of all this, there is something irrepressible in methodological discussion. As new work unfolds, as changes in emphasis occur in the objectives of economics, and as fresh tools come into use, the desire for exchange of views on methodology recurs irresistibly. Thus, Harrod's essay is one of three highly perceptive methodological discussions contained in a single volume of the *Economic Journal*,[1] in a year following a period of drastic changes of emphasis in economic thought.

More recently, changes in the content and direction of economic analysis have been more gradual, in a period of both consolidation and broadening of economic ideas and research. However, while there have been no other substantive revolutions in economic thinking comparable to the "Keynesian revolution," there has been a cumulative change in the tools of theory as well as of empirical research (to be discussed more in detail in the third essay of this collection), which is bound to have repercussions in methodology. The present essay is a plea for methodological recognition of the potentialities of the tools that have come to the fore. If I in turn defy the low regard for methodological discussion, the motive is again best expressed by a quotation from Harrod's article:

> My substantial excuse for choosing methodology today is that I feel a strong inner urge to say something.

2. THE DIPLOMATIC STYLE OF DISCOURSE

As in any empirical science, progress in economics comes about through continual interaction of observation, proceeding from the

[1] The other two are E. F. M. Durbin, "Methods of Research—A Plea for Cooperation in the Social Sciences," pp. 183–195, and L. M. Fraser, "Economists and Their Critics," pp. 196–210 (a reply to Barbara Wootton, *Lament for Economics*, G. Allen, London, 1938).

casual to the systematic, and reasoning, proceeding from the incidental to the more general and formal. In some of the physical sciences a considerable degree of differentiation has developed between experimental work, devoted to observation, and theoretical work, devoted to reasoning and to the construction of premises from which to reason. In economics, such a separation of activities has so far not developed to the same extent. In those writings representing the best achievements of economics, we find and expect to find pieces of reasoning and references to facts closely intertwined.

This informality of economics (as one might call the simultaneous preoccupation with all aspects of knowledge-building) is strongly rooted in the nature of its subject matter. The "facts" of economic life are all around us. Hence much of the factual background of economics can be presupposed without extensive examination or discussion. Furthermore, in a democratic environment, policy recommendations in economic matters need to be understood by the enlightened citizen in order to meet with acceptance. We have excellent testimony[1] indicating that this consideration moved Alfred Marshall to establish by his shining example a highly effective style of writing, in which the technical aspects of reasoning are somewhat concealed between the lines, or relegated to appendixes. The effectiveness of this form of communication in economics was enhanced by the fortunate circumstance that some of the most important insights achieved by economic analysis— such as the efficiency of resource allocation by competitive markets in a predictable world in which technology permits perfect competition —can be at least strongly suggested through a form of discourse which demands from its readers genuine intellectual effort, it is true, but not a high degree of technical training.

It is gradually becoming apparent that the mundane and diplomatic approach to economic writing also has its disadvantages. Perhaps these can be epitomized in the observation how extraordinarily difficult it is to uncover the foundations on which our economic knowledge rests. How much of it is derived from observation, how much from reasoning? From what assertions does the reasoning start? The puzzle

---

[1] J. M. Keynes, "Alfred Marshall, 1842–1924," in A. C. Pigou (ed.), *Memorials of Alfred Marshall*, Macmillan, London, 1925.

presented to us by the very persuasiveness of economic analysis is wittily described by Hicks in the following quotation:

> Pure economics has a remarkable way of producing rabbits out of a hat—apparently *a priori* propositions which apparently refer to reality.[1]

3. THE POSTULATIONAL STRUCTURE
OF ECONOMIC THEORY

In preparation for further comment on this puzzle, it may be useful to describe briefly, and without claim to originality,[2] the logical structure of our economic knowledge discernible underneath the polished prose. Since it is impossible to say which comes first, observation or reasoning, the chicken or the egg, our description may start with either. We shall start with, and in fact place most emphasis on, the reasoning merely because most of our comments in this essay are concerned with that compartment of economic analysis. Some comments on observation are made in the third essay of this volume.[3]

Explicitly or implicitly, any logically valid chain of reasoning starts from certain premises. We shall use the term *postulates* for any premises used in any piece of economic analysis, which are not themselves conclusions from earlier parts of the reasoning in the same piece of analysis. If often these postulates are not formally introduced, but referred to or implied at the point where they are used, this does not change their logically recognizable character of basic premises.

The postulates contain certain *terms* that are the representatives or counterparts in the analysis of persons, organizations, things, actions, or states such as are found in the world of experience. Often the adoption of terms is effected by the use of certain key words, such as con-

---

[1] J. R. Hicks, *Value and Capital*, Clarendon Press, Oxford, 1946, 2d ed., p. 23.

[2] At the time this essay was nearing completion I became aware of the similarity of the point of view here adopted with some of the ideas expressed in somewhat stronger terms by T. W. Hutchison in *The Significance and Basic Postulates of Economic Theory*, London, 1938, quoted hereafter as "*The Significance* . . . ." There is some difference in emphasis in that the present essay gives more attention to the detachability of the chains of reasoning from the interpretation of the postulates. In so far as there is duplication or repetition, there seems to be no harm done by it, since the practical consequences of the views expressed have not yet been generally realized or accepted.

[3] See especially Sections 7 and 8.

sumer, worker, enterpreneur, commodity, production process, output, consumption, probability, climate. The associations that have come to cling to these terms through extensive use in the literature are sometimes sufficient for practical purposes. However, if one wishes to get down to fundamentals, it is clear that a meaningful analysis presupposes that the language used is or has been explicitly established by definitions, statements or descriptions connecting the terms with observable phenomena. We shall call these descriptions the *interpretations* of the terms.

Whether these interpretations are expressly provided or borrowed by tacit consent from the stream of literature, they lend relevance and economic meaning to the postulates. Without the interpretations, the postulates are bare statements establishing logical relations between unspecified entities represented by the symbols we have called *terms*. Through the interpretations, the postulates become statements that specify the range of choices open to the various persons introduced (often one man's range of choice is circumscribed by other men's choices); the effects of these choices on the things, processes, and states represented by the terms; and the rules or principles from which actual choices are derived in the light of the individual's evaluation of the known or presumed effects of these choices. However, from the point of view of the logic of the reasoning, the interpretations are detachable. Only the logical contents of the postulates matter. We shall return below to the importance of this circumstance.

Once a set of postulates has been adopted, the reasoning itself develops, by the rules of logic and, where appropriate, with the help of other mathematical techniques, those implications that are verifiable or otherwise interesting. The reasoning is often helped by the introduction of additional terms through definitions that use terms already established. Terms such as utility, price, income, capital, savings, efficiency, strategy, often occur in this role, although some of them may in other pieces of analysis be "primitive" terms.

The reasoning may prove the postulates to be in contradiction with each other. Or it may reveal that the postulates are not sufficiently specific or numerous to have the kind of implications one is looking for. In a "successful" analysis, the reasoning leads to conclusions that are interesting for one or both of two reasons which are connected with the purposes the analysis is to serve. A distinction needs to be made here between *explanatory* and *normative* analysis. Synonymous designations such as *descriptive*, or *positive*, versus *prescriptive* analysis are also in use. These two types of analysis do not necessarily differ in the interpretations placed on the terms. They differ only in the motivation of the search for conclusions, and in the use made of those that are found. In explanatory analysis, what one looks for in a conclusion or prediction is the possibility of testing, that is, of verification or refutation by observation. Of course, the interpretations of the terms used in the postulates form the connecting link through which observation is brought to bear on the statements that represent conclusions. Verification, or absence of refutation, lends support to the set of postulates taken as a whole. Refutation indicates that at least one of the postulates is inadequate for the purpose of "explaining" the phenomena to which the conclusions refer.[1]

In normative analysis, the purposes of the analysis are not limited to the empirical testing of the set of postulates, and need not even include the latter objective. The new purpose is that of recommending, to one or more of the persons or organizations represented in the analysis, a choice or course of action which can be expected to serve his or their objectives better than, or at least as well as, alternative actions open to them. If the recommendation is implemented, this may provide an opportunity for testing the postulates on which it is based. However, it may also happen that, because of the continual impact of factors disregarded in the analysis, or because of the all-pervasive effect of the action implemented, no opportunity remains for observing the effect of not taking the recommended action or of taking some alternative action. In such cases, the recommendation is as good as the postulates from which it is correctly derived, but the analysis need not be less worthwhile for that reason.

Although our distinctions have been illustrated by terms taken from economics, it would seem that the above description fits general scientific procedure. Nor is the distinction between explanatory and normative analysis limited to the social sciences. It is paralleled, for instance, in

---

[1] In this discussion we follow what appears to be the accepted view: that the validity of the reasoning from postulates to conclusions is entirely a matter of logical rather than empirical test.

the distinction between physical sciences and engineering. However, there is a difference with regard to opportunities for what might be called "direct" verification of the postulates. This leads us to consider further the puzzling question on what foundations economic knowledge rests.

4. THE SEARCH FOR THE FOUNDATION
OF ECONOMIC KNOWLEDGE

The basic postulates of modern physics and chemistry are concerned with entities so far removed from daily experience that long chains of reasoning, mostly of a highly mathematical character, are involved in linking the postulates with observable phenomena that can substantiate or refute them. The postulates of economics are concerned with human ends and choices of means, and with technological and physiological possibilities for production and consumption. As pointed out already, these are matters in which each of us has some opportunities for rather direct observation. It was undoubtedly considerations of this order that led Lionel Robbins, in his classical *Essay on the Nature and Significance of Economic Science*, to attach a quality of almost immediate obviousness to the postulates of economic theory. The following passage, which was introduced into the second edition of the essay, seems so well to summarize his thought that we shall reproduce it almost in full.[1]

The propositions of economic theory, like all scientific theory, are obviously deductions from a series of postulates. And the chief of these postulates are all assumptions involving in some way simple and indisputable facts of experience relating to the way in which the scarcity of goods which is the subject-matter of our science actually shows itself in the world of reality. The main postulate of the theory of value is the fact that individuals can arrange their preferences in an order, and in fact do so. The main postulate of the theory of production is the fact that there are more than one factor of production. The main postulate of the theory of dynamics is the fact that we are not certain regarding future scarcities. These are not postulates the existence of whose counterpart in reality admits of extensive dispute once their nature is fully realized.

[1] Lionel Robbins, *An Essay on the Nature and Significance of Economic Science*, Macmillan, London, 1935 (2d ed.), pp. 78–80 of the reprinting of 1946.

We do not need controlled experiments to establish their validity: they are so much the stuff of our everyday experience that they have only to be stated to be recognised as obvious. Indeed, the danger is that they may be thought to be so obvious that nothing significant can be derived from their further examination. Yet in fact it is on postulates of this sort that the complicated theorems of advanced analysis ultimately depend. And it is from the existence of the conditions they assume that the general applicability of the broader propositions of economic science is derived.

Now of course it is true, as we have already seen, that the development of the more complicated applications of these propositions involves the use of a great multitude of subsidiary postulates regarding the condition of markets, the number of parties to the exchange, the state of the law, the *minimum sensibile* of buyers and sellers, and so on and so forth. . . . But while it is important to realise how many are the subsidiary assumptions which necessarily arise as our theory becomes more and more complicated, it is equally important to realise how widely applicable are the main assumptions on which it rests. As we have seen, the chief of them are applicable whenever and wherever the conditions which give rise to economic phenomena are present.

Thus reassured about the validity of their premises, economists have constructed on them an impressive body of theory. The intellectual prestige of this theory is enhanced by the fact, referred to in the above quotation from Hicks, that so much is derived from so little. Nevertheless, the beauty and persuasiveness of Professor Robbins's prose do not quite overcome a certain statesmanlike vagueness in the description of the postulates, a vagueness which lingers on in those passages[1] in which the postulates are discussed at greater length. As many economists have pointed out in various instances, the attempt to spell out literally and in detail the basic postulates of economic theory soon reveals limitations to their obviousness.

To illustrate this point let us consider for a moment the postulate that each consumer has a complete preference ordering of all commodity bundles the consumption of which is possible to him, and compare it with our direct knowledge of consumption decisions. In one interpretation, the postulate is applied to explain consumption levels adopted in response to given circumstances, where these levels are

[1] *Ibid.*, pp. 75–78.

maintained for as long as the determining circumstances remain the same. We note immediately that this interpretation denies the consumer such privileges as the joy in random variability in consumption, as well as its opposite, the comfort of consumption habits somewhat rigidly maintained under varying circumstances. In another interpretation, in which the choice to be explained is that of a consumption program extending over a sequence of time periods in response to an anticipated sequence of circumstances, the postulate by holding him to that program if the circumstances materialize as anticipated denies him the opportunity to learn about his own preferences by experience. It thus ignores his willingness to forego some immediate satisfaction if he can thereby postpone some decisions about consumption in a more distant future until more learning has taken place. Finally, in either interpretation, the postulate denies him the noble urge to respond with sacrifices to the distress of others, as well as the less highly regarded gratification in levels or conspicuous forms of consumption outdoing those of others. Nevertheless, almost every consumer values these privileges, and regards them as part of his normal experience and motivation.

Similar "realistic" objections have so frequently been made with regard to the two postulates of entrepreneurial behavior known as "profit maximization" and "perfect competition," that they need not be repeated here. Milton Friedman has attempted to meet such objections with an argument diametrically opposite to that of Robbins. In his view, the question of the "realism" of the premises of economic analysis is irrelevant to its validity, and preoccupation with that question at times definitely harmful:

> The difficulty in the social sciences of getting new evidence for this class of phenomena [i.e., which the hypotheses (or postulates) are designed to explain, T.C.K.] and of judging its conformity with the implications of the hypothesis makes it tempting to suppose that other, more readily available, evidence is equally relevant to the validity of the hypothesis—to suppose that hypotheses have not only "implications" but also "assumptions" and that the conformity of these "assumptions" to "reality" is a test of the validity of the hypothesis *different from* or *additional to* the test by implications. This widely held view is fundamentally wrong and productive of much mischief. Far from providing an easier means for sifting valid from invalid hypotheses, it only confuses the issue, promotes

misunderstanding about the significance of empirical evidence for economic theory, produces a misdirection of much intellectual effort devoted to the development of positive economics, and impedes the attainment of consensus on tentative hypotheses in positive economics.[1]

Since any statement is implied by itself, one could interpret Professor Friedman's position to mean that the validity or usefulness of any set of postulates depends on observations that confirm or at least fail to contradict (although they could have) *all* their implications, immediate and derived. This entirely acceptable view would circumscribe and qualify Robbins's belief in the obviousness of the postulates, by requiring that not only the postulates themselves, but also their derived implications meet the test of observation. Such an interpretation receives further support from Friedman's remark[2] that, in many systems of related propositions, one has a certain freedom of choice as to which statements one wishes to regard as premises, and which ones as derived implications. It also seems to be supported by the following quotation:

> To put this point less paradoxically, the relevant question to ask about the "assumptions" of a theory is not whether they are descriptively "realistic," for they never are, but whether they are sufficiently good approximations for the purpose in hand. And this question can be answered only by seeing whether the theory works, which means whether it yields sufficiently accurate predictions. The two supposedly independent tests [i.e., through the realism of the assumptions and through their derived implications, T.C.K.] thus reduce to one test.[3]

But this interpretation of Friedman's position does not seem to lead to the extreme inferences he draws from it in the next paragraph:

> The theory of monopolistic and imperfect competition is one example of the neglect in economic theory of these propositions. The development of this analysis was explicitly motivated, and its wide acceptance and approval largely explained, by the belief that the assumptions of "perfect competition" or "perfect monopoly" said to underlie neoclassical economic theory are a false image of reality. And this belief was itself based

---

[1] Milton Friedman, "The Methodology of Positive Economics," in *Essays in Positive Economics*, University of Chicago Press, Chicago, 1953, pp. 1–43. The quotation is from p. 14. Copyright 1953 by the University of Chicago.

[2] *Ibid.*, p. 26.

[3] *Ibid.*, p. 15.

almost entirely on the directly perceived descriptive inaccuracy of the assumptions rather than on any recognized contradiction of predictions derived from neoclassical economic theory. The lengthy discussion on marginal analysis in the *American Economic Review* some years ago is an even clearer, though much less important example. . . .

Here the "direct" implications of the postulates, their accuracy in describing directly observed individual behavior, are placed in a category with which we need to be less concerned.

There are several objections to such a concept of theory construction. In the first place, in order that we shall have a refutable theory at all, the postulates then need to be supplemented by a clear description of the class of implications by which the theory stands or falls. Otherwise, every contradiction between an implication and an observation could be met by reclassifying the implication as a "direct" one.

This objection is met by Friedman's suggestion that there should in each case be "rules for using the model," that is, a specification of the "class of phenomena the hypothesis is designed to explain." But a second objection arises out of this answer to the first. To state a set of postulates, and then to exempt a subclass of their implications from verification is a curiously roundabout way of specifying the content of a theory that is regarded as open to empirical refutation. It leaves one without an understanding of the reasons for the exemptions. The impression of ingeniousness that this procedure gives is reinforced by the fact that in each of Professor Friedman's examples he knows more about the phenomenon in question than he lets on in his suggested postulates. He is willing to predict the expert billiard player's shots from the hypothesis that the player knows the mathematical formulae of mechanics and computes their application to each situation with lightning speed, even though he (Friedman) knows that most experts at billiards do not have these abilities. He is willing to predict the distribution of leaves on a tree from the hypothesis that each leaf seeks a position of maximum exposure to sunlight (given the positions of all other leaves), although no one has reported observing a leaf change its location on a tree.

One cannot help but feel uneasy in the face of so much ingenuity. Truth, like peace, is indivisible. It cannot be compartmentalized. Before we can accept the view that obvious discrepancies between behavior postulates and directly observed behavior do not affect the predictive power of specified implications of the postulates, we need to understand the reasons why these discrepancies do not matter. This is all the more important in a field such as economics where, as Friedman also emphasizes, the opportunities for verification of the predictions and implications derived from the postulates are scarce and the outcome of such verification often remains somewhat uncertain. The difficulties of verification seem in large part due to the virtual impossibility of experiments under conditions approaching those of real life, and to the presence of many factors simultaneously influencing actual economic developments. In such a situation, we have to exploit all the evidence we can secure, direct and indirect. If, in comparison with some other sciences, economics is handicapped by severe and possibly unsurmountable obstacles to meaningful experimentation, the opportunities for direct introspection by, and direct observation of, individual decision makers are a much needed source of evidence which in some degree offsets the handicap. We cannot really feel confident in acting upon our economic knowledge until its deductions reconcile directly observed patterns of individual behavior with such implications for the economy as a whole as we find ourselves able to subject to test.

Friedman himself indicates an important step in this direction when he points out,[1] in parallel with Alchian,[2] that the postulate of profit-maximizing behavior by entrepreneurs is supported by the fact that those who do not manage to maximize profits are likely to be eliminated by competition in the course of time. Here a postulate about individual behavior is made more plausible by reference to the adverse effect of, and hence penalty for, departures from the postulated behavior. The reality of the penalty is documented by technological and institutional facts, such as the reproducibility of production processes and the operation of accounting procedures and bankruptcy laws, facts which are a degree less elusive to verification than mere behavior postulates. But if this is the basis for our belief in profit maximization, then we should postulate that basis itself and not the profit maximization which it

[1] *Ibid.*, pp. 21–22.
[2] Armen A. Alchian, "Uncertainty, Evolution and Economic Theory," *Journal of Political Economy*, vol. 57, June 1950, pp. 211–221.

implies in certain circumstances. We should then postulate that entrepreneurial policies unsuitable for economic survival are applied by only a minority of enterprises which exhibit a high rate of economic mortality.

Such a change in the basis of economic analysis would seem to represent a gain in realism attributable to a concern with the directly perceived descriptive accuracy of the postulates. It would lead us to expect profit maximization to be most clearly exhibited in industries where entry is easiest and where the struggle for survival is keenest, and would present us with the further challenge to analyze what circumstances give to an industry that character. It would also prevent us, for purposes of explanatory theory, from getting bogged down in those refinements of profit maximization theory which endow the decision makers with analytical and computational abilities and assume them to have information-gathering opportunities such as are unlikely to exist or be applied in current practice.[1] It seems that nothing is lost, and much may be gained, in thus broadening the postulational basis of economic theory.

Let us sum up the puzzle. After more than a century of intensive activity in scientific economics, two economists who have made outstanding substantive contributions to our science, and whose positions on questions of economic policy are moreover not far apart, seek the ultimate basis of economic knowledge in considerations which (a) contradict each other and (b) are each subject to strong objections. One is led to conclude that economics as a scientific discipline is still somewhat hanging in the air.

There is no harm in this admission. The positions which our two authors so strongly (but contradictorily) embrace have in common that, in so far as either is adopted, its effect is a conservative one. This word is used in a scientific, not a political sense (although scientific conservatism may also have politically conservative effects). Whether the postulates are placed beyond doubt, or whether doubts concerning their realism are suppressed by the assertion that verification can and should be confined to the hard-to-unravel more distant effects—in either

---

[1] For an exploratory discussion of limitations to the decision-making process, see Herbert A. Simon, "A Behavioral Model of Rational Choice," *Quarterly Journal of Economics*, vol. 69, February 1955, pp. 99–118.

case the argument surrounds and shields received economic theory with an appearance of invulnerability which is neither fully justified nor at all needed. The theories that have become dear to us can very well stand by themselves as an impressive and highly valuable system of deductive thought, erected on a few premises that seem to be well-chosen first approximations to a complicated reality. They exhibit in a striking manner the power of deductive reasoning in drawing conclusions which, to the extent one accepts their premises, are highly relevant to questions of economic policy. In many cases the knowledge these deductions yield is the best we have, either because better approximations have not been secured at the level of the premises, or because comparable reasoning from premises recognized as more realistic has not been completed or has not yet been found possible. Is any stronger defense needed, or even desirable?

5. ECONOMIC THEORY AS A SEQUENCE OF MODELS

We have thus been led to the realization that neither are the postulates of economic theory entirely self-evident, nor are the implications of various sets of postulates readily tested by observation. In this situation, it is desirable that we arrange and record our logical deductions in such a manner that any particular conclusion or observationally refutable implication can be traced to the postulates on which it rests. This will help in designing and collecting observations of greatest discriminating power with respect to those postulates regarded as least established. It will also help us keep in mind, in sifting or evaluating policy recommendations, on what body of experience supporting specific combinations of postulates each recommendation rests. Considerations of this order suggest that we look upon economic theory as a sequence of conceptional *models* that seek to express in simplified form different aspects of an always more complicated reality. At first these aspects are formalized as much as feasible in isolation, then in combinations of increasing realism. Each model is defined by a set of postulates, of which the implications are developed to the extent deemed worthwhile in relation to the aspects of reality expressed by the postulates. The study of the simpler models is protected from the reproach of unreality by the consideration that these models may be prototypes of more realistic, but also more complicated, subsequent models. The card file of successfully completed pieces of reasoning represented by these models can then be looked upon as the logical core of economics, as the depository of available economic theory.

It may appear at first sight as if we are here advocating the very compartmentalization of truth which we have rejected in the preceding section. But in the present section we are not concerned with empirical truth, with the verification of theories. We are concerned with the prior question of their logical truth and clarity, with the correct tracing of the implications of given postulates, and with the efficient arranging and recording of the conditional, tautological but useful, truths so found. What is not permissible in verification—the intentional ignoring of obviously important aspects of reality—is indispensable for the gradual unfolding of a body of logically valid implications of economically relevant (but not necessarily by themselves valid) postulates.

It is by adopting this concept of economic theory that we can resolve the apparent conflict between rigor and realism noted at the end of the first essay of this volume. Perception of additional aspects of reality must necessarily precede their recognition in model formulation. Hence realism will always be ahead of rigor in the gradual extension of the range of economic knowledge. But unless rigor follows along to consolidate the gains in realism, we shall not know which conclusions or recommendations depend on which postulates, and which postulates depend for their validity on which verifications of their implications by accumulated experience.

The ideas here advocated are in no way a new proposal, or a new conception of the substance of economic theory. Most economists when pressed will agree to one formulation or another of such a view of the logical structure of economic knowledge, and of the incomplete but progressing state of verification of this knowledge. It is in the practice of our professional activities that we do not live up to it. Often we are more preoccupied with arriving at what we deem to be true statements or best predictions, in the light of such knowledge as we have of the phenomena in question, than in exhibiting the postulational basis, and thereby the ultimate observational evidence, on which our statements rest. Undoubtedly, this is the right preoccupation in those situations in which an urgently needed policy recommendation, backed mainly by the feeling of confidence in it held by experienced advisers, is the main objective of the professional activity. However, for the purpose of the cumulative process of building knowledge that is transferable to other minds and open to general scientific scrutiny, more precautions are required. Undoubtedly progress in economics is slowed down by the inextricable intermingling of facts and reasoning found so often in published writings, and even more frequently in verbal professional discussion. We can best keep track of the foundation for each statement, and of the degree of assurance with which it can be held, if facts are recognized at the beginning of each piece of analysis by explicitly formulated postulates, and where appropriate at the end by confrontation of conclusions or predictions with additional observations, but are not permitted to enter through a side door when the reasoning proper is in progress.

6. CONSIDERATIONS OF SCIENTIFIC EFFICIENCY

While the need for clarity as to the ultimate basis for each economic proposition is the main, and a sufficient, ground in favor of the explicit postulational approach to economic theory, considerations of economy of thought strengthen the case. Sometimes quite different economic phenomena are expressible by sets of postulates of which the logical content is similar or even identical. As already observed, the reasoning itself depends only on that logical content, and not on the interpretations of the terms used. An economy of effort is thus achieved and insight into logical unity under substantive diversity is gained, if the piece of reasoning is allowed to stand in the record as such, detached from the substantive context which may have led to its original construction. This point may be illustrated by the several interpretations of the model of competitive equilibrium which we have encountered in the first essay of this volume, and which differ in the treatment of time, in the character of the economic agents considered, and in the presence or absence of uncertainty. This example also shows how the same chains of reasoning may serve in explanatory as well as in normative economic theory.

More explicit use of the postulational approach is favored also by considerations of communication between the sciences. Specialists in reasoning outside economics such as mathematicians, logicians, statisticians, and philosophers, will more readily contribute from their experience in other fields if they are enabled to examine the reasoning on which economics rests in isolation from the welter of facts, circumstances, and interpretations, which the economist must have in mind when appraising the value to him of these pieces of reasoning. I can testify from personal experience about the obstacles encountered by one trained in another field who embarks on the study of economics and seeks to absorb its substance from Wicksell's *Lectures* or Marshall's *Principles*—perhaps the best guidebooks handed down to us from the period in which the basic ideas of current economic theory were conceived. By reducing the body of facts to be recognized to a set of postulates, logical and mathematical skills can be more effectively brought to bear on the deductive aspects of economic theorizing. Likewise, cross-fertilization between different social sciences is facilitated by concise formalization of the essential ideas of the models developed in these sciences.

If economics develops along such lines, it is somewhat inevitable, though not without risks, that the differentiation of skills within the economics profession will go somewhat further than it has already gone. The task of linking concepts with observations demands a great deal of detailed knowledge of the realities of economic life as well as of processes of measurement. On the other hand, the reasoning from postulates to conclusions, and the appraisal of the postulates with regard to their suitability as a basis for reasoning, increasingly demands logical and mathematical skills not often found united in the persons most suited for the first category of tasks. The testing of conclusions, besides requiring the skills involved in aligning concepts and phenomena, also depends in many cases on the handling of subtle procedures of statistical inference. Finally, and most important of all, the appraisal of postulates with regard to their plausibility, their realism and the relevance or usefulness of the conclusions they lead to, demand a type of allover evaluation and judgment for which the specialist in definition and measurement, in reasoning, or in statistical inference is not necessarily equipped. If the combination of all requisite skills in one person remains an ideal that should guide the training of at least some future economists, intensive communication between differently formed minds is a prerequisite for the ultimate approach to that ideal.

7. CONSIDERATIONS OF PSYCHOLOGY OF SCIENTIFIC EFFORT

The case for an explicit postulational approach to the construction of economic knowledge has now been argued on general grounds of clarity and efficiency. It could logically be rested at this point. This, however, may leave the reader with an impression that we have been laboring the obvious, or, as the Dutch say, have been kicking at an open door. For this reason—and subject to all the risks of methodological discussion so well described by Harrod in our opening quotation—we may be allowed to discuss some psychological pitfalls which beckon the economist who does not keep the postulational and observational basis of his convictions continually in mind.

As long as economic theory is regarded as concerned with economic reality in general, and is built up by absorbing bits of observation as the need arises, a tendency results to overestimate the scope of the conclusions. Results correctly reached for two or three models in succession may grow into beliefs about the world instead of theorems resting on postulates that express certain traits of the world, and of which some implications have not been refuted by observation. Perhaps the outstanding example is the overextended belief of the liberalist school of economic thought in the efficiency of competitive markets as a means of allocating resources in a world full of uncertainty.[1] To my knowledge no formal model of resource allocation through competitive markets has been developed, which recognizes ignorance about all decision makers'

---

[1] This overextension is strikingly illustrated by the proposal, advanced by F. A. von Hayek in two articles in *The Banker* of September and October 1939, suggesting that the allocation of resources to the British war effort in World War II be arranged for preponderantly through price incentives. The first article, concerned with the allocation of materials, is almost convincing. The second article, dealing with the allocation of capital through an appropriate rate of interest is much less so. There is no discussion of the difficulties of appraising the return on a particular capital investment arising from uncertainties about the future course of war and about future relative demands for the various means with which it is to be fought. It is not clear whether these risks can at all, and if so should in Professor Hayek's view, be shifted to private firms through a price system. A third article, announced as to be concerned with problems of equity and of government finance, was never published.

future actions, preferences, or states of technological information as the main source of uncertainty confronting each individual decision maker, and which at the same time acknowledges the fact that forward markets on which anticipations and intentions could be tested and adjusted do not exist in sufficient variety and with a sufficient span of foresight to make presently developed theory regarding the efficiency of competitive markets applicable. If this judgment is correct, our economic knowledge has not yet been carried to the point where it sheds much light on the core problem of the economic organization of society: the problem of how to face and deal with uncertainty. In particular, the economics profession is not ready to speak with anything approaching scientific authority on the economic aspects of the issue of individual versus collective enterprise which divides mankind in our time. Meanwhile, the best safeguard against overestimation of the range of applicability of economic propositions is a careful spelling out of the premises on which they rest. Precision and rigor in the statement of premises and proofs can be expected to have a sobering effect on our beliefs about the reach of the propositions we have developed.

If overestimation of the range of validity of economic propositions is the Scylla of "informal" economic reasoning, a correct appraisal of the limited reach of existing economic theory may cause us to swerve into the Charybdis of disillusionment with economic theory as a road to useful knowledge. The temptation to identify the results of existing economic theory with economic theory as such—and to disqualify both in one breath—is strongest for the experienced economic adviser to government or business, to whom the limitations of existing theory are most painfully apparent. One can hear such feelings reverberate in statements made at professional meetings by outstanding leaders of the economic profession, who in their younger days made important contributions to economic theory. If the concept, here advocated, of economic theory as a sequence of models is more widely accepted, however, dissatisfaction with the relevance of available models will provide the necessary stimulus for cumulative refinement of models to take into account more and more relevant aspects of reality.

There is another but related difficulty of the psychology of scientific effort which has arisen from time to time in the development as distinct from the application of economic theory. This is the difficulty of perceiving at what point, in the recognition of further phenomena to be "explained" by reasoning, the postulates used so far become impotent and need supplementation or replacement by other postulates that recognize aspects of reality essential to the explanation of the next group of phenomena. The problem of the optimum size of the firm, whether from the private producer's or from the social point of view, may serve as an example because it gives rise to precisely this difficulty.

The model of linear activity analysis described in Section 3 of the preceding essay can be looked upon as a "pre-firm" theory of allocation of resources. It recognizes the technology of production in a highly simplified form, and it takes as given the identity of those commodities the making of which constitutes the purpose of production. The main service it renders is to show that value theory—that is, the theory of prices as guides to allocation of resources and of the relations between these prices and the technology—is of such a fundamental character that it can be constructed without reference to institutional postulates regarding the existence and the behavior of firms and of consumers.

The model of competitive equilibrium described in Section 2 of the same essay comes a step closer to the individual enterprise economy by recognizing producers and consumers and endowing them with simplified behavior patterns. However, the characteristics of the producing firms are again specified only to the extent and in a form needed to establish the logical possibility and the Pareto optimality of competitive equilibrium. If the postulates about production possibilities used imply constant returns to scale, the productive establishment (which embodies the function of the firm recognized in that model) is of indeterminate size. The only alternative postulate compatible with the model, that of a convex production set with decreasing returns to scale, does imply an optimum size for each firm, which is both a private and a social optimum (in the Pareto sense), and which is uniquely determined if the production set is strictly convex.[1] But, as we have already argued,[2] the aspects of reality that actually could explain a departure from constant returns to scale are still abstracted from in that model. Thus the model has no

---

[1] See Section 1.6 of the first essay of this volume. In the case of a production process with a single output, strict convexity of the production set implies a decreasing marginal productivity of equal successive increments to the bundle of inputs.

[2] See Section 2.9 of the first essay of this volume, pages 64–66.

real bearing on the question of the size of the firm, either normatively or in an explanatory way. Attempts to deal with that question within its framework cannot produce much useful insight.

Prominent among the aspects of reality that have been recognized as important in determining the size of the firm are indivisibilities in the physical and entrepreneurial inputs to production, the effects of location and transportation costs, and uncertainty with regard to future decisions of consumers and producers. We have not mentioned such obvious departures from perfect competition as product differentiation in order to emphasize that recognition of the "physical" aspects of reality mentioned above already destroys the basis of the theory of competitive equilibrium described in the preceding essay. Indivisibilities entail increasing returns to scale and thus favor relatively large productive establishments. Location and cost of transportation limit the market, and thus work in the opposite direction. Recognition of these two aspects alone could perhaps produce a determinate theory of the sizes and geographical distribution of productive establishments, but such a theory would be quite different from, and mathematically more complicated than, the model of competitive equilibrium. As argued cogently by Professor Kaldor,[1] the recognition of uncertainty would introduce another limiting factor to the size of the firm as a decision-making unit.

Of course the various aspects of reality mentioned are important to many other economic problems besides that of the size of the firm, which has served us merely as an illustration. In the remainder of this essay we shall therefore discuss some of the difficulties met with in the attempt to recognize these various factors in further developments of economic theory. Meanwhile the remarks already made suggest that the problems of economic theory can fruitfully be classified in accordance with the aspects of reality that need to be recognized by suitable postulates to make discussion of each problem possible or meaningful.

8. WHAT MODELS NEXT?

Let us therefore now ask ourselves, in the highly tentative way befitting any such discussion, whether we can glimpse some directions in

[1] Nicholas Kaldor, "The Equilibrium of the Firm," *Economic Journal*, vol. 44, March 1934, pp. 61–76, hereafter quoted as "The Equilibrium . . . ."

which greater realism can be attained by the introduction of further refinements or improvements into the system or systems of postulates underlying economic analysis. In particular, we should seek greater clarity on the question whether the class of postulates that impressed Professor Robbins by their obviousness has perhaps by now been exhausted. If so, the "casual" empiricism which has seemed for a time to be a sufficient basis for economic analysis would have to be superseded to an increasing extent by more systematic observation and direct or indirect testing of postulates. The latter view has been strongly expressed by Hutchison,[1] who sees in the recognition of uncertainty the turning point beyond which empirical verification of postulates should become the main preoccupation of economists. Any discussion of this nature is likely to be fragmentary and to reflect particular preoccupations of its author. Our main concern will be to show by a few examples that the relative need for theoretical versus empirical work is likely to vary with the phenomenon or aspect of reality to be recognized. In particular, there is a clearly discernible difference between the two main classes of postulates, those concerning production possibilities, and those concerning economic behavior.

9. INDIVISIBLE COMMODITIES, INCREASING RETURNS TO SCALE, AND LOCATION PROBLEMS

No elaborate empirical investigation is needed to establish that the indivisibility of some commodities is a very fundamental aspect of technology and indeed of human existence. At the same time the importance of indivisibilities for the phenomenon of increasing returns to the scale of the individual productive establishment and of the industrial conglomeration are generally realized. So are the implications of this phenomenon for the life expectancy of perfect competition in any given industry. In spite of this, the incorporation of indivisible commodities in formal economic theory has hardly begun.

There has been an interesting exchange of views between Nicholas Kaldor and E. H. Chamberlin on the question whether increasing re-

[1] *The Significance* . . . , chap. IV. (See footnote 2 on page 132.)

turns to scale are entirely or necessarily due to indivisibilities. Kaldor wrote rather briefly that—

> . . . it appears methodologically convenient to treat all cases of large-scale economies under the heading "indivisibility." This introduces a certain unity into analysis and makes possible at the same time a clarification of the relationships between the different kinds of economies. Even the cases of increasing returns where a more-than-proportionate increase in output occurs merely on account of an increase in the amounts of the factors used, without any change in the proportions of the factors, are due to indivisibilities; only in this case it is not so much the "original factors," but the specialised functions of those factors, which are indivisible.[1]

Chamberlin takes issue with this view, and sees instead as the main sources of increasing returns

> (1) increased specialization made possible in general by the fact that the aggregate of resources is larger, and
> (2) qualitatively different and technologically more efficient units of factors.[2]

In spite of Professor Chamberlin's firmly expressed conviction that this is a different "explanation," it seems that both his sources of increasing returns exhibit the characteristic that may conveniently be used as defining an indivisible commodity. The relevant aspect of worker specialization appears to be that, up to a certain degree of specialization, the undivided attention given by a specialized worker to a full-time task of a sufficiently challenging character produces not exactly (but presumably more than) twice as much as half-time attention (with half the training!) given to the same task, if the other half of the worker's time (and training) is applied to a different productive activity. Similarly, many pieces of capital equipment have the characteristic that the ratios of inputs into their manufacture to outputs from their use cannot be reproduced at a smaller scale. In both cases there is a commodity, labor, or equipment, with which one cannot realistically associate a parameter expressing its amount, in such a way that this amount can be reduced below a natural unit without qualitative change,

---

[1] Nicholas Kaldor, *The Equilibrium* . . . ." p. 65, ftn. 1.

[2] Edward H. Chamberlin, *The Theory of Monopolistic Competition*, 6th ed., Harvard University Press, Cambridge, 1948, Appendix B, p. 235.

that is, without change in the ratios of inputs to outputs in at least one of the processes in which it is made or used.

If this is a valid description, Chamberlin's disagreement with Kaldor is merely a terminological one, arising from the use of words and their intuitive connotations as the conceptual raw material of analysis. In a postulational approach, indivisible commodities can be introduced through the suppression of the proportionality postulate[1] for all activities in which one of the commodities in question enters. Professor Chamberlin's objection that this reduces the "explanation" of increasing returns to a tautology misses the point. As Hutchison has emphasized,[2] all pure theory, that is, all study of the implications of given postulates is tautological in character. Accordingly, the reproach of tautology has been leveled against many propositions of economic theory. What matters is that a model which differs from the linear activity analysis model in that it omits the proportionality postulate, or at least excepts from it all activities involving certain commodities, seems to express those aspects of reality that have been recognized as responsible for increasing returns to scale. Such a model may therefore be a suitable vehicle for a first exploration of this phenomenon, and of its effect on the suitability of prices as guides to allocation.[3] So far, mathematical difficulties have been the main obstacle to such an exploration.

Additional complications arise if the locational aspects of production are combined with the indivisibility of workers and equipment. It has

---

[1] Preceding essay, Section 3, Postulate (page 76).

[2] *The Significance* . . . , chap. III.

[3] I have not found one example of increasing returns to scale in which there is not some indivisible commodity in the surrounding circumstances. The oft-quoted case of a pipeline whose diameter is continuously variable can be seen as a case of choice between alternative pieces of capital equipment, differing in diameter, used to carry oil from Tulsa to Chicago, say. No matter what diameter is selected, one entire pipeline of the requisite length is needed to render this service. Half the length of line does not carry half the flow of oil from Tulsa to Chicago.

A case mentioned by C. Palm where increasing returns are due to the operation of the laws of probability governing machine breakdown also involves, as Arrow points out, the indivisibility of the individual workers and machines. See Kenneth J. Arrow, "The Allocation of Risk-Bearing," unpublished manuscript. Abstract in *Econometrica*, July 1955, vol. 23, p. 342. William Feller, *An Introduction to Probability Theory and Its Application*, Wiley, New York, 1950, vol. I., pp. 379–383; and C. Palm, "The Distribution of Repairmen in Servicing Automatic Machines" (in Swedish), *Industritidingen Norden*, vol. 75, 1947, pp. 75–80, 90–94, 119–123.

been remarked in the preceding essay[1] that the models there considered are subject to two different interpretations with regard to time, one in terms of constant commodity flows for an indefinite period, the other in terms of dated commodities and of production and consumption programs for a number of successive time periods. A similar choice in interpretation exists with respect to location in space. In a spaceless interpretation, qualitatively the same commodities in different locations are regarded as identical commodities, and the resources absorbed in transportation are ignored. In a more realistic spatial model of the economy, commodities are distinguished by location as well as by qualitative characteristics, and transportation services between given pairs of points are treated as productive activities that require inputs of resources.

Just as indivisible commodities can be introduced in a spaceless model, so also can locational problems be studied without recognizing indivisible commodities. Much of the literature on location problems is of that character. The data that define the location problem in this case are the geographical distributions of various mineral deposits, geographical variations in the suitability of land for the production of various crops, and costs (or input requirements) of transportation between pairs of points. If, as in most of these studies, location problems are looked at from the point of view of the individual firm, the geographical distribution of markets is an additional datum. In models, descriptive or normative, which are concerned with the location of all economic activities, this distribution becomes itself a variable.

As long as indivisibility of commodities is not recognized, these models fail to grasp the essential character of the problems posed by urban conglomerations. The manner in which the various activities of a metropolitan area are (or could best be) arranged in space has very little relation to mineral deposits or grades of agricultural land, although the particular collection of activities represented in any such area may well be strongly influenced by the character of these factors in the surrounding country. If we imagine all land to be of the same quality, both agriculturally and in amount and accessibility of mineral resources, then an

---

[1] See Section 2.6, page 60.

activity analysis model of production that includes the proportionality postulate would show a perfectly even distribution of activities to be most economical. Each square inch of area would produce the same bundle of commodities from its own resources by the same bundle of activities, and all transportation would thus be avoided! If this model is modified so as to reflect continuous distributions of soil fertility and of mineral content, transportation does become economical if its resource requirements are not too high in relation to the advantages to be gained by transportation. However, even then there will be no reason for having concentrated cities unless mineral deposits (or possibly soil infertility) were to be highly concentrated. This suggests that without recognizing indivisibilities—in the human person, in residences, plants, equipment, and in transportation—urban location problems, down to those of the smallest village, cannot be understood.

Preliminary exploration of models in the location of indivisible plants throws serious doubt on the possibility of sustaining an efficient locational distribution of economic activities through a price system.[1] The decisive difficulty is that transportation of intermediate commodities from one plant to another makes the relative advantage of a given location for a given plant dependent on the locations of other plants. This dependence of one man's decision criterion on other men's decisions appears to leave no room for efficient price-guided allocation.

Again, there is no doubt about the existence and importance of transportation cost or of intermediate commodities. One may conclude from these observations that, in regard to the allocation problems raised by indivisible commodities, with or without locational distinctions, theoretical analysis still has not yet absorbed and digested the simplest facts establishable by the most casual observation. This is a situation ready-made for armchair theorists willing to make a search for mathematical tools appropriate to the problems indicated. Since the mathematical difficulties have so far been the main obstacle, it may be desirable in initial attempts to select postulates mainly from the point of view of facilitating the analysis, in prudent disregard of the widespread scorn for such a procedure.

[1] See T. C. Koopmans and M. Beckmann, "Assignment Problems and the Location of Economic Activities," *Econometrica*, vol. 25, January 1957, pp. 53–76.

10. SINGLE DECISION MAKER FACED WITH UNCERTAINTY

Considerable progress has been made in recent years in the logic of one person decision making under uncertainty.[1] The studies in question explore the implications of simple postulates about the behavior of the decision maker when choosing between actions having different but uncertain sets of consequences. These studies have derived surprisingly strong and detailed conclusions from postulates that seem unobjectionable as a statement of mere consistency and sharpness of preferences, and of a certain continuous variability in the objects of preference. Thus, von Neumann and Morgenstern[2] have considered a decision maker who chooses between prospects of which some, possibly a finite number, are available with certainty (commodity bundles, sums of money, or whatever is being valued), while the others constitute all probability mixtures of the sure prospects. A probability mixture is defined by specifying the sure prospects represented in it and the objectively given probabilities associated with these in a lottery that determines which sure prospect will become available. We let follow an approximate paraphrase of the Herstein-Milnor version[3] of the postulates in question.

(1) There is given a preference ordering which completely orders all prospects.[4]

(2) If A, B, and C are prospects ranked in that order, there is a probability mixture of A and C to which B is equivalent.

---

[1] For a survey of these developments, see Kenneth J. Arrow, "Alternative Approaches to the Theory of Choice in Risk-Taking Situations," *Econometrica*, vol. 19, October 1951, pp. 404–437, quoted hereafter as "Alternative Approaches. . . ."

[2] John von Neumann and Oskar Morgenstern, *Theory of Games and Economic Behavior,* Princeton University Press, Princeton, N.J., 1947, chap. 9, sec. 3, and Appendix on "The Axiomatic Treatment of Utility." For later simpler versions of the axioms and proofs, see Jacob Marschak, "Rational Behavior, Uncertain Prospects, and Reasonable Utility," *Econometrica*, vol. 18, April 1950, pp. 111–141, and I. N. Herstein and John Milnor, "An Axiomatic Approach to Measurable Utility," *Econometrica*, vol. 21, April 1953, pp. 291–297. For two expository discussions see Armen A. Alchian, "The Meaning of Utility Measurement," *American Economic Review*, vol. 43, March 1953, pp. 26–50, and Robert H. Strotz, "Cardinal Utility," Papers and Proceedings, *American Economic Review*, vol. 43, May 1953, pp. 384–397.

[3] See footnote 1 above.

[4] For the definition of a complete preference ordering, see Section 1.4 (page 18) of the first essay of this volume.

(3) The replacement of a prospect in a probability mixture by another prospect equivalent to it does not affect the ranking of that mixture among other prospects.

These postulates (or the original von Neumann-Morgenstern version) are shown by their respective authors to imply the existence of a cardinal utility scale, which consciously or unconsciously guides the choices. The emphasis here is on the word "cardinal." The result is not merely that the preference ordering is representable[1] by a continuous utility function of the probabilities associated with the various sure prospects in a probability mixture. The new and stronger result is that in addition the utility of each probability mixture is found to be equal to the expected utility of its outcome, that is, to a weighted sum of the utilities of the sure prospects represented in the mixture, in which the weights are the objectively given probabilities with which these prospects occur in the mixture. Due to this property, the utility function is cardinal in the sense that all that remains necessary to make it numerically determinate is to specify arbitrarily a prospect of zero utility and a pair of prospects differing in utility by one unit. While von Neumann and Morgenstern chose for historical reasons to attach the established term "utility" to this function, it will be clear that its existence depends on stronger postulates, hence implies more about actual choices, than is the case with the classical notion of a utility function.

A choice situation as postulated by this model would be approximately realized, for instance, for an isolated and self-sufficient farmer who has a sufficient record of past experience to enable him to estimate fairly accurately the probability distribution of the outputs resulting from given inputs to any given activity. It would apply to a farmer working for the market only if he felt that a probability distribution of the prices of future inputs and outputs could be estimated at decision time with comparable accuracy. Even in regard to uncertainty about future output quantities only, however, the model would hardly apply, for instance, to decisions about research and development, of which the outcome depends on as yet unrevealed properties of nature not susceptible to objective probability statements. Actually, such decisions

[1] See Section 1.4 of the first essay, page 19.

are and have to be made continually, on the basis of subjective hunches and beliefs of the decision makers.

The implications of consistent and discriminating choice, suitably defined, in situations of this latter kind have been studied by Savage,[1] among others. He considers choice between acts of which the consequences relevant to the choosing individual also depend in a known manner on the (future) state of nature, which itself is unknown and possibly incapable of description by an objective probability distribution at time of choice. We present a paraphrase of the postulates used.[2] Where appropriate we insert a tabular illustration of the postulate in question, in which the symbols $a, b, c, \ldots$ represent consequences.

(1) There is a complete preference ordering of all acts.

(2) If two acts have identical consequences in certain states of nature the preference between them shall not depend on what these identical consequences are, but only on a comparison of consequences in those states of nature where they are different from each other.

	STATES OF NATURE				
	1	2	3	4	. . . .
ACTS I	a	b	c	d	. . . .
II	a	b	e	f	. . . .

The ordering of acts I and II does not depend on a and b.

(3) In particular, if two acts have identical consequences in some states of nature, while the consequences of each act in all remaining states are independent of the state but different for the two acts, then the preference between the acts is the same as it would be if this same pair of different consequences resulted in all states of nature. (This requirement is not imposed if the states in which the two acts have different consequences are together deemed so improbable by the individual that he is indifferent

[1] Leonard J. Savage, *Foundations of Statistics*, Wiley, New York, 1954. Some earlier studies along the same lines are mentioned by Savage, and some by Arrow, "Alternative Approaches . . . ," pp. 431–432. (See footnote 1 on page 155.)

[2] What follows is a verbal translation (with all the inaccuracies of such) of the list of definitions and postulates printed inside the cover of Savage's book.

as between any two acts of which the consequences differ only in those states.)

	STATES OF NATURE				
	1	2	3	4	5
ACTS I	a	b	c	c	c
II	a	b	d	d	d
III	c	c	c	c	c
IV	d	d	d	d	d

I is preferred to II whenever III is preferred to IV.

(4) Consider further two given sets of states, with each of which a particular act is associated as follows. The act (I) associated with the first set of states (1 and 2 in the table) has one and the same consequence, a, in all states of that set, and another consequence, b, in all states not in that set. Likewise, the act (II) associated with the second set of states (2, 3 and 4) has the consequence a in each state of the second set and b in each state not of the second set. It is then required that the preference between these acts is governed by only two circumstances, (i) the preference between two acts (III and IV) which would result in a and b, respectively, in all states of nature and (ii) the two given sets of states of nature.

	STATES OF NATURE				
	1	2	3	4	5
ACTS I	a	a	b	b	b
II	b	a	a	a	b
III	a	a	a	a	a
IV	b	b	b	b	b

Which way the preference goes in the case posed by Postulate 4 defines which of the two sets of states, taken as a whole, is deemed more probable by the individual. In order that such a discrimination be possible at all, it is also postulated that

(5) the individual is not indifferent as between every two conceivable acts.

A probability ordering between sets of states can be established on the basis of Postulates 1–5. In order that numerical subjective probabilities can be associated with states of nature (or sets thereof) one additional postulate is needed, which expresses the possibility of arbitrarily fine subdivision of the set of states of nature.[1]

(6) If one set of states is deemed less probable than another, then the set of all conceivable states can be exhaustively subdivided into mutually exclusive "small" states of nature such that, if any one of the small states is included with the less probable set of states, the so augmented set will nevertheless remain less probable than the other (unchanged) set of states.

These requirements of consistency and discriminating power in the behavior of an individual faced with uncertainty are shown by Savage to imply both the existence of a subjective numerical probability (with all the properties of probability) associated with each state of nature, and the existence of a utility associated with each consequence, such that preference between acts is governed by maximization of the expected utility of the consequences, as determined by using subjective probabilities as the weights of the various states of nature in evaluating expectations.[2] Hence the theory of von Neumann and Morgenstern is contained in Savage's theory, if we interpret the probabilities occurring in it as subjective probabilities.

The results described so far, apart from their intrinsic interest as studies in the pure logic of choice under uncertainty, have considerable normative value. They suggest that consistency of choices, even among decisions of a single decision maker, is best achieved by making beliefs as well as valuations numerically explicit. Whether or to what extent these results have descriptive value is an empirical question to which the answer is not obvious. It may be felt that the surprisingly far-reaching implications of simple postulates of consistency and sharpness of preferences concerning objects capable of a particular type of continuous variation throw some doubt on their descriptive accuracy. On the other hand, the situations described in the model are, at least in their most direct interpretation, still so far removed from those met with in reality, that verification by observation of actual economic decisions appears difficult, whereas verification in experimentally created conditions may well be of limited relevance for explanatory theory.

[1] We paraphrase the simpler version labeled P6', Savage, *op. cit.*, p. 38.

[2] One further postulate (7) and a slightly stronger version of (6) above are needed if this conclusion is to hold also for acts that can have an infinite number of different consequences.

One complicating aspect of actual decision making can in principle be recognized by reinterpretation of the model. Directly interpreted, the model refers to one-shot decisions, of which all the consequences are consummated before another decision is called for. Actually, most decisions are staggered over time, with later components of decisions being made in the light of more information than earlier ones. The new information may, for instance, include such things as the outcome of production processes or of research and development completed in the meantime. Or, in the case of a consumer, it may represent a change in his preference structure resulting from the experience of consumption in the meantime. In both cases, a cascading of decisions that maintains useful flexibility seems called for.[1]

Conceptually, this complication can be incorporated in the model by interpreting a decision as a strategy which spells out the action to be taken in each future contingency after it is revealed. But such an interpretation would strengthen another "realistic" objection to the decision models under discussion. Most real-life decisions have widely ramifying effects, even within one productive establishment, on the circumstances relevant to future decisions. In order to make a correct initial decision, one would need to ascertain in what manner the circumstances for later decisions are modified thereby. Hence, in many cases, the cost of collection, processing, and use in decision making of information about all circumstances relevant to such a family of interdependent decisions can no longer be neglected. One would expect cost of information handling to limit the amount and detail of information that it is worthwhile to relate to any given initial decision. Problems of balancing the cost of information against its value in decision making are only in the beginning of their formulation.[2] Yet one feels that in realistic models this balance should be treated as an important aspect. The models of decision making under uncertainty described above are likely to represent valuable starting points for such an endeavor.

[1] For producers, this point has been emphasized particularly by Albert Hart in *Anticipation, Uncertainty and Dynamic Planning*, University of Chicago Press, Chicago, 1940. For consumers, it was emphasized by the present author in "Utility Analysis of Decisions Affecting Future Well-Being," abstract, *Econometrica*, vol. 18, April 1950, pp. 174–175.

[2] See, for instance, Jacob Marschak, "Towards an Economic Theory of Organization and Information," chap. XIV of *Decision Processes*, R. M. Thrall, C. H. Coombs, and R. L. Davis (eds.), Wiley, New York, 1954.

Another obstacle to verification, already present in the classical model of a preference ordering of sure prospects only, has not yet been removed. While the present model makes the decision maker recognize uncertainty in the external world, it does not allow him in his turn to indulge in a certain randomness in his response to (subjectively appraised) given circumstances.[1] His rules of behavior are formulated in such a way as to leave no room for exceptions. A single observed inconsistency would suffice to defeat the theory. Verification will therefore need to be preceded by a certain relaxing of the postulates sufficient to accommodate natural variability of response but not going so far as to deprive the theory of all empirical content and predictive value. Work in this direction has been reviewed and carried further by Marschak.[2]

11. INTERACTING DECISION MAKERS UNDER UNCERTAINTY

We come closer to the core of dynamic economics when decision makers of the kind just described are placed in interaction with each other through markets. This would change only the dimensions but not the character of the problem as long as each decision maker took his clues about concurrent and future decisions of the others merely from a study of records of their past decisions as reflected in historical market data. Markets would exist only for present commodities, and each decision maker would base his plans for the future on his own guesses about the future actions and responses of others without any communication about such actions taking place.

At the other extreme is the interpretation of the model of competitive equilibrium referred to in Section 2.6 of the preceding essay.[3] In this case, information about everybody's future plans would circulate to the precise extent necessary for Pareto-optimal decisions, through the operation of markets in which claims are traded on a specified commodity,

---

[1] Except that the postulates do not prescribe a choice from among acts between which he is indifferent.

[2] J. Marschak, "Norms and Habits of Decision Making under Certainty," in *Mathematical Models of Human Behavior*, Dunlap and Associates, Stamford, Conn., 1955, pp. 45–53.

For an experiment that allows for variability of behavior, see Donald Davidson and Patrick Suppes, "Experimental Measurement of Utility by Use of a Linear Programming Model," abstract, *Econometrica*, vol. 24, April 1956, pp. 201–202.

[3] See page 60.

for delivery at a specified future date, valid only in the event of a specified future contingency. The contingencies include in Arrow's version all future natural events and discoveries of characteristics of nature, and in Debreu's version future changes in preferences as well. These contingencies may be looked upon as primary sources of uncertainty that should receive first recognition. The model referred to then constitutes a first exploration in which only these sources of uncertainty are recognized.

Undoubtedly the real world finds itself somewhere between these two extremes. Markets for unconditional future delivery exist only for securities and for a few highly standardized commodities. In addition, insurance against loss of life, property damage, or crop failure, as well as the variety of bets that can be placed at Lloyd's in London, provide examples of contracts involving conditional commodities where the motivation for the contract is the reduction of economic risks through transfer and consolidation, rather than the assumption of a risk for the sake of the gamble. Few of these contracts go beyond the range of experience within which objective actuarial risks can be estimated.

Other contingencies important for economic planning are not readily expressible in a contract clause. This is true for changes in technology as well as for changes in consumers' preferences. Arrow has pointed out[1] that securities are themselves quite similar to conditional commodities. While dividend payments are not contractual obligations contingent upon stated conditions, they are in practice dependent in a highly predictable degree on the states of nature and of technical knowledge that affect the profitability of production processes financed by the shares of stock in question. Even in the case of financing by bonds, there is a chance of default dependent on the "state of nature." It is therefore conceivable that the hedging opportunities offered by markets in securities make up to some extent for the nonexistence of the markets in conditional commodities that are presupposed by the model in its literal interpretation.

While this idea is highly suggestive for further research, it is in fact doubtful that such hedging opportunities as there are come anywhere near to being sufficient. In a rough and intuitive judgment the secondary

[1] For references, see footnote 5 on page 61.

uncertainty arising from lack of communication, that is from one decision maker having no way of finding out the concurrent decisions and plans made by others (or merely of knowing suitable aggregate measures of such decisions or plans), is quantitatively at least as important as the primary uncertainty arising from random acts of nature and unpredictable changes in consumers' preferences. Observed flucutations in specific markets,[1] in inventories,[2] and in investment generally are of a kind suggesting that the information-circulating function which economic theory attributes to competitive markets is not discharged by any existing arrangements with the detail and forward extension necessary to guide decisions of which the desired benefit depends on future developments to the extent inherent in modern technology. There is, of course, an optimum residual level of "secondary" uncertainty beyond which cost of information processing exceeds further potential benefits from the circulation of more detailed information. By current indications, secondary uncertainty has not been brought down to this level. Such existing devices as surveys of investment plans or of consumers' intentions to buy durable goods are only first beginnings in a direction in which substantial further improvements in the allocative efficiency of the economy seem possible.[3]

Cost of information processing is only one out of several factors in the more general problem of how to limit the time horizon of economic planning, or perhaps better of how gradually to decrease the amount of detail and definiteness in the specification of preferences and production plans, as the periods to which they refer recede into a more distant future. Among other factors relevant to this problem are the limited life of specialized labor and equipment and the multiplicity of their uses.[4] In permitting the more distant future needs to be arranged for at

[1] M. Ezekiel, "The Cobweb Theorem," *Quarterly Journal of Economics*, vol. 52, February 1938, pp. 255–280; J. Tinbergen and J. J. Polak, *The Dynamics of Business Cycles*, University of Chicago Press, Chicago, 1950, chaps. VIII and XIV; Ruth P. Mack, *Consumption and Business Fluctuations*, publication of the National Bureau of Economic Research, Princeton, N.J., 1956.

[2] M. Abramowitz, *Inventories and Business Cycles*, National Bureau of Economic Research, New York, 1950.

[3] For further discussion of the survey method, see Sections 7 and 8 of the third essay of this volume.

[4] For a study of the effect of storage cost in limiting the horizon for production planning see F. Modigliani and F. E. Hohn, "Production Planning over Time and the Nature of

a later time, these features of physiology and technology reduce the relevance of the needs and preferences of a distant future to present decisions. Finally, there is the desire for flexibility in consumers' preferences already mentioned, which at the same time reduces the willingness of consumers to commit themselves to choices for distant periods. The concept of choice over time as a strategy does not in its present form exhibit such a tapering off of detail.

It cannot be said that the research needed to explore further the problems of dealing with uncertainty in a sequence of decisions will have to be preponderantly theoretical or preponderantly empirical. Important empirical problems include relevant traits of technology, such as the frequency distribution of life expectancy of manpower and equipment, physically and as circumscribed by the rate of technological change—and such as the range of alternative uses of given labor, equipment, or materials. They include the study of actual flows of information, and of the cost of potential additional flows. They include principles, rules, habits, and beliefs that consciously or unconsciously guide entrepreneurs and consumers in making decisions under uncertainty, and the changes over time in these rules and beliefs.

The list could be extended much further. Without a concurrent theoretical effort, however, the fact finding or statistical testing runs a risk of proliferation or maldistribution. The processes of interaction are sufficiently complicated that study of hypothetical models is needed for us to see which hypotheses about individual behavior have first claim to verification or testing, because of their relevance to questions concerning the entire economy or large segments of it to which we seek answers. As an example, consider the possible effects of risk aversion in the behavior of entrepreneurs. At first sight, one might expect that a general increase in risk aversion could lead to the technologically more risky fields of endeavor being neglected, and could result in reduced efficiency in the allocation of resources, manifested for instance by reduced growth for given levels of consumption. However, further analysis may show that the main effect is distributional, namely, a rise

the Expectation and Planning Horizon," and Francois Morin, "Note on an Inventory Problem Discussed by Modigliani and Hohn," *Econometrica*, vol. 23, January 1955, pp. 46–66 and October 1955, pp. 447–450, respectively.

in the profit of those thereby induced to engage in the riskier ventures, with little effect on efficiency of allocation in the narrow sense. This is not the kind of problem on which empirical analysis is likely to have a direct hold. It needs to be studied in conceptual models, initially as simple as permit such study, before we would know which hypotheses about the behavior of the individual firms we should attempt to test empirically.

Reverse situations also come to mind. For instance, with respect to the problem of how to taper off the details of economic foresight into a more distant future, empirical studies of the durability and flexibility of equipment and of experienced rates of change in technology and in consumers' preferences can prevent the theorist from going off on the wrong tack. Conversely, the theorist may suggest suitable measuring rods for these phenomena.

Conceptual work is needed in particular with regard to the notion of information. The scalar measure of the amount of information suggested by Shannon[1] from the point of view of the communication engineer is suggestive in this regard, but seems for the present purpose too closely tied to the words in which the information is expressed as distinct from its relevant contents. If the cost of information processing is to be balanced against its contribution to decisions, a more general method for quantifying the several relevant aspects of the intuitive notion of information is needed.

12. INTERACTION OF PREFERENCES

Changes in consumers' preferences would be a much less important source of uncertainty if in fact such changes occurred for different consumers independently of each other. The law of large numbers would in that case cut down the variability in the distribution of aggregate demand at constant prices over the various commodities. It is through waves of imitation in fashions and in the introduction of new gadgets that interacting preferences become an important source of uncertainty.

More important even than this quantitative effect of the emulative

[1] Claude E. Shannon and Warren Weaver, *The Mathematical Theory of Communication*, University of Illinois Press, Urbana, Ill., 1949.

formation of preferences is the doubt it throws on the criterion of allocative efficiency employed in the models discussed so far. What is the good of "efficient" utilization of resources to satisfy preferences created by advertising and propagated by competitive and conspicuous consumption? If beyond a certain stage above the bare subsistence level welfare is comparative rather than absolute, should not criteria of fairness in the distribution of opportunities rank above criteria of efficient allocation?

Such questions about the objectives of economic organization exceed the limits of the present essay. However, it may be conjectured that if it will be possible to give a precise meaning to the idea of fairness in the distribution of opportunities there is likely to be no unresolvable conflict between the objectives of fairness and of allocative efficiency. If this were found to be true, the "ethically" higher criterion of fairness would provide a basis for a further choice between states characterized by allocative efficiency, rather than demand a sacrifice in efficiency.

III

THE INTERACTION
OF TOOLS AND PROBLEMS
IN ECONOMICS

Tremendous spurts in the progress of the various sciences are almost always connected with the development of a new technique or the sudden emergence of a new concept. It is as though a group of prospectors were hunting in barren ground and suddenly struck a rich vein of ore. All at once everyone works feverishly and the gold begins to flow. [JAMES B. CONANT, *On Understanding Science*, YALE UNIVERSITY PRESS, NEW HAVEN, CONN., 1947, P. 81].

THE INTERACTION

OF TOOLS AND PROBLEMS

IN ECONOMICS

1. THE NEED FOR DISCUSSION

When we set about defining a field of scientific inquiry, such as economics, we identify a class of phenomena to be studied. For instance, in defining descriptive economics, we may say that we study the satisfaction of wants in human society. Or, in defining normative economics, we may say that we seek clarification as to what are, according to some suitable criterion, best ways of satisfying human wants, starting from a given state of technological knowledge and experience.

The particular formulation of these definitions is of no great importance here, and other forms may be more accurate or more informative. But we observe that quite properly the definition specifies only the problems to be studied, and not the tools of observation and analysis to be applied to these problems. In principle, tools have a servant's status. The best choice of tools depends on the problem area selected and on the extent to which at least partial answers have been found. The tools that should be developed for future use depend on the precise nature of the problems that seem most likely to be demanding or promising further answers.

If we look with a historian's interest at the development of a science, however, we find that tools also have a life of their own. They may even come to dominate an entire period or school of thought. The solution of important problems may be delayed because the requisite tools are not perceived. Or the availability of certain tools may lead to an awareness of problems, important or not, that can be solved with their help. Our servants may thus become our guides, for better or for worse, depending on the accidents of the case. But in any case changes in tools and changes in emphasis on various problems go together and interact.

The present phase in the development of economics provides vivid examples of the manifold interactions between tools and problems. To attempt to discuss these in specific terms is a hazardous undertaking. While "problems" are to some extent posed by conditions and needs of society, "tools" and states of training in the use of tools are part of the personal equipment of the investigator. It is true that it is already difficult, at best, to be objective about what are valid answers to a given social or economic problem. Society is all around us, and we are involved in it in many ways other than as observers and students. But it is even harder to be objective about what are promising tools for unsolved problems: the usefulness of our own individual minds and of the investments of personal effort sunk in our training and direction of interest are involved.

At the same time, new choices about tools and their relation to problems need to be made continually in connection with research, study, and instruction. In these circumstances, a pooling of the judgments and intuitions of people with widely differing orientation and equipment is perhaps the best procedure for gaining the insights which, as a profession, we need. The observations in this essay are submitted in this spirit, as one man's tentative opinions on some of the questions involved in the choice of tools for current and future economic research.

The present phase of economics is indeed one of turbulence and transition in the domain of tools, more so than in the domain of problems and suggested solutions. Perhaps the most conspicuous development is the increasing use of a growing number of mathematical concepts, theories, and theorems in economic reasoning. But several other important developments demand attention. There is the revolutionary increase in the capabilities of computing and data-processing equipment; the increased application of methods of statistical inference, including methods specifically designed for economic problems; the opportunities afforded by systematic application of sample survey methods of observation.

These changes in tools—and undoubtedly additional changes outside these four categories could be identified—have brought about serious difficulties of communication within the economics profession. There are risks and frustrations in a situation where separate and esoteric languages seem to spring up, among mathematical economists (including as a partly separate category the linear programmers), among econometricians, among designers and users of surveys, and among specialists in computing—thus inhibiting communication between these groups, and between them and the profession at large.

Most of the frustrations are likely to be of a temporary character. When new activity springs up around a tool development, the need most urgently felt by those engaged in the activity is for communication among themselves. The choice of language is strongly influenced by the immediate needs of this communication, and shows little regard for informing "outsiders." The suspicion of outsiders is then aroused, and may also be fanned by evidence of overestimation of the potential contribution of the new tool on the part of their developers—evidence that somehow seeps through the barriers to communication. At this point, the need for more effective communication is realized by both camps, and bridges are built from both sides. This is bound to lead ultimately to a better appraisal of the usefulness of the tools in question. If a specialization remains after this process has run its course, it is likely to be one that is accepted by the profession.

These observations apply in varying degrees to the four specific tool developments which we have selected for comment. They apply with particular force to the developments in the use of mathematics and of techniques of statistical inference.

2. THE USE OF MORE FUNDAMENTAL MATHEMATICS

The explicit use of mathematics in economics is more than a century old. So is the discussion of the contributions made by the use of this tool. The lively round of discussion[1] of the role of mathematics in economics that we have witnessed in the last ten years was presumably touched off by the two new developments noted above: the increase in the amount of economic writing in mathematical form, and the variety of mathematical concepts and theories newly introduced into economics. Started off by challenges issuing from the wisdom and experience of E. B. Wilson and J. M. Clark, and recently flaring up again in a somewhat organized response to a passionate and heroic revival of the challenge by David Novick, the discussion has reasonably well clarified the general issues involved. The essential logical equivalence of mathematics and language (Samuelson) as against the greater efficiency and conciseness of mathematical reasoning in a number of important problems (Samuelson, Stigler, and others) has been brought out. The point that the mathematical method when correctly applied forces the investigator to give a complete statement of assuredly noncontradictory

[1] E. B. Wilson, Review of T. Haavelmo, "The Probability Approach to Econometrics," *The Review of Economic Statistics*, vol. 28, August 1946, pp. 173–174.

J. M. Clark, "Mathematical Economists and Others: A Plea for Communicability," *Econometrica*, vol. 15, April 1947, pp. 75–78, extended reprint of a section of "Some Cleavages among Economists," *American Economic Review, Proceedings*, vol. 37, May 1947, pp. 1–11.

J. Marschak, "On Mathematics for Economists," *Review of Economic Statistics*, vol. 29, November 1947, pp. 169–273.

George J. Stigler, "The Mathematical Method in Economics," the fourth of *Five Lectures on Economic Problems*, London School of Economics and Political Science, Macmillan, New York, 1950.

Richard Ruggles, "Methodological Developments," (especially Section IIA), chap. 10 of *A Survey of Contemporary Economics, II*, B. Haley, ed., Irwin, Homewood, Ill., 1952.

Paul A. Samuelson, "Economic Theory and Mathematics—An Appraisal," *American Economic Review, Proceedings*, vol. 42, May 1952, pp. 56–66.

Wassily Leontief, "Mathematics in Economics," *Bulletin of the American Mathematical Society*, vol. 60, May 1954, pp. 215–233.

M. Allais, "L'Utilization de l'outil mathematique en economique," *Econometrica*, vol. 22, January 1954, pp. 58–71.

David Novick, "Mathematics: Logic, Quantity, and Method," with discussion by Klein, Duesenberry, Chipman, Tinbergen, Champernowne, Solow, Dorfman, Koopmans, Samuelson, and Harris, *Review of Economics and Statistics*, vol. 36, November 1954, pp. 357–386.

Diran Bodenhorn, "The Problem of Economic Assumptions in Mathematical Economics," *Journal of Political Economy*, vol. 64, Feburary 1956, pp. 25–32.

assumptions (Marschak, Samuelson[1]) has been generally conceded as far as the relations of the assumptions to the reasoning is concerned. To this may be added that the absence of any natural meaning of mathematical symbols, other than the meaning given to them by postulate or definition, prevents the associations clinging to words from intruding upon the reasoning process.[2] However, as has been pointed out by several of the authors quoted (Clark, Ruggles, Bodenhorn) nothing in the mathematical method per se forces the investigator to specify operational criteria that link the postulated concepts with observable entities. This task, essential for interpretation and verification of the conclusions drawn from economic analysis, is often left undone by mathematical economists when they concentrate on the reasoning.

Warnings against overemphasis on formal reasoning as an apparent end in itself have also been sounded (Stigler, Allais). There is substantial agreement that mathematical economists—if not individually, then as a group—should do their utmost to communicate the assumptions and the conclusions of their analyses in verbal form, although similar translation of their reasoning will often be impracticable. Differences of opinion remain as to where sterile "formalism" begins, and as to the relevance and pervasiveness of those parts of economics in which mathematics is an essential tool.

Since the questions on which differences of opinion subsist can be conclusively answered only by future developments, it seems unnecessary to add further to the discussion in the general terms in which it has been conducted. However, it may be worthwhile to have a closer look at some specific developments in the variety of mathematical tools used, and at the problems they pose for the general economist.

Perhaps the oldest mathematical tools in economics are the numerical example and the diagram. The use made of the numerical example has changed in character through time. In the older literature one finds the numerical example used as a tool of analysis, that is, applied without

---

[1] *Foundations of Economic Analysis*, Harvard University Press, Cambridge, Mass., 1948, p. 92.

[2] For an illustration of the manner in which words may conceal a conceptual void see the discussion of the altitude of Longs Peak in Herman Weyl, "The Mathematical Way of Thinking," address delivered at the Bicentennial Conference of the University of Pennsylvania, reprinted in J. R. Newman, (ed.), *The World of Mathematics*, vol. 3, Simon and Schuster, New York, 1956, pp. 1832–1849.

backing up the conclusions suggested by it with the help of another tool of greater power or generality of application. Later on, the numerical example has been demoted to the role of a tool of exposition. Diagrammatic or explicit mathematical analyses came to be used to provide more conclusive proof of the propositions suggested by numerical examples. It will be argued below that the power of modern computing equipment may well restore the numerical example to a position of honor among tools of analysis in regard to problems too difficult for more general solution.

Diagrammatic representation, by its nature most suitable as a tool of exposition, has long occupied a dominant position among tools of analysis in spite of the availability of more reliable tools. Ease of apprehension has made the diagram appear a tempting short cut to insight. It is true that a problem involving two or even three variables can often be correctly reasoned with a diagram as the only formal means of analysis. The logical justification of this use of diagrams lies in the fact that the postulates underlying the analytical description of space[1] are identical with those used to represent the joining and separating of commodity bundles[2] and the multiplication of such bundles by numbers. Arguments involving only a few variables can therefore often be visualized in two- or three-dimensional space. But the eye is essentially an organ of perception rather than of reasoning. Nothing in the process of reading a diagram forces the full statement of assumptions and the stepwise advance through successive implications to conclusions that are characteristic of logical reasoning. Assumptions may be concealed in the manner in which the curves are "usually" drawn, and conclusions may be accepted unconditionally although they actually depend on such unstated assumptions.

These risks may seem greater when the diagrammatic tool is being handled by our students than when it is being used by experienced analysts. However, the habit of looking at diagrams drawn in a particular way can act as blinders for long periods of time. How else, for example, can it be explained that the important implications of the nonnegative character of many economic variables were overlooked for so long?

[1] See footnote 1 on page 9.
[2] See the last sentence of Postulate 6 on page 72.

The proper uses of diagrams are in heuristic or expository discussion of relatively simple problems. For proving propositions, there is nothing a diagram can do that cannot be done with greater cogency by explicit symbolic mathematical reasoning. Mathematicians beginning with Descartes have found it rewarding to reestablish geometry on an analytical basis. It would seem that economics still suffers from the delayed consequences of the high position afforded to geometry in the Euclidean manner in the educational systems of those countries in which the decisive contributions to modern economics were made.

To the unreliability of diagrams as a guide to reasoning—a psychological rather than a logical matter—one must add the confining effect that this tool has on the choice of problems studied. The blackboard and the printed page offer only two dimensions to our gaze. A third may be added by skillful projection or by constructing a solid exhibit, but that is about the limit. In contrast, the central problems of economics concern the interaction of many variables. Only unnecessary and self-imposed tool limitations can explain why, for instance, almost the entire literature on the theory of international trade has been confined to models of two countries trading in two commodities.

We come now to the more formal mathematical concepts and theories that have come to be used in economics. The last twenty years have seen a considerable widening of the mathematical horizon of the economist. We have already commented in the first essay of this collection[1] on the trend away from calculus in analyzing how the price system can serve to decentralize the efficient allocation of resources. Several considerations have motivated this trend. In the first place, as we have seen, calculus used as a scanning device for optimal positions is myopic; it permits comparison only with neighboring positions. We have also seen that the criteria suggested by such an application of calculus need modification and supplementation whenever inequalities come to be limiting. Finally, it was found that differentiability of utility and production functions, whether or not plausible on other grounds, is irrelevant to the problems referred to and hence should not clutter up its discussion.

This particular development is one instance of a more general phenomenon which has by no means run its full course: the emancipation

[1] See, in particular, Sections 1.1 (page 6) and 1.7 (page 37).

of the social sciences, in the choice of mathematical tools, from the precedents of the more classical parts of the physical sciences.

Many other instances come to mind. A utility function of a consumer looks quite similar to a potential function in the theory of gravitational or electrical fields. But there is no counterpart apparent in physics to the more general concept of a preference ordering, not necessarily representable by a utility function. The concept of a preference ordering can be further weakened to that of a partial ordering, in which one recognizes the possibility of incomparable objectives, or at least of objectives that need not be forced into comparison for the analysis at hand.

The theory of games of von Neumann and Morgenstern[1] provides another instance. It deals with a situation, arising only in social phenomena, where each of two or more individuals controls only some of the variables which together determine the outcome of a process in which these individuals have at least partly opposed interests. The central concept of this theory is that of a strategy, a rule by which the individual determines his own response to any conceivable set of actions of his adversaries. While "games against nature" have also been studied, particularly in the theory of statistical decision making, the notion of a strategy is the key to the study of competitive or antagonistic social situations. It is used in the theory of games to determine (where possible) what strategy on the part of each participant ensures him the highest possible gain that no strategies of the other participants can deprive him of. This formulation constitutes an advance in consistency over the earlier analyses of oligopoly that relied on asymmetric rules of response whereby each participant imputes to his adversaries a more automatic, less calculating, behavior than he himself is following.[2]

Further examples could be added. Basic topological theorems have been used in studying the possibility of equilibrium in a perfectly competitive economic system[3] where the range of choices available to each

---

[1] J. von Neumann and O. Morgenstern, *Theory of Games and Economic Behavior*, 2d ed., Princeton University Press, Princeton, N.J., 1947.

[2] Whether the theory of games is to the same extent an advance in realism in the explanation of oligopolistic markets is still a somewhat open question. The theory in its present form may be assuming a greater ability and willingness to make complicated calculations and the availability of more information than is found in reality. However, any improvement in realism is likely to retain the concept of a strategy.

[3] See the studies by Arrow, Debreu, Gale, McKenzie quoted in footnotes 8–12 on page 39.

economic agent depends on the choices made by the other agents. The methods of symbolic logic have been used to study the possibilities of deriving a social preference ordering from the individual preferences of members of a group.[1] While further examples could be cited, these instances are sufficient to indicate a trend toward the use of what for lack of a better word may be called more fundamental mathematics. It is found repeatedly that needed mathematical concepts and propositions can be built up and derived from the basic postulates used to represent the phenomena studied. The postulational structure of the mathematical tool parallels that of the substantive theory to be constructed, and the two are studied and apprehended simultaneously. The welcome result is that "mathematical" and "literary" economics are moving closer to each other. They meet on the ground of a common requirement for good hard thought from explicit basic postulates, rather than for manipulative skills in calculus, differential equations, or determinants. To illustrate: in some intuitive sense the "distance" between A. P. Lerner's *The Economics of Control*[2] and the mathematical formulations of the propositions of welfare economics reviewed in the first essay of this book is, I believe, not large. If there is a difference, it is one of succinctness of expression rather than of content, concepts, or objective.

If these observations have some validity, they lead to a concept of mathematical training and self-training of economists rather different from present practice. Instead of a course in calculus, followed in a minority of cases by differential equations, the economist's primary need is for a course or reading in fundamental mathematics. The purpose of such a course would be to introduce him to the postulational structure and the first few theorems of each of a number of different mathematical theories. While the particular bundle of theories selected is not crucial, the theories of sets, of relations, of the real number system, of functions,

---

[1] Kenneth J. Arrow, *Social Choice and Individual Values*, Cowles Commission Monograph 12, Wiley, New York, 1951; Clifford Hildreth, "Alternative Conditions for Social Orderings," *Econometrica*, vol. 21, January 1953; pp. 81–94; Kenneth O. May, "A Set of Independent Necessary and Sufficient Conditions for Simple Majority Decision"; "A Note on the Complete Independence of the Conditions for Simple Majority Decisions"; "Transitivity, Utility, and Aggregation in Preference Patterns"; *Econometrica*, vol. 20, October 1952, pp. 680–684; vol. 21, January 1953, pp. 172–173, and vol. 22, January 1954, pp. 1–13, respectively.

[2] Macmillan, New York, 1946.

calculus and integration, of probability, of linear spaces and matrix algebra, of combinatorial topology and a few results of general topology, have all been found suitable and useful in one part or another of economic analysis.[1]

The main benefit to be reaped from exposure to a few of these theories is likely to be an increase in the economist's sensitivity to the basic postulates of the economic theories he constructs or examines. In addition, he will be better equipped to decide, on the basis of his area of interest in economics, in which mathematical tools, if any, he should seek a modicum of technical proficiency.

3. THE TOOL NEEDS OF ECONOMIC DYNAMICS

It is not accidental that a convergence of literary and mathematical economics is most clearly perceivable in the rather abstract area of welfare economics, in which only a few aspects of economic reality are recognized. The two are as yet much further apart in the more complicated and concrete subjects of dynamic analysis: business cycles and economic growth. To illustrate again, let us select more or less at random a recent literary essay in this area, R. A. Gordon's highly stimulating discussion of investment behavior and business cycles.[2] In reading this study, one is immediately struck by a wealth of suggestive terms and perceptive distinctions that seem to identify important links in the various chains of causation of cyclical fluctuations and economic growth. Terms such as "the stock of investment opportunities," "attitudes toward liquidity," suggest a much richer conceptual content than the two-dimensional curves of the marginal efficiency of capital and of liquidity preference found in mathematical formulations of Keynesian theory. At the same time, one realizes that the translation of these terms into concepts both sharp enough for mathematical reasoning and concrete enough for accessibility to observation will require a major effort of formal theory construction. It is no reflection on Professor Gordon's work to observe that at the present stage of our knowledge it

[1] For a discussion of a desirable mathematics curriculum for social scientists, see "Recommended Policies for the Mathematical Training of Social Scientists. Statement by a Committee of the Social Science Research Council," reproduced in *Econometrica*, vol. 24, January 1956, pp. 82–86.

[2] Robert A. Gordon, "Investment Behavior and Business Cycles," *Review of Economics and Statistics*, vol. 37, February 1955, pp. 23–34.

can only be so perceptive and so rich in distinctions because words are cheap. Having chosen a means of expression which is most suitable for an exploration of problems, Gordon achieves just that and no more. Needless to say, this is fully worthwhile achieving.

One enters a different, and in many ways poorer and more rigid, world when one examines the mathematically expressed literature of economic dynamics. The choice of assumptions in this field has for most of the last twenty years been dominated by two main limitations of the tools used, operative separately or in combination: the linearity of the behavior equations and the highly aggregative character of the variables occurring in them.

An example of linearity without economy-wide aggregation is the discussion of stability of an individual commodity market or of a system of interconnected markets. The various assumptions that have been used[1] to describe the adjustment of price or quantity in a commodity market clearly show their parentage in the laws of the physical sciences. If, for instance, the net rate of increase in price is assumed to be proportional[2] to the excess of demand over supply, whose behavior is thereby expressed? And how is that behavior motivated? And is the alternative hypothesis, that the rate of increase in supply is proportional to the excess of demand price over supply price any more plausible, or any better traceable to behavior motivation?[3]

It is hard to say whether such difficulties are covered up or circumvented in those aggregative models[4] in which commodity bundles are represented by total money values rather than by a quantity and a price for each item. The Keynesian assumption that total consumption expenditure in the economy is a simple linear function of total consumers' income which is largely independent of the prices of individual com-

---

[1] See, for instance, Oskar Lange, *Price Flexibility and Employment*, Principia Press, Bloomington, Ill., 1944, Appendix, sec. 2, and Paul A. Samuelson, *Foundations* . . . , chap. IX.

[2] That is, for small amounts of excess demand, to permit discussion of stability "in the small."

[3] Apart from the lack of a clear connection with economic motivation, there are also difficulties of definition and accessibility to observation in some of the concepts used in these formulations.

[4] See, for instance, Paul A. Samuelson, "Interaction between the Multiplier Analysis and the Principle of Acceleration," *The Review of Ecconomic Statistics*, vol. 21, May 1939, pp. 75–78, reprinted in *Readings in Business Cycle Theory*, American Economic Association, Philadelphia, 1951; and Lloyd A. Metzler, "The Nature and Stability of Inventory Cycles" and "Factors Governing the Length of Inventory Cycles," *The Review of Economic Statistics*, vol. 23 (1941), pp. 113–129 and vol. 29 (1947), pp. 1–15, respectively.

modities has an appeal of simplicity that makes both its continued testing and the study of its implications appear worthwhile and important. It may even be claimed that this simple assumption recognizes the social and emulative aspects of consumption better than the more detailed theories of individual choice have done so far. One might also feel that the introduction, as an additional causal factor, of the preceding year's income or of the highest previous income[1] (making the equation nonlinear!) again is a simple way of recognizing the partly social, partly technological, inflexibilities of consumption.

However this may be, models that are either linear or highly aggregative or both certainly break down with regard to production, inventory, and investment decisions. With regard to linearity, the difficulty is not only that these decisions by their nature often relate to quantities and not to money values. Even in terms of relations between quantities, a linear model would either have production always below capacity or always at capacity, but cannot express alternation between these two states. Neither can a linear model express the simple fact of experience that inventories can be carried forward in time but not backward, or the equally basic fact that disinvestment is not a physical reversal of the investment processes that produce plant and equipment.

These elementary considerations have of course not escaped the attention of economists. They have led to the development of a number of highly instructive nonlinear but still aggregative models of economic fluctuations,[2] some of which have been strongly influenced by proto-

---

[1] See James S. Duesenberry, *Income, Saving and the Theory of Consumer Behavior*, Harvard University Press, Cambridge, Mass., 1949; and Franco Modigliani, "Fluctuations and the Saving-Income Ratio: A Problem in Economic Forecasting," *Studies in Income and Wealth*, vol. 11, pp. 271–438, National Bureau of Economic Research, New York, 1949.

[2] Ph. Le Corbeiller, "Les Systèmes auto-entretenus et les oscillations de relaxation," *Econometrica*, vol. 1, July 1933, pp. 328–332.

L. Hamburger, "Note on Economic Cycles and Relaxation Oscillations," *Econometrica*, vol. 2, January 1934, p. 112.

N. Kaldor, "A Model of the Trade Cycle," *Economic Journal*, vol. 50, 1940, pp. 78–92.

J. R. Hicks, *A Contribution to the Theory of the Trade Cycle*, Clarendon Press, Oxford, 1950, especially chaps. VII and VIII.

R. M. Goodwin, "The Nonlinear Accelerator and the Persistence of Business Cycles," *Econometrica*, vol. 19, January 1951; pp. 1–17, and "Econometrics in Business Cycle Analysis," chap. 22 in A. H. Hansen, *Business Cycles and National Income*, Norton, New York, 1951.

Nicholas Georgescu-Roegen, "Relaxation Phenomena in Linear Dynamic Models," chap. V (pp. 116–131) in T. C. Koopmans (ed.), *Activity Analysis of Production and Allocation*, Cowles Commission Monograph 13, Wiley, New York, 1951.

types in engineering analysis. The main limitation to the direct applicability of these models has been that recognition of the nonlinearities mentioned at the same time increases the need for disaggregation. There is no reason why production should reach the limit of capacity simultaneously in all industries, why inventories should be depleted simultaneously for all commodities, or why disinvestment should become equal to depreciation simultaneously in all industries.

How is it to be explained that mathematical models in dynamic economics should have remained so distant from technological and motivational realities? The main reason seems to reside in the particular questions asked of the analysis. Perhaps again on the basis of precedent in classical physics, the laws of motion were conceived as deterministic in character.[1] In one class of cases, the question asked was to chart the complete future course of the model economy from given initial conditions. In another segment of the discussion, the question was asked whether there exists a level or future course of the model economy which will be approached more and more closely in a more and more distant future by any future course, no matter what initial conditions it starts from—or at least whenever it starts within a certain range of initial conditions.

The requirement that questions of this kind can be answered in explicit mathematical form has so far placed severe limitations on the number and kinds of nonlinearities that can be recognized in a model of the economy. At the same time, for at least two reasons, these questions are not important for the understanding of the economy. In the first place, one cannot help feeling that models for which these questions can be answered are bound to give a poor image of reality precisely with respect to the predictability of developments in a distant future. Recognition of the role of accident and of elements of chance in economic decisions, in invention, and in innovation suggests that the predictability of the future fades away with increasing distance in time. Within presently available techniques of prediction it fades quite rapidly.

Secondly, economic policy provides a means of influencing, and where desired counteracting, the movements exhibited by the economy. The

---

[1] With two exceptions, Samuelson's discussion of stochastic models, *Foundations* . . . , pp. 342–349, and the "econometric" models that recognize random elements for statistical purposes. We return to the latter category of models in Sections 6 and 8 below.

need for prediction is therefore strongest for that limited yet sizable time span required for the perception, discussion, formulation, adoption, and implementation of appropriate economic policies. This is the idea of the "economics of the steering wheel," forcefully presented by Lerner,[1] and developed in quantitative terms by Orcutt[2] and by Tinbergen.[3]

It does not follow that a model which implies predictability of an indefinitely long future is for that reason unsuitable as a guide to prediction for the time span involved in the application of policy (although it is unsuitable for assessing the degree of error in such prediction). But the question whether a model has this trait is worth examining only so that we may understand the implications and limitations of the mathematical tools it uses. Possession of this trait is no merit in itself. It becomes a disadvantage if it is attained at a cost of ignoring or distorting important features of reality that are likely to be relevant also for short-term prediction.

The present train of thought can best be continued after some further discussion of tools of computation, of statistical inference, and of observation. Meanwhile, lest some of the preceding remarks be misunderstood, it should perhaps be said that the success of a mathematical tool or theory in one field (such as physics) creates no presumption either for or against its usefulness in another field (such as economics). But each transfer of a tool between fields is attended by a risk which was clearly described, in a context quite different from the present one, by Festinger and Katz:[4]

> The real problem is not that techniques cannot be adapted to a variety of problems but that they tend to carry with them the type of thinking and even the concepts of the area in which they were developed.

The test of suitability of a tool of reasoning is whether it gives the most logical and economical expression to the basic assumptions appropriate to the field in question, and to the reasoning that establishes

---

[1] Abba P. Lerner, *Economics of Employment*, McGraw-Hill, New York, 1951, chap. I.

[2] Guy H. Orcutt, "Toward Partial Redirection of Econometrics," followed by comments from T. C. Koopmans, J. Tinbergen, and N. Georgescu-Roegen, *The Review of Economics and Statistics*, vol. 34, August 1952, pp. 195–213.

[3] J. Tinbergen, *On the Theory of Economic Policy*, North-Holland Publishing, Amsterdam, 1955.

[4] L. Festinger and D. Katz, eds., *Research Methods in the Behavioral Sciences*. The quotation is from the Foreword, by permission of The Dryden Press, Inc. Copyright 1953 by The Dryden Press. New York.

their implications. The difficulty in economic dynamics has been that the tools have suggested the assumptions rather than the other way around. Until we succeed in specifying fruitful assumptions for behavior in an uncertain and changing economic environment, we shall continue to be groping for the proper tools of reasoning.

4. COMPUTING TECHNIQUE AND MANAGEMENT SCIENCE

Others are more competent than the present author to describe the capabilities and probable further improvements of modern computing and data-processing equipment. Even the layman in this field can see, however, that the advances that have been made are revolutionary in character. They have already found application in many areas of quantitative research, and have great potentialities in others as well. In any exploration of the tools of economics, a discussion, however speculative, of the possible contributions to be obtained from the new equipment is appropriate.

In one area in which economics is strongly involved, the use of the new equipment has already proved its value. This is the area of the practical problems of operation, scheduling, programming, and allocation that arise within the business firm or government agency. The remarkable recent developments in this area are largely a delayed result of war experience in the analysis, planning, and performance of military operations, of their logistic support, and of the sustaining production programs. The analytical side of these tasks drew to it personnel from many different sciences, conceptual (logic, mathematics, statistics) as well as substantive (physical sciences, engineering, psychology, economics, law, etc.). After the war, the application of similar interdisciplinary techniques spread to business and to nonmilitary government problems. In the United States alone, three new professional societies and four new journals devoted themselves to the new field, expressing by their chosen names[1] their concept of the field or of their role in it to which they adhere.

[1] "Operations Research Society of America," founded in 1952, and its journal, now named *Operations Research;* "The Institute of Management Sciences," founded in 1953, and its journal, *Management Science;* "Society for Industrial and Applied Mathematics," founded in 1953, and its journal, *Journal of the Society for Industrial and Applied Mathematics;* and the *Naval Logistics Research Quarterly.* In addition, older journals such as *Econometrica* and the *Journal of Farm Economics* have brought out articles in the area of management science.

Two aspects can be distinguished in practically all the problems with which "operations research" or "management science" is concerned. One is the presence of a purpose or valuation, often expressed by an objective function to be maximized—output, or profit, or the probability of winning an engagement. The other is the description of the circumstances or obstacles limiting the possible degree of attainment of the objective. These circumstances are expressed by relationships between or constraints on suitably chosen variables. Impressed by the problems of establishing the circumstances and determining the relationships, the physical scientists who have entered operations research have looked on it as an extension of the methods of the physical sciences to a new range of problems. On the other hand, impressed by the pervasiveness of valuation, economists have looked on the new field as an application of economic thinking in a wider range of circumstances, specified in greater detail than has been usual in traditional economic analysis. Both views are valid.

Some of the problems to which operations research has addressed itself, such as the congestion problems of traffic, telephone exchanges, or other service systems, while having a strong economic aspect have traditionally been the concern of engineers and probability theorists. To these problems operations research brought an intensification of a line of work already flourishing before the war. On the other hand, postwar management science produced something of a break-through in regard to problems of long standing in one branch or another of economics proper: problems of production scheduling, inventory control, transportation programming, oil refinery operations, animal feeding, portfolio selection, contract awarding, etc. Important new insights in decision making, bargaining, incentive systems, were also brought to bear on economic problems. The question naturally arises how it came about that a spurt of progress on problems central to economics had to await an influx of talent from other fields.

Two circumstances stand out among possible causes: a different direction of main interest, and lack of the decisive tools. The different direction of interest was clearly expressed by Pigou in an incidental statement in his famous debate with Clapham about the "empty economic boxes":

. . . it is not the business of economists to teach woollen manufacturers how to make and sell wool, or brewers how to make and sell beer, or any other business men how to do their job. If that was what we were out for, we should, I imagine, immediately quit our desks and get somebody— doubtless at a heavy premium, for we should be thoroughly inefficient— to take us into his woollen mill or his brewery . . . .[1]

The idea underlying this statement is, presumably, that the economist's primary task is to explain the interplay of forces in the market and in the entire economy. While this task requires assumptions about business behavior, the quotation suggests that the assumption of business efficiency in the maximization of profits was deemed a sufficient first approximation for that purpose.

While Professor Pigou's statement is perhaps typical of an era in Anglo-Saxon economics, in some other countries economists did indeed make important contributions to the economics of production. There was in the thirties a lively discussion among Scandinavian and German economists concerning problems of production economics.[2] The Nordisk Tidsskrift for Teknisk Økonomi is a forerunner of management science and operations research. In particular, one can find in its pages ideas that came later to be associated with activity analysis and linear programming.[3] Similarly, in France mathematical economics was always close to engineering.

Language barriers were not the only reason why this work hardly affected economics in the United States and England in the interwar period. A controlling reason is that important tools were not available to or not prominent in the awareness of most economists concerned

---

[1] A. C. Pigou, "Empty Economic Boxes; A Reply." *Economic Journal*, vol. 32, December 1922, pp. 458–465. The quotation is from p. 463.

[2] See, for instance, Erich Schneider, *Theorie der Produktion*, J. Springer, Vienna, 1934; H. von Stackelberg, *Grundlagen einer reinen Kostentheorie*, J. Springer, Vienna, 1932; Sune Carlsen, *A Study on the Pure Theory of Production*, Stockholm Economic Studies no. 9, King, London, 1939. These authors were directly or indirectly stimulated to a considerable extent by unpublished work of Ragnar Frisch.

[3] B. Gloerfelt Tarp, "Den økonomisk definerede Produktions-funktion og den heterogene Fremstillingsprocess;" Erik Schmidt, "Økonomisk definerede Produktionsfunktioner" *Nordisk Tidsskrift for Teknish Økonomi*, 1937, pp. 225–272 and 1939, pp. 275–296, respectively. See also F. Zeuthen, *Økonomisk Teori og Metode*, Copenhagen, 1942 (English translation; *Economic Theory and Method*, Harvard University Press, Cambridge, Mass., 1955), especially chap. 15. I am indebted to Dr. Sven Danø for these references.

with business and production problems. Neither advanced mathematics nor high-powered computing equipment is essential for all problems of management science. Most of the techniques in use can be presented and understood with elementary mathematical concepts and without computing equipment other than pencil and paper. However, many of the practical decision problems of government and business are both sufficiently complicated and of sufficiently frequent recurrence to make systematic mathematical analysis and modern computing equipment important tools for reaping the full economic benefit of the new techniques. Thus the promise of substantial savings from the application of mathematical and computing tools has acted as a spur to the development of the concepts and methods involved.

We have already commented on an inclination among economists to regard the developments in management science as outside the range of economics proper.[1] Without pressing that comment further here, it is worth examining for a moment whether we may perhaps look forward to a useful feedback from management science into the problems of the economy as a whole. One finding already stands out: the practical implementation of profit maximization is a great deal more complicated than the traditional textbook formula of equating marginal cost with marginal revenue would suggest. In those situations where businessmen have indeed come close to applying profit maximization or other more general behavior maxims, management science may therefore give the economist more realistic hypotheses about business behavior. In those situations in which the complications of the problem have so far prevented business from approximating optimal policies, the advice of management science if heeded may help bring theory and practice closer together and thus make the economy more understandable and possibly more predictable than it would otherwise have been. Finally, to the extent that the advice of management science is not heeded— either because it fails to take important objectives into account or because business decisions themselves are not fully rational—it will help bring to light additional rational or irrational elements of business motivation and decisions. In sum, better understanding of what is involved in the application of explicit maxims is likely to increase our knowledge of actual behavior in one way or another.

[1] In Section 3.2 of the first essay of this volume, see page 70.

5. COMPUTING AND THE PREDICTION
OF PRODUCTION POTENTIAL

The application of high-speed computing to management problems was preceded by two parallel and large-scale development efforts directed to its use for government problems. One of these was the development of programming methods for the manifold activities of the United States Air Force by Wood, Dantzig, and associates.[1] In this work the linear programming model discussed in Section 3.13 of the first essay of this volume was used primarily as a framework for information handling, and secondarily, to the extent permitted by computing and information processing capacities, for optimization. The other development was directed at the assessment of the production potential of an entire economy. The particular model that has been used most extensively to guide data collection and computation for this problem is the open input-output model of Professor Leontief.[2] In both developments the data collection was the more costly part of the undertaking. At the same time, high-speed computing was essential for utilizing these data in the manner envisaged by the models used. Work on the input-output model was cut back in 1953 by the incoming federal Administration. Work on Air Force programming was reoriented to smaller problems of immediate applicability, such as transportation, production scheduling, or contract awarding. Currently, Air Force interest in more inclusive scheduling is again increasing.

There is no published account or appraisal of experience with programming methods in the Air Force. Experience with input-output models for testing the feasibility of production programs has been reported on more fully though by no means completely, and has also been the subject of evaluative studies. For this reason, and because of the importance of this experience for our present discussion of the tools of economics, we shall briefly review the problems it has raised,

[1] See Marshall K. Wood and George B. Dantzig, "The Programming of Interdependent Activities: General Discussion," and Marshall K. Wood and Murray A. Geisler, "Development of Dynamic Models for Program Planning," chaps. I (pp. 15–18) and XII (pp. 189–215), respectively, of T. C. Koopmans (ed.), *Activity Analysis of Production and Allocation*, Cowles Commission Monograph 13, Wiley, New York, 1951.

[2] Wassily W. Leontief, *The Structure of the American Economy, 1919–1939*, 2d ed., Oxford University Press, New York, 1951.

even though this requires introducing a certain amount of technical detail.

The basic assumptions of the input-output model have already been described in Section 3.14 of the first essay of this volume. In its application to the prediction of production potential, the productive system is subdivided into a number of "sectors," or "industries." The output of each industry is measured by its value in a base year, and thereafter treated as a homogeneous "commodity." The inputs into this industry of the various "commodities," each of which is the output of one other industry, are again measured by their values in that base year. The ratios of the various inputs to the output of any one industry are computed and are thereafter used as if they were technical input-output coefficients, specific to the method of production of that industry. This method is treated as the only process available to that industry, subject to variation only in the scale of application—that is, proportional variation in all inputs and in the unique output. The entire technology is thus represented by an almost-square matrix of input-output coefficients.[1] In successive computations, the number of industries has increased from 9 through 38, 44, 95, 192, to 450. The data used in some of these stages were obtained as condensations of matrices representing more highly disaggregated stages.

It will be clear from this description that, while input-output analysis involves extensive statistical measurement, it does not involve statistical inference in the sense of employing observations to confirm, reject, or screen individual assumptions of the model used. Empirical testing is delayed until the entire model is assembled with numbers filled in, at which time the model can be given "trial runs" before actual use, to which we shall return below.

The main use of the model consists in computing for each industry the total output level implied, through the assumptions stated, in a given "commodity" composition of final demand, also called the "bill of goods." Depending on the application, the bill of goods may be built up from one or more of the following constituents: consumption, net exports, investment, and net government demand for general purposes, defense, or war. If one desires the answer in a form that permits varia-

---

[1] There may be one or more extra rows for the input coefficients of primary factors, such as labor, which are not treated as outputs of an industry.

tion of the bill of goods, the computation involves primarily one matrix inversion, which constitutes a technical problem requiring high-speed computing equipment only because of the size (or "order") of the matrix in question.

As pointed out among others by Dorfman,[1] information of the kind sought in this manner can be useful for many purposes, provided it can be supplemented by other methods for predicting the amount and composition of consumption, investment, and other items, if any, in the bill of goods. However, there is one use in which this supplementary information is itself approximately given by the nature of the problem. This situation arises in assessing the feasibility of a production program for war or for preparedness for war, under circumstances where consumption and investment can to a large extent be thought of as controllable, or at least foreseeable. The feasibility test then consists in comparing the output levels of the various industries implied in a given bill of goods with known or planned capacities of the industries and of their labor force. It is with this use of the model in view that substantial resources have been devoted in the United States to the data collection and computation required by the model. Various European countries have likewise developed input-output tabulations, preponderantly with a view to their use in general economic policy determination, along with other procedures for predicting or influencing the bill of goods.[2]

The literature on input-output analysis is by now substantial, with increasing attention being paid to the evaluation of the method. The Conference on Research in Income and Wealth of the National Bureau of Economic Research devoted an entire conference to this purpose in 1952, the proceedings of which are now available.[3] In particular, the article by Carl Christ in that volume,[4] and the article by Robert Dorf-

[1] Robert Dorfman, "The Nature and Significance of Input-Output," *The Review of Economic Statistics*, vol. 36, May 1954, pp. 121–133.

[2] For accounts of this work, see two volumes of proceedings of conferences held in Driebergen, Netherlands, in 1950, and in Varenna, Italy, in 1954. The references are *Input-Output Relations*, Stenfert Kroese, Leiden, 1953; and *The Structural Interdependence of the Economy*, T. Barna (ed.), Wiley, New York, 1956.

[3] *Input-Output Analysis: An Appraisal*, Studies in Income and Wealth, vol. 18, National Bureau of Economic Research, Princeton University Press, Princeton, N.J., 1955, and a Technical Supplement issued directly by the N.B.E.R.

[4] "A Review of Input-Output Analysis," pp. 137–168.

man already referred to represent, between them, as good, as fair, and as penetrating an evaluation as can be made from publicly available evidence. There is no need to add further to the discussion here, except to emphasize one point relevant to the debate on the input-output analysis—as well as to our present topic of the relations between tools and problems in economics—a point which is not emphasized by either Christ or Dorfman, and which was definitely overlooked by the several critics[1] at the Conference in their understandable zeal to whittle down the exaggerated claims that had been made for the input-output model by some of its protagonists. Since this point arises in connection with the question what is to be regarded as a crucial empirical test of the usefulness of the input-output model, we must first review briefly the available tests.

"Trial runs" carried out by Leontief,[2] Hoffenberg, Barnett,[3] and Evans and Hoffenberg are described and reviewed by Christ.[4] To these we should add a further test by Selma Arrow.[5] All these tests are of the same general type. The directly measured actual[6] bill of goods for one or more experienced "test years" different from the "base year" is combined with a matrix of input-output coefficients derived from the base year (with or without corrections for easily recognizable technological changes between base and test year) to form estimates of the total outputs of each industry in the test year. These estimates are then compared with directly measured industry outputs in the test year. The discrepancies between "estimated" and "measured" industry outputs are in turn compared with similar discrepancies obtained by applying more mechanical or naïve methods of estimating specific industry outputs from a given bill of goods, methods that are intended primarily

---

[1] Especially Rutledge Vining, *op. cit.*, pp. 31–46, and Milton Friedman, *op. cit.*, pp. 169–174.

[2] *The Structure of the American Economy, 1919-1939*, pp. 216–218.

[3] Harold J. Barnett, "Specific Industry Output Projections," in *Long Range Economic Projection*, Studies in Income and Wealth, vol. 16, National Bureau of Economic Research, Princeton University Press, Princeton, N.J., 1954, pp. 191–226.

[4] Christ, *op. cit.*, pp. 159–167.

[5] "Comparisons of Input-Output and Alternative Projections," unpublished memorandum P–239 of the RAND Corporation, April 1951.

[6] Except in the Barnett test, which uses two alternative projections of the 1950 bill of goods prepared in 1947 by Cornfield, Evans and Hoffenberg. As a result, the Barnett test does not discriminate between the errors of these projections (which their authors did not regard as predictions) and the errors of the various methods of tracing the specific industry output implications of a given bill of goods.

as standards of comparison. The naïve methods that have been used are the "final demand blowup," which "assumes" that the total output of each industry is a constant multiple of final demand for its product, the "GNP blowup," which "assumes" that the ratio of each industry's output to (real) gross national product is a constant, and a regression method, used only by Barnett and by Mrs. Arrow, which predicts each industry's output (a degree less naïvely) from a multiple regression over a recent period of that output on gross national product and on time.

Subject to the one exception of Leontief's test using 1939 as the base year and 1919 and 1929 as test years, the tests by and large show the regression method to be the most accurate one and final demand blowup to be about on a par with the input-output technique, with GNP blowup trailing behind. This must be looked upon as a preliminary result, subject to all the qualifications about the biases of the methods compared, about the defects of the data used, and about the timing of the availability of similar data in future applications, which have been brought out by the authors of the tests and by their discussants in two conferences.[1] In particular, all publicly available tests are based either on an early 38–industry matrix for 1939 or on condensations of it. Mrs. Arrow attributes the better showing of the regression method in part to the inclusion of a time variable representing gradual change in technology and in consumers' preferences.[2] It should not be too difficult to make allowances for gradual change in technology in an input-output matrix, and perhaps also for gradual change in preferences in an estimated bill of goods. One should therefore perhaps be equally concerned with the failure of the input-output model in most of the tests to do better than the final demand blowup in deriving specific industry outputs from the bill of goods. Disappointment on this score is expressed specifically by Barnett.[3]

Although provisional and incomplete, the few available test results give renewed importance to the question raised above, which has so far received insufficient discussion: What is a crucial empirical test for the input-output model's usefulness in predicting the productive

---

[1] See the references in footnote 3 on page 189 and in footnote 3 on page 190.

[2] And in part to the fact that the test years used by her fall within the period to which the regressions have been fitted.

[3] *Op. cit.*, sect. D, pp. 212–213.

potential of an economy? It is here that our point comes in. All the test years selected are peacetime years. These are years in which the composition of the bill of goods changes only gradually, and in a manner exhibiting a rather regular relationship with total productive activity as measured, for instance, by gross national product. Industry outputs will accordingly also exhibit a rather regular covariation with gross national product. These circumstances favor the simple methods, and give them a chance to match or outdo the input-output model through their comparative advantages: the inclusion of a time variable and a constant term in the regression method, and dependence on a comparatively small number of relatively aggregative observations (in which percentage error has been reduced by aggregation) in the final demand blowup as well as in the regression method. But these are not the circumstances at which the large-scale development of input-output analysis was aimed. A defense or war production program is likely to involve drastic shifts in the composition of the bill of goods that depart from peacetime relationships to total activity. The regression method yields no information on the consequences of such shifts for specific industry outputs. The final demand blowup is likely to go wrong particularly for those industries whose output goes in the main into inputs to other industries producing the "commodities" for which the shifts in demand are strongest. It could give approximately correct answers only through some statistical accident that would steer the shifts in the composition of final demand in such a manner that the induced demand for the product of each industry for use as inputs in other industries would happen to change in proportion to final demand. Whether such an accident is a possibility for some given or planned shift in the bill of goods cannot be ascertained in advance within the "assumptions" of the final demand blowup "model." In some sense, the input-output model with a moderate degree of disaggregation is the simplest, and one might well say the crudest, model of which the assumptions at all have a bearing on the problem of feasibility testing of an industrial mobilization program that cuts across peacetime relationships of the various demands to income.

This point has come up at various occasions in the debate on input-output analysis. It is made very clearly in Mrs. Arrow's unpublished memorandum.[1] The distinction on which it rests is also made by

[1] *Op. cit.*, p. 7.

Alexander Henderson[1] when he warns that, if input-output analysis were found to be successful in predicting the industrial impact of largely proportional peacetime changes in final demand, this would not guarantee similar success in regard to disproportional wartime changes in demand. While this is undoubtedly true and needed saying, the distinction also cuts the other way. The naïve and seminaïve methods are at their best for quasi-proportional changes in final demand. Failure of input-output analysis to improve on these methods for such changes does not imply similar relative failure under the shifts in demand, unrelated to consumers' and business incomes, that arise in industrial mobilization. Neither success nor failure in the one set of conditions prejudges the outcome of a test under the other set of conditions.

These considerations show the extraordinary difficulty of testing the suitability of the input-output model for the purpose for which it was developed on a large scale. It is conceivable that the experience data for World War II are found to be sufficiently detailed and accurate to make a useful trial run possible, should there be a sponsor for such a project. But even if in this fearful age the world were to go through the horrors of another major war, the very destructiveness of the new weapons would be likely to make the data assembled in an input-output model irrelevant. The information requirements for national survival after a major atomic attack are of a different character, with greater emphasis on location, vulnerability, and prompt determination of damage sustained.[2] It is only in the event of a major war in which the most destructive weapons are withheld from use that the model could receive an all-over trial run. The resulting experience would come too late to contribute to preparedness for such an eventuality.

Neither can one be confident on a priori grounds that the relative structural superiority of the input-output model over its naïve competitors would give it a decisive advantage if events were to subject it to such a test. We have argued that the input-output model embodies some notion of the repercussions of changes in the composition of final demand down the production hierarchy of intermediate demands, where

---

[1] *Input-Output Analysis: An Appraisal*, pp. 22–29, especially pp. 26–27. See footnote 3 on page 189.

[2] See Marshall Wood, "Industry Must Prepare for Atomic Attack," *Harvard Business Review*, vol. 33, May–June 1955, pp. 115–128.

the naïve models have none. But the input-output model in its turn fails to recognize essential aspects of this chain of repercussions. The output of each industry, treated as a homogeneous commodity, actually consists of physically different commodities made by processes with different input requirements. The approximation on which the model rests disregards the differences between these input requirements. This approximation can presumably be improved by disaggregation. But disaggregation at the same time increases the distortion created by another specification of the model. The recognition of only one method of production for each industry blinds the model to all possible changes in processes that modify the participation of the different supplying industries in producing the input bundle to that industry. As the industry classification is made finer, there will be more such alternative processes that are important.

Both defects are aggravated by the shifts in demand arising from industrial mobilization. Relative shifts in the commodity composition of demand for the products of one industry—not perceived by the model—may well be as large as the shifts between industries that are recognized by the model. The scarcities created by both types of shifts are likely to entail changes in methods of production not perceived by the model. Thus the very circumstances that require a structural approach are likely to demand a more thoroughgoing structural approach, one that recognizes more aspects of the industrial system than the input-output model does.

All these considerations strengthen the case—argued by several commentators at the Conference—for more testing of the individual pieces of a model of the production system under a variety of circumstances, rather than depending on all-over trial runs of the entire model. This actually means going more deeply into the technological structure of specific production processes than can be done by measurement of value flows between industries in one year.

The direct study of technological processes has been taken up by Leontief and his collaborators in a recent volume[1] containing among other contributions a number of quantitative studies of the production

---

[1] Leontief, Chenery, Clark, Duesenberry, Ferguson, A. P. Grosse, R. N. Grosse, Holzman, Isard, Kistin, *Studies in the Structure of the American Economy*, Oxford University Press, New York, 1953.

functions of several industries.[1] Studies of this kind draw on information about production possibilities at the level of disaggregation at which it is available to the production engineer or to the designer of equipment. Markowitz has proposed,[2] under the name "process analysis," a refinement of the input-output model in which the commodities are identified by their physical characteristics rather than by the industry that produces them, and in which production processes are identified with particular types of equipment or even particular uses thereof rather than with the using industry. The model may recognize several alternative processes for the production of one commodity. Processes of joint production are also permitted. Maintaining the assumptions of proportionality of the inputs and outputs of each process, and of noninteraction between processes, Markowitz is thereby led to use the model of linear activity analysis described in Section 3 of the first essay of this volume. Production possibilities are represented by a rectangular matrix of input-output coefficients for which estimates are obtained directly from engineering knowledge of the processes in question. The computing techniques of linear programming then permit computation of interesting alternative production programs situated on the efficient boundary that separates feasible from infeasible programs —assuming that the assumptions of the model apply and that the data used are sufficiently accurate for the purpose. They also permit associating with each such program a system of efficiency prices indicating marginal rates of substitution between different outputs, applicable to limited modifications of that program. The use of direct engineering knowledge is regarded by Markowitz as the essential characteristic of process analysis, the use of the mathematical model of linear activity analysis as a choice imposed by presently available mathematical and computational techniques. His article summarizes[3] a process analysis study of the United States petroleum industry involving 109 commodities and 350 processes, which was developed by Alan Manne and will be published by its author in greater detail. This represents a degree

---

[1] Including the cotton textile, air transportation, and gas pipeline industries.

[2] Harry Markowitz, "Industry-wide, Multi-industry and Economy-wide Process Analysis," in T. Barna (ed.), *The Structural Interdependence of the Economy*, Proceedings of a conference at Varenna in 1954, Wiley, New York, 1956, pp. 121–150.

[3] He also refers to similar studies contemplated or in process for the iron and steel, metalworking, fuel and power, and chemical industries.

of disaggregation far in excess of that contemplated by input-output analysis.

Markowitz and Manne visualize process analysis as a method of recording and scanning the production possibilities of an economy in which the industrial coverage and the degree of technological detail can be adjusted to the questions to be answered. The reader may well ask whether, if moderate disaggregation and crude recognition of the structure of production did not in the tests made so far give input-output analysis an edge over more naïve and mechanical models, further dis-aggregation and better recognition of the structure of production is more likely to produce the desired accuracy of prediction.

To this the developers of process analysis would reply first that their model can be tested separately for each sector or industry covered by it, and that each segment of the model that stands such a test has usefulness in itself. They would argue further that the recognition of choice in methods of production, of substitution among materials used, and of multiple products of a process avoids distortions of reality that have been recognized as sources of error in the application of the input-output model. Finally, they would add that the degree of disaggregation used in process analysis is unavoidable if one wishes to tap the knowl-edge about production technology and capacities possessed by those in charge of the processes in question. To integrate this knowledge and to test it against statistical data on achieved rates of production contributes to the analysis of the efficiency of our productive system in the handling of information and in the making of production decisions.

The desirable degree of recognition of detail and fine structure in empirical model construction is a central problem of econometrics. Since we shall encounter it again in the next section in connection with the measurement of economic behavior, its discussion will be resumed in Sections 8 and 9 below.

As in the case of input-output analysis, the possible uses of process analysis are not limited to problems of industrial mobilization. They include all problems in which one wishes to foresee the effects of rather drastic changes in the rates of use of quantitatively known or predict-able production processes. There are important problems of economic development that fall in this category. In considering such applications, it should be kept in mind that both input-output analysis and process analysis concentrate on the quantitative description of technological possibilities, and give little attention to the effect of economic behavior on the utilization of these possibilities. Since the input-output model does not recognize choice in the utilization of technology, it can in particular not describe inefficient utilization except in the crude form of unemployment of the limiting primary factor of production, whether labor or an industrial capacity. The process analysis model does recognize choice and therefore can also be used to describe inefficient allocation of fully used resources. However, it has so far been applied only under the assumption of efficient allocation. These may be good first approximations for problems of industrial mobilization. In problems of economic development or of business fluctuations, the description of technological possibilities will need to be supplemented by the study of economic behavior as it affects the utilization of resources.

In the study of economic behavior, the element of unpredictable variation is even more prominent than in the description of technology. It is in this central area of economic research that there has been considerable growth in the application of formal methods of statistical inference.

6. STATISTICAL INFERENCE AND THE MEASUREMENT OF ECONOMIC BEHAVIOR

Modern statistical theory has greatly increased the flexibility, the power, and the precision of our procedures for drawing inferences from observations, and for assessing the power or precision achieved by these procedures. The tool of statistical inference becomes available as the result of a self-imposed limitation of the universe of discourse. It is assumed that the available observations have been generated by a probability law or stochastic process about which some incomplete knowledge is available a priori. Technically this knowledge is expressed by specifying a class of probability laws of which the law that has generated the observations is postulated to be a member. The term "universe" may be used for this class (with a slight extension of its usual meaning). In the theory of testing hypotheses, developed by J. Neyman and E. S. Pearson, the universe then constitutes the maintained hypothesis, and a designated subclass of probability laws (possibly a single law) constitutes the hypothesis under test. The theory attempts to answer the question whether or not the "true law" is a member of that subclass in such a way as to minimize the risks of error in that answer, and studies how those minimal risks of error depend on what the true law really is. The theory of estimation, which in its modern form goes back to R. A. Fisher, presupposes that a concept of continuity or proximity applies to the way in which the probability laws are arranged in the universe. Estimation then consists in determining from the available observations a particular law which has a good chance (or better: does not fall far short of the best attainable chance) of coming close to the "true law."[1] The theory of decision making initiated by Abraham Wald adjoins to the universe of probability laws a class of possible actions or decisions and presupposes knowledge of how the "reward" or "pay-off" to be expected from each decision in that class depends on the unknown "true law." The theory then specifies, and shows how to implement, criteria for making a good decision in the light of whatever information about the identity of the true law can be extracted from the available observations. Finally, the theories of sampling and of the design of experiments deal with those situations in which the observer has an influence on the number and character of the observations. These theories tell how to choose the number of observations and the conditions under which they are obtained so as to raise the precision of the inferences or the benefit expected from the actions up to a point of balance between cost and return.

It should be kept in mind that the sharpness and power of these remarkable tools of inductive reasoning are bought by willingness to adopt a specification of the universe in a form suitable for mathematical analysis. Considerable progress has been made in recent years, particularly in connection with so-called nonparametric or distribution-free methods and the use of order statistics, toward a widening of the universes for which statistical methods have been or can be developed. Generally and naturally, one finds that the larger the number of observa-

---

[1] More generally, estimation determines one subclass out of a predesignated, exhaustive family of nonoverlapping subclasses of the universe, so as to have a good chance that the subclass so determined contains a law close to the "true" one.

tions, and the greater one's influence on the conditions under which they are obtained, the less restrictive can be the universe chosen and still permit useful inferences. Nevertheless, the problem of specification error, or more broadly of the consequences of incorrect specification, is always present in the trail of every application of statistical methods. Thus in any particular field of applicability of statistical methods progress depends on taking more observations, or on exercising greater control over the conditions under which observations are obtained, or on making more use of plausible a priori knowledge (that is, knowledge not contained in the observations) in specifying the universe—or on a combination of these.

The various approaches to empirical economics that have been developed for a variety of purposes can be classified, among other ways, by the relative emphasis placed on one or another of these avenues of progress. The input-output and process analysis models for assessing the production potential of an economy depend on a priori knowledge or assumption to such an extent that formal procedures of statistical inference have so far not found application in these models. At the other extreme, the approach of the National Bureau of Economic Research to the empirical study of business cycles, developed by Mitchell, Burns,[1] and their associates, emphasizes the number and wide coverage of observations to the virtual exclusion of explicit a priori specification—again thereby precluding the use of formal techniques of statistical inference.[2] The "econometric" approach to the measurement of behavior equations, whether for individual markets or for an entire economy, emphasizes the combination of a priori knowledge or assumption with observation. While initially the observation was largely a "passive" use of accumulated records, the increased use of the sample survey as a method of observation has more recently strengthened the element of choice in the making of observations.

In the light of these remarks, it is not surprising that statistical methods have been used most extensively in the econometric measure-

[1] See, in particular, A. F. Burns and Wesley C. Mitchell, *Measuring Business Cycles*, National Bureau of Economic Research, New York, 1946.

[2] For further discussion of this point, see Tjalling C. Koopmans, "Measurement without Theory," *Review of Economics and Statistics*, vol. 29, August 1947, pp. 161–172, and a discussion between Rutledge Vining and Tjalling C. Koopmans on "Methodological Issues in Quantitative Economics," *Review of Economics and Statistics*, vol. 31, May 1949, pp. 77–94.

ment of behavior equations. The objectives of this effort have ranged from the measurement of demand or supply equations for markets of individual rather homogeneous commodities,[1] through systems of such equations for a few related and usually more aggregated markets,[2] to the more ambitious equation systems attempting to represent the dynamic properties of an entire economy.[3] The latter category is of particular interest from our present point of view because the degree of complication and the data requirements of these studies call for extensive use of observation, data processing, statistical methods, and computation. Again some technical discussion is needed for our purpose. However, the wide range of economic ideas that have been utilized in the more ambitious models of an entire economy make it difficult to summarize their content. The observations made in the remainder of this Section 6 are therefore addressed primarily to those readers who have some familiarity with the economic assumptions on which the models in question have been based.

In accordance with what has been said above, these assumptions are introduced through specification of the universe of possible laws of generation of the observations. The investigator specifies a number of behavior equations, the variables entering into each, a simple mathematical form for each equation, and a rather wide class of probability distributions for the disturbances of the various equations. The disturbance in any one equation is here looked upon as the aggregate effect of many individually unimportant or random variables not explicitly recognized in setting up the behavior equation in question.

Because of the relative importance of systematic or a priori factors

---

[1] Representative studies are Henry Schultz, *The Theory and Measurement of Demand*, University of Chicago Press, Chicago, 1938; Herman Wold and Lars Juréen, *Demand Analysis*, Wiley, New York, 1953; and Richard Stone, *The Measurement of Consumers' Expenditure and Behavior in the United Kingdom, 1920–1938*, vol. I, Cambridge University Press, Cambridge, Eng., 1954.

[2] Examples are A. R. Bergstrom, "An Econometric Study of Supply and Demand for New Zealand's Exports," *Econometrica*, vol. 23, July 1955, pp. 258–276, and C. Hildreth and F. G. Jarrett, *A Statistical Study of Livestock Production and Marketing*, Wiley, New York, 1955.

[3] The principal studies in this category are J. Tinbergen, *Statistical Testing of Business Cycle Theories*, vol. I, *A Method and Its Application to Investment Activity*, vol. II, *Business Cycles in the United States of America, 1919–1932*, League of Nations, Geneva, 1939; *Business Cycles in the United Kingdom, 1870–1914*, North-Holland Publishing, Amsterdam, 1951; Lawrence R. Klein, *Economic Fluctuations in the United States, 1921–1941*, Cowles Commission Monograph 11, Wiley, New York, 1950; and L. R. Klein and A. S. Goldberger, *An Econometric Model of the United States, 1929–1952*, North Holland Publishing, Amsterdam, 1955.

as against random factors, the term *structure* has come to be used instead of the "probability law" of general statistical terminology, and the term *model* instead of what above we have called "universe," although as far as the logic of statistical inference goes no change in meaning adheres to the change in terms. Economic theory or intuition about the motivation of individual firms or households has been used in specifying the variables in those equations that are to represent the aggregate outcome of similar decisions taken by large groups of firms or households. Two important advantages are bought by a willingness to confine the investigation to the implications of a priori assumptions about the form of the equations and the participating variables of each. They relate, respectively, to the two different purposes of the models in question.

The first of these purposes, which has been emphasized most in the work of Lawrence Klein, is the conditional prediction of endogenous variables from hypothetical or projected contemporaneous values of exogenous variables and from observed past values of both exogenous and endogenous variables. Here exogenous variables are defined as variables that are assumed to be independent (in a probability sense) of the random elements in behavior. They are thought of mostly as noneconomic or semieconomic variables such as population, technology, government policies, and sometimes also as "external" economic variables such as world prices or exports. An obvious alternative prediction method that could serve this same purpose would be to fit a suitable regression of the predictand on all the predictors. The existence of such a regression relationship is of course implied in the model. It can be estimated with at least some precision if the exogenous variables in question have shown enough independent variation over the period of observation. However, *if* the model contains a sufficient number[1] of *valid* a priori specifications, the advantage of the use of these specifications in estimating the structural equations lies in the greater accuracy of the predictions thereby obtained, as compared with those obtained from a mere regression fitted to observations of the same period. Usually, there is a computational cost connected with the use of the a priori specifications. Even more serious, of course, is the risk of error introduced by possibly erroneous specifications.

---

[1] Technically this means that the specifications should be "overidentifying."

The second purpose of model construction of the type indicated—a purpose emphasized more strongly in the earlier work of Tinbergen although not disregarded by Klein—is that of predicting the quantitative effects of policies which have not been subject to change in the past, or which have not changed enough or independently enough to allow a forecast to be made from a regression on past experience. The policies may be changes in tax regulations, in government expenditure policies, or in the stimulation of private consumption or investment, or any other known changes in structure. The same economic reasoning that has suggested the choice of variables and the form of the behavior relationships often also suggests which of the relationships are changed by given policies, in which direction, and sometimes also by how much they are shifted or otherwise modified. But there is no way of tracing such knowledge through to its quantitative consequences for the economy as a whole except on the basis of estimated structural equations that represent the behavior of the relevant parties in the economy, however approximated and aggregated. Thus the advantage of the use of a priori specifications about the form and the participating variables of each behavior equation, for the purpose of predicting the effects of "new" policies, is an absolute rather than a relative advantage. Usually, this purpose cannot be served in a meaningful way by simpler procedures resting on decisively fewer assumptions. The importance of this consideration was first clarified by Hurwicz.[1] Its implications were subsequently restated and elaborated by Marschak.[2] These ideas have motivated the development of a methodology of identification and estimation of structural equations of which the technical aspects need not be discussed in the present context.[3]

[1] Leonid Hurwicz, "Prediction and Least Squares," chap. VI of *Statistical Inference in Dynamic Economic Models*, T. C. Koopmans (ed.), Cowles Commission Monograph 10, Wiley, New York, 1955. See especially pp. 266–274.

[2] Jacob Marschak, "Economic Structure, Path, Policy and Prediction," *American Economic Review, Proceedings*, vol. 37, May 1947; pp. 81–84; and "Economic Measurements for Policy and Prediction," chap. I in *Studies in Econometric Method*, William C. Hood and Tjalling C. Koopmans (eds.), Cowles Commission Monograph 14, Wiley, New York, 1953.

[3] For summaries see the Monograph quoted in the preceding footnote, and L. R. Klein, *Econometrics*, Row Peterson, Evanston, Ill., 1953. The development was sparked by Trygve Haavelmo, "The Statistical Implications of a System of Simultaneous Equations," *Econometrica*, January 1943, pp. 1–12, and *The Probability Approach in Econometrics*, Supplement to *Econometrica*, July 1944.

Obviously the question of testing the performance of these aggregative models of interacting economic decisions is again crucial. One contrast with the input-output model should be brought up at this point. A certain amount of statistical testing and screening of the assumptions of the behavior model can be and usually is performed along with the estimation procedure. Whenever the specifications concerning a given equation are more detailed than the minimum needed for its identification (that is, for distinguishing it from the collection of relationships implied in all other equations of the structure), these specifications taken together are subject to statistical test, and can be revised if the tests so require. For the same reason, a wider range of alternative specifications of the form of the relationships in question can often be permitted a priori. In comparison with the input-output model, these advantages arise from having more observations per parameter to be estimated.

Clearly such preliminary testing does not do away with the need for an allover performance testing of the models in question. Tinbergen's models were not tested in the latter sense.[1] Carl Christ made one test of Klein's 16-equations model for 1921–1941,[2] modified by Christ to fit data for 1946 and 1947. He compared the forecasting performance of that model for the relatively quiet year 1948 with that of two "naïve" models suggested by Friedman[3] as standards of comparison. The first of the naïve models "forecasts" each endogenous variable for a given year by the observed value in the preceding year. The second "forecasts" the rate of increase between two successive years by the observed rate of increase similarly measured one year earlier. For the "structural" forecasts Christ uses two alternative procedures that (for reasons of

---

[1] The study made by H. J. Witteveen (*Loonshoogte en Werkgelegenheid*, De Erven F. Bohn, Haarlem, 1947, chap. XII), in which extrapolations to the New Deal period of equations based on Tinbergen's analysis and fitted to pre-New-Deal data for the U.S. economy were compared with New Deal experience, do not constitute a straight test, because they are in part an attempt to estimate effects of New Deal policies on the relationships in question.

[2] See footnote 3 on page 200.

[3] Carl Christ, "A Test of an Econometric Model for the United States, 1921–1947," with comments by Milton Friedman, Lawrence R. Klein and others, in *Conference on Business Cycles*, National Bureau of Economic Research, New York, 1951, pp. 35–130. See also, in the same volume, Jan Tinbergen, "Reformulation of Current Business Cycle Theories as Refutable Hypotheses," with comments by Tjalling C. Koopmans and David McCord Wright.

computational economy) are both intermediate between the complete use of all a priori information specified by the model, on the one hand, and the regression of endogenous on concurrent exogenous variables and on preceding variables mentioned above, on the other. He compares the two naïve model forecasts for 1948 of each of 13 endogenous variables with the two structural forecasts,[1] and he finds that the naïve model forecasts are closer to the observed values of the variables in a majority of the 13 cases. The majority is narrow in the case of the "structural" forecast using the smaller amount of a priori information and larger in the case of the more highly "structural" forecast.

In his comments[2] Klein has contested the significance of these results, objecting to the choice of data used, the particular modifications made to his model, and the incomplete use made of a priori information. Since these objections carry some weight (as anticipated or acknowledged by Christ), it is of interest to examine the outcome of a similar test applied to a more recent 20–equations model fitted by Klein and Goldberger[3] to data for 1929–41 and 1946–50. The authors do not apply such a test, but the information they provide has made it possible for Christ, in a recent review article,[4] to apply it to their forecasts of 14 endogenous variables for 1951 and 1952, and to those of 5 important such variables for 1953 and 1954. The forecasts for 1951 and 1952 are "ex-post" forecasts that use observed values for exogenous variables of the same years. Out of the 14 variables, the ex-post structural forecasts are better than those of the naïve model that assumes no change from last year in 8 cases (plus one tie) in 1951, in 4 in 1952. The successes include gross national product, the private wage bill and the money wage rate in both years, national income and the price level in one, gross investment in neither year. As a second crude test, the directions of change are found to be correctly predicted in 9 cases (plus one tie) in 1951, in 10 cases in 1952.

---

[1] The term "forecast" is not literally applicable to the structural forecasts because observed 1948 values of exogenous variables are used in their computation.

[2] See footnote 3 on page 203.

[3] L. R. Klein and A. S. Goldberger, *An Econometric Model for the United States, 1929–1952*, North-Holland Publishing, Amsterdam, 1955. Again the fit uses most but not all of the a priori information specified by the model.

[4] "Aggregate Econometric Models," *American Economic Review*, vol. 46, July 1956, pp. 385–408.

The forecasts for 1953 and 1954 are based on a reestimated structure using data for 1929–41 and 1946–52. In addition, they are ex-ante forecasts using the authors' anticipations of concurrent exogenous variables, as well as recent experience of discrepancies between structural equations and facts. In both years, out of the 5 variables examined by Christ, the structural forecasts are better than the naïve model forecasts in the cases of gross national product, consumption (both in real terms) and employment, and not as good in the cases of (real) gross investment and the price level. Of the 6 successful forecasts 5 fall within 1 per cent of the observed variables (the sixth one deviates $1\frac{1}{4}$ per cent). Investment is overestimated in both years by a little over 10 per cent, the price level by about 5 per cent. The predicted direction of change fails in only one case in one year.[1]

While the results for the 1951 and 1952 ex-post forecasts are ambivalent, those for the 1953 and 1954 ex-ante forecasts are encouraging. It should be noted in particular that 1954 was a year of a mild downturn in economic activity as measured by gross national product. A structural model which does no better than naïve models in years of continuing growth but succeeds in calling a downturn justifies for that reason alone the efforts invested in its construction. It is therefore important that structural estimation and prediction and the testing of its results be continued and extended, so that we may know whether this most recent forecasting experience is due to luck or to a genuine advance in quantitative knowledge.

We need to ask ourselves again how possible tests bear on the two purposes of the model we have distinguished, that of "straight forecasting" and that of assessing the effects of previously unused policies or of other known or given structural changes. Here it is clear that in years in which there are no important changes in policy or in structure, the straight forecasting ability of the models can be tested by itself alone. However, an isolated test of the ability to predict the effect of

[1] The impression of partial success of the forecasts for 1953 and 1954, conveyed by this test for a small number of relatively the most important variables, is confirmed and elaborated by comparisons for a larger number of variables. Data for the 1953 forecast supplied to the author by Dr. Goldberger indicate 9 out of 14 variables for which the forecast is better than the naïve model. Data for the 1954 forecast contained in a table on p. ix of the preface to the book of Klein and Goldberger indicate 8 or 7 such cases out of 11 variables, for the forecasts announced in December 1953 and in June 1954, respectively.

policies would be possible only in the rare case in which two countries of highly similar structure and in highly similar initial conditions apply different policies, or in which one country applies different policies at two different times at which it is in highly similar states. Discounting this unlikely possibility, the ability to predict the effect of policies cannot be tested separately from straight forecasting performance. Thus we shall not know how well these models serve the purpose for which structural estimation is indispensable until they render satisfactory service in straight forecasting.

7. THE SAMPLE SURVEY

We have reserved comment on the third avenue of improvement of econometric studies, better control of the conditions under which observations are obtained, because it merits discussion especially in connection with the fourth important tool development that we have distinguished, the sample survey. Together with the various types of census, of which it can be considered a refinement, the sample survey represents the main tool of *active* observation of the quantitative or the classifiable qualitative variables in the economy. This stands in contrast to most other economic data which are obtained largely as byproducts of administrative processes of revenue collection, law, regulation, trade or industry. The survey based on a probability sample in turn distinguishes itself from the complete enumeration of the census type by greater flexibility in the type of information collected and in the degree of precision sought, greater speed of collection and processing, and finally lower cost for given precision because the quality of interviewing can be better controlled. For these reasons, the sample survey may well attain an importance in the study of economic behavior similar to that of the microscope in the study of biological phenomena.

Valuable demonstrations and discussions of the possibilities and limitations of survey data for economic analysis have become available[1] as a result of the work of the Survey Research Center at the University

---

[1] See, for instance, Katona, Klein (ed.), Lansing and Morgan, *Contributions of Survey Methods to Economics*, publication of the Survey Research Center of the University of Michigan, Columbia University Press, New York, 1954.

of Michigan, and of various committees of consultants that have reported to the Board of Governors of the Federal Reserve System.[1] The sample survey is practically the only suitable instrument for the measurement of buying intentions, of attitudes, and of expectations. It has been found in particular that the information on buying intentions has definite value for forecasting purchases.

The sample survey method can also contribute to the structural knowledge of economic behavior, although difficulties of interpretation or identification similar to those that arise in inference from aggregate time series must also be faced here. An example is given by the way in which the effect of assets on saving depends on income, as found and explained by Morgan and discussed also by Klein.[2] At low-income levels, larger assets are associated with smaller savings, ostensibly because in that case a reserve is available to draw on for needed expenditures. At high-income levels, larger assets are found associated with larger savings. The probable explanation is that both accumulated assets and current savings reflect a persistent trait of thriftiness. Thus entirely different chains of causation are presumed to be operative at the two ends of the income scale.

Identification difficulties of this kind are most pronounced in completely random samples of the population. They can be reduced by sample designs that exercise control on some variables while retaining randomness in all remaining directions. The relative oversampling of high-income groups exhibiting a more variable behavior, applied by the Survey Research Center, is one example of this technique. It would seem that the idea of sampling from subpopulations selected to have predesignated values or value ranges for some variables could be carried further with fruit. In a field where experimental control over the objects of observation can usually not be established, careful exercise of choice over the classes of objects singled out for closer observation is perhaps the nearest one can come to the conditions more commonly associated with experiments. To illustrate, in the example of the association of larger assets with larger savings among high-income groups, a further

[1] Committees on Saving Statistics, on Consumer Expectations, on Inventory Statistics. on General Business Expectations, and on Business Plant and Equipment Expenditure Expectations.

[2] *Op. cit.*, pp. 112 and 201, respectively.

distinction between inherited wealth and accumulated wealth in a sample concentrated in this group might clinch the tentative explanation that has been advanced. Establishment of quasi-experimental control of this kind through sample design may also permit the simpler methods of statistical inference that were developed primarily for use in experimental situations—such as analysis of variance or regression analysis—to be validly applied to the estimation of structural behavior characteristics.

Obviously, data from a single survey can only elucidate the response to variables that are actually different among members of the population sampled. If, for instance, the general climate of opinion about economic prospects should have an influence on decisions independent of the decision maker's own anticipations, or if all anticipations were found to vary more or less in unison, a sequence of surveys would be needed both for measuring the variation over time in the climate of opinion, and for studying its causal connections with other variables. The difficulties inherent in structural estimation from time series can then not be avoided.

8. IMPLICATIONS OF TOOL DEVELOPMENTS
FOR FUTURE RESEARCH

The discussion so far has perhaps overstressed the more heroic research ventures addressed to questions that can only be answered through models of economy-wide coverage. Concurrent with these ventures, there has been a great deal of quantitative research devoted to individual markets or types of decisions. The tool developments we have reviewed are equally important to these more concentrated studies.[1] Taken as a whole, econometric work in this broad category has been more clearly successful and cumulative, and the individual pieces of knowledge so gained have often been useful by themselves. Undoubtedly, this experience has added force to what appears to be the prevailing current of professional opinion: that in the present stage

---

[1] Besides the examples quoted in footnotes 1 and 2 on page 200, we may mention S. Prais and H. S. Houthakker, *The Analysis of Family Budgets*, Cambridge University Press, Cambridge, Eng., 1955, in which electronic computation was used to enable more detailed data to be brought to bear on the problem.

research resources are best channeled into concentrated studies of specific types of economic behavior. The following two quotations, both from discussions of desirable directions of future research, put the issue clearly. The first is from an unpublished memorandum by James Tobin.

> In particular, given the present state of economics, I believe that a "subject" organization around the major types of decision-making institutions is appropriate. What is wrong with economics is not so much the putting together of the pieces. Economists have become skilled practitioners of the art of building "models" expressing economic interdependence. These models enable us to perceive the ultimate implications of any set of assumptions about economic behavior. Advances in recent years in the application of mathematical methods to economic theory and developments in high-speed calculating machines make it possible to work with models of much greater complexity, scope, and detail than was formerly thought possible. What is wrong is the poor quality of the pieces that we put together in such models. We do not know which basic assumptions about the behavior of the strategic decision-making units are empirically relevant. Until we do, model-building will be a branch of mathematics and logic rather than a powerful tool for an empirical science.[1]

The second quotation is from a report by Howard Bowen.

> Second, as a matter of practical research strategy, it is recommended that encouragement and substantial resources be given to research on specific and detailed aspects of business behavior. It is, of course, important to explore big questions and to formulate all-embracing theories. However, the writer suspects that the greatest need at this time is for careful scholarly investigations of a more limited type, in which the purpose is to explain particular aspects of business, for example, goals, expectations, investment, inventories, dividends. Indeed, there may be practical advantages in studying business decisions on specific matters which are of minor importance in the life of enterprises—on charitable contributions, introduction of particular labor-saving machines, responses to small changes in excise taxes, or responses to the growing custom of the morning break for coffee. Subjects such as these can be discussed by businessmen objectively and without fear of disclosing confidential information, whereas it is more difficult for them to discuss more vital

---

[1] James Tobin, "Research on Full Employment and Inflation," memorandum prepared for the Social Science Research Council, July 1953.

decisions with outsiders. The main point is that substantial research energy should be directed toward explaining specific types of behavior, whether of minor or major importance. A large number of such studies, especially if conducted within the framework of a consistent set of objectives, would be very fruitful in conclusions on such fundamental questions as the decision-making process, the values of firms, responses to changes in costs, or reactions to changes in the social milieu.[1]

These may well be counsels of wisdom. It is certainly true that poor pieces cannot make good models. It is likewise true that for many aspects of economic behavior, the best pieces we have are pretty poor pieces. However, lest the trend of opinion expressed in our quotations lead to a complete swing away from attempts to construct the best economy-wide models possible from current knowledge, a few considerations may be brought up on the other side.

The first consideration arises from the question how to choose the pieces that we shall try to improve. Like all questions of the objectives of basic research and of the priorities arising therefrom, it is best solved through professional discussion and a great deal of individual initiative. In such discussion, it has often been noted that the selection of economic research problems has been subject to wide swings of emphasis in delayed response to economic events. The great depression brought about a decade of almost exclusive preoccupation with problems of stability and full employment. The war led to an emphasis on efficient allocation of resources. A decade of postwar prosperity in industrially advanced countries has allowed a broadening out of professional attention over a greater variety of problems of theory, fact, and policy. The growth problems of underdeveloped countries have claimed a great deal of exploratory effort. Inequalities between regions or industries, in income or in opportunities for growth, have been studied. Institutional aspects of competition, of the labor market, of invention and innovation, have been investigated. At the same time, abstract theory has been widened and deepened in a number of directions.

It should be realized that this increased wealth of research orienta-

[1] Howard R. Bowen, *The Business Enterprise as a Subject for Research*, Pamphlet 11 of the Social Science Research Council, New York, 1955. The quotation is from p. 77. Only the second recommendation is quoted. The first, for greater emphasis on empirical as against theoretical studies, and the third, for more frequent communication between scholars of the business enterprise, do not involve issues in the present context.

tions, this increased concentration on in the long run more fundamental problems, are the fruits of our postwar freedom from even moderate depressions, and from immoderate inflations. The occurrence of either such event would again tend to narrow down the attention of economists, and even more the public discussion and governmental appraisal of their recommendations. We shall therefore be able to continue advancing on many fronts only if we at least hold the line on one front, that of assuring to the economy a course of reasonably full employment with a reasonably stable, or at least not too rapidly rising, price level.

Current professional opinion holds that the knowledge needed to cope with this problem is at hand, although its prompt application when needed is not equally assured. It is also felt that the problem has been made less difficult by the elements of flexibility and stability that have been introduced into the economic system since the great depression. Without attempting to make quantitative comparisons, it may be noted in passing that the need for flexibility has also increased. If the fluctuating production and manpower needs of national security in a two-power world are to be determined on their own merits, we need to be able to absorb their dynamic repercussions on the economy. At the same time, an element of instability has been added to private demand through the increased importance of durable goods in production and in consumption. Finally, the avoidance of depressions has in itself become an even more important objective in a world in which many new nations are forming judgments about alternative systems of economic organization on the basis of their performance characteristics.

Whatever weight attaches to each of these various considerations, it will not be disputed that relevance to the problems of ensuring stability in the growth of the economy remains an important criterion in the allocation of research resources. One feels intuitively that a study of the morning break for coffee has a low score in this value scale. But there are other choices to which the criterion is harder to apply. The problem of stability is essentially one of balance between many types of decisions. We therefore need to go on fitting together the best pieces of analysis we have, if we are to make good judgments as to which gaps in our knowledge most inhibit progress on the problem of steadying our rate of economic growth. This is point one in favor of a continued research interest in economy-wide models.

It will be objected that experience with the model construction efforts we have already reviewed has not been encouraging. In spite of the differences in purpose between the input-output model and the economic behavior models, there is a remarkable similarity in the testing record. We must face the fact that models using elaborate theoretical and statistical tools and concepts have not done decisively better, in the majority of available tests, than the most simple-minded and mechanical extrapolation formulae. There is little consolation in the thought that the tests of either model have not involved situations of drastic change in policies or external events, in which they might reveal a comparative advantage for the structural analysis underlying the model in question. The quality of the disaster insurance afforded by structural models is uncertain until either a disaster occurs and provides a test, or until the models are improved to the point where their performance in response to milder stimuli is more accurate. The outcome of the most recent predictions of Klein and Goldberger is a ray of hope in this regard.

It may be further objected that experience with the two models under review has not shown the existence of a definite pay-off to further disaggregation. In the light of this outcome, should we at all contemplate going farther on the road toward more disaggregative models?

In answer to both objections, we can point to another striking similarity between the two models. They did not show an increase in flexibility commensurate with their gradual increase in size and in detail. This is particularly true for the input-output model, in which a simple theoretical scheme was impressed on a larger and larger body of defenseless data. But we shall argue below that the economic behavior models we have described encounter similar difficulties in recognizing obvious aspects of reality and in utilizing relevant information. Professor Tobin is right in saying that the new tools have made it possible to recognize and incorporate more information in our models. But we have not yet learned how to do so to best effect. A further trying out of the new tools for this purpose seems as important as a further increase in our understanding of individual behavior.

This is point number two in favor of continuing work on models with wide coverage. To clarify it further we shall consider, in relation to behavior models of this kind, the three avenues of possible improvement recognized in Section 6: more observations, better use of available a priori knowledge, and better control of observations. At the same time, we shall spot some suggestions contained in research developments of the last decade that may help in one or another of these directions.

It so happens that, in the present context, all three avenues point toward further disaggregation. To begin with, apart from the slow annual accumulation of new data of the types collected and studied earlier, the number of observations can be drastically increased only by further breakdown of aggregates: use of quarterly or monthly instead of annual data in the study of dynamic responses, breakdown by industries or even processes in the study of technology, of production and of investment, and breakdown by types of consumers and by commodity classes in the study of consumption.

A mere increase in the volume of data fed into econometric analysis is no guarantee of an increase in resulting knowledge of economic behavior. However, such a priori knowledge as we have applies to individual situations. In the discussion of models of production, we found that a high degree of disaggregation was needed to use engineering knowledge which by its nature relates to individual processes rather than to industries. At the same time, the greater flexibility of the assumptions of process analysis was needed to make such a degree of disaggregation meaningful.

Similar observations have been made about behavior models by Karl Fox in a recent article,[1] which gives particular attention to the agricultural sector of the economy. He explains that the degree of disaggregation of the Klein-Goldberger model is not sufficient to permit use of a great deal of available information about agricultural markets relevant to the state of the general economy, or to answer questions about the effects of important agricultural policies such as the determination of support prices.

The information to which Fox refers consists primarily of demand and supply relationships and other knowledge concerning individual commodities. The argument can be carried further with regard to individual decision makers. Introspective knowledge or direct observation of economic motivation applies strictly only to individual firms or

---

[1] Karl Fox, "Econometric Models in the United States," *Journal of Political Economy*, vol. 64, April 1956, pp. 128–142.

households. While it has been the practice in econometric studies to apply such knowledge directly and somewhat mechanically in specifying the form of aggregative behavior relations, there is a long line of studies in which this practice has been questioned or its implications scrutinized.[1] It has transpired from these studies that in most circumstances estimates of behavior parameters obtained from aggregate data do not have the direct and exclusive relationship to individual behavior parameters that one wishes. An aggregate price elasticity of demand so measured depends not only on individual price elasticities of demand, but also to some extent, for instance, on individual income elasticities of demand. The extent of such distortions is controlled by the correlation between the two elasticities in the population.

Our increasing awareness of nonlinearities and inequalities as essential elements in the description of microeconomic phenomena strengthens the case for more disaggregation. All the nonlinearities present in the Klein-Goldberger model are of the mild and smooth type arising from identities such as "value = price $\times$ quantity," or "labor input = number of hours worked $\times$ number of workers," and from the use of a percentage rate of change of a variable in one case. The treatment of production does not recognize "ceilings" set by capacity limits in specific industries or processes. Neither does the treatment of investment place a "floor" at zero gross investment. We have already seen that the recognition of these sharper forms of nonlinearity requires a relatively high degree of disaggregation. Thus, the degree of aggregation used does not permit us to exploit the simplest types of a priori information we possess.

These remarks are not intended as criticisms of the pioneering work

[1] Jacob Marschak, "Personal and Collective Budget Functions," and "Money Illusion and Demand Analysis," *Review of Economic Statistics*, vol. 21, November 1939, pp. 161–170 and vol. 25, February 1943, pp. 40–48, respectively.

P. de Wolff, "Income Elasticity of Demand, a Microeconomic and Macroeconomic Interpretation," *Economic Journal*, vol. 51, 1941, pp. 140–145.

Trygve Haavelmo, "Family Expenditure and the Marginal Propensity to Consume," *Econometrica*, vol. 15, October 1947, pp. 335–341.

Sten Malmquist, *A Statistical Analysis of the Demand for Liquor in Sweden*, Uppsala, 1948, especially chap. II, sec. 5.

James Tobin, "A Statistical Demand Curve for Food in the U.S.A.," *Journal of the Royal Statistical Society*, ser. A, part II, 1950, pp. 113–149.

M. J. Farrell, "Some Aggregation Problems in Demand Analysis," *Review of Economic Studies*, vol. 21 (3), 1954, pp. 193–202.

H. Theil, *Linear Aggregation of Economic Relations*, North-Holland Publishing, Amsterdam, 1954.

of Klein and Goldberger. Their main intent is to argue that in future empirical work we should seek to use the power of the new tools to achieve an increased concentration on more highly disaggregative studies. The individual parts of such studies can often be tested within their own sphere of relevance, and are useful within that sphere whenever they stand the test. The point to be made here, however, is that an increasing degree of disaggregation in empirical work is also necessary for progress in the study of movements of the economy as a whole.

The amount of detail that can be recognized and utilized in any model is of course limited by the capacity of available computing and data processing equipment and by the state of the art of programming the computations to be performed by such equipment. There have been a number of interesting experiments in the use of computing equipment to make possible greater flexibility and greater receptivity to available information in dynamic models of the economy or its parts. Analog and digital computers have been used to determine and study the solutions to simple nonlinear equation systems suggested by dynamic economic theories.[1] These studies constitute a rehabilitation of the numerical example as a tool of analysis in situations where general mathematical analysis either is too difficult, or shows the outcome to be highly dependent on the numerical values of the parameters of the model. So far these studies have used hypothetical values for the parameters, or values obtained by analogy (rather than measurement) from a few aggregative statistics. Some of them have been directed to tracing out implications of a deterministic model for a few variables far into the future, ignoring the stochastic elements in economic events. There is no reason why similar methods could not be used to compute the implications of a stochastic model for a larger number of variables over the shorter time span of predictability implied in such a model.

The processing of a larger number of observations places a premium on simple methods of statistical inference, possibly at some sacrifice in

<hr>

[1] See, for instance, N. F. Morehouse, R. H. Strotz, and S. J. Horwitz, "An Electro-Analog Method for Investigating Problems in Economic Dynamics: Inventory Oscillations," *Econometrica*, vol. 18, October 1950; pp. 313–328; R. H. Stortz, J. C. McAnulty, and J. B. Naines, Jr., "Goodwin's Nonlinear Theory of the Business Cycle: An Electro-Analog Solution," *Econometrica*, vol. 21, July 1953, pp. 390–411; A. S. Manne and J. M. Frankovich, "Electronic Calculating Methods for Handling the Excess Capacity Problems," *Review of Economics and Statistics*, vol. 35, February 1953, pp. 51–58.

information extracted. Suggestions in that direction are contained in the work of the National Bureau of Economic Research, which has studied various order statistics such as leads and lags in turning points, and amplitudes and periods of fluctuation, for a large number of available time series. Used originally mainly as a means of measuring past cyclical experience,[1] similar techniques have been studied by Moore as a possible means of prognosis in his work on diffusion indices.[2] The selection of the particular order statistics used has been made largely on intuitive grounds. At first sight, the selection of just a few items out of a time series, or the utilization of directions of change rather than magnitudes of change may appear as a somewhat wasteful use of information. However, in regard to nonlinear models that recognize ceilings and floors to the movements of some variables, the theory of statistical inference might show such measures to be reasonably efficient summaries of a large part of the relevant information contained in the series. If this were to be the case, the intuitions that led to the adoption of such measures would be vindicated.

Methods of this kind could well be combined with planned selection of the observation points at which time series are collected, in order to increase the value of the information contained in them. This leads us to the third avenue of improvement, better control over the conditions under which observations are made. The results obtained with the sample survey justify further development of this tool both for observation of current conditions and for the measurement of behavior parameters. The methodology of combining current information from this source with systems of structural equations fitted to time series also needs further development.

A model of the economy which utilizes these and other suggestions contained in the literature will need to be not only more detailed, but also more flexible in its concepts and in the statistical techniques to which it gives rise. Here is a challenge to economic, statistical, and

---

[1] See A. F. Burns and Wesley C. Mitchell, *Measuring Business Cycles*, National Bureau of Economic Research, New York, 1946.

[2] Geoffrey H. Moore, "The Diffusion of Business Cycles," a chapter in *Economics and the Public Interest*, R. A. Solo (ed.), Rutgers University Press, New Brunswick, N.J., 1955; also *Statistical Indicators of Cyclical Revivals and Recessions*, Occasional Paper 31, National Bureau of Economic Research, New York, 1950. See further the discussion between Moore and Arthur L. Broida in *The American Statistician*, April-May 1954, June 1955, and October 1955.

mathematical ingenuity. While our imagination could easily run ahead of us in this regard, one could think of a conceptually highly disaggregative model, containing many individual behavior equations for most of which the variables are not measured individually, and the parameters are not estimated individually. One type of observation, represented by more or less aggregative time series, could be employed to estimate suitably defined aggregate equations, of which the coverage might be made to vary with the state of the economy, more specifically with the proximity to floors or ceilings observed in various industries. Current survey data on the other hand would apply directly to the states, plans, behavior, and anticipations of individual firms or households, such that the model would permit inferences from these data to aggregative variables not yet measured or not yet formed.[1]

Much more experience and knowledge than we now possess must be acquired before we shall be able to balance the cost of observation by survey methods against the value for economic stability of the information secured. However, there seems to be no reason why we cannot look forward ultimately to a situation in which the amount and kind of current economic information to be regularly collected is determined in the same way in which the number, locations and observation programs of weather stations are determined on the basis of the contribution expected to be made to weather forecasting.

9. THE APPRAISAL AND SUPPORT OF RESEARCH VENTURES

There is thus both scope and need in the future for experimentation with more flexible, more disaggregative, model formulations with greater data requirements, met in part through surveys designed to collect information of those kinds and at those points where the contribution made per dollar spent is thought to be greatest. It is believed that projects of this character will form an increasing part of economic research activity, regardless of the distribution of emphasis between

[1] Presumably some such model was in the mind of Professor Arnold Tustin when he presented an engineer's challenge to the economic profession. In a highly stimulating book (*The Mechanism of Economic Systems*, Heinemann, London, 1953), he has expressed the view that the experience accumulated by engineers in the design of automatic control systems is relevant to the problem of stabilization of economic growth. His proposals merit careful examination, even though the individual economic decision maker is not so dependable as the individual part or circuit in a control mechanism.

studies of economy-wide coverage and intensive studies of particular types of decisions.

Such research ventures are costly. They require organized teams of personnel with widely different skills. They demand data-processing services and equipment. In so far as they use data not already collected for other purposes, they may involve very substantial expenditures for data gathering. The question naturally arises from what sources support for such ventures is best sought, and by what processes their prospects and results are best evaluated. Experience to date with sizable research ventures of the type considered allows a few observations to be made on these points.

The starting point in these observations is that the ventures in question are risky. There is no advance assurance that the results will justify the costs. It follows from this that government agencies of an operating character—as distinct from agencies set up to support basic research—are not the best sources of funds for analysis, for data processing, and for collection of data that do not already have a recognized usefulness for governmental purposes, independent of the purposes of the study contemplated. In the present state of our knowledge, the use of such sources is likely to be dependent on an overestimation of the chances of success of the venture, and may also be conducive to an oversimplified choice of the body of premises on which the model rests.

The preferable source of support for the type of ventures we are discussing is therefore found in the risk capital made available by society for attempts to increase basic knowledge. In the "Western" form of society this capital is allocated by private foundations and other private donors, by government agencies for the support of basic research, and in much smaller amounts by a larger number of universities. Support from these sources has been extremely important to empirical work in economics. What is needed for a full exploration of the potentialities of the new tools in economics is more of such support, and greater continuity of it. A higher amount of support is required because of the higher costs of the new tools. Continuity is important in particular from the point of view of testing the models constructed.

In all model developments that have taken place so far, testing has been the weakest aspect. This is in part explainable by an understandable reluctance on the part of developers of models to face tests that are perhaps premature, or to face tests that may be not quite appropriate to the purposes of the model. They may also find it difficult to set aside resources from their research budgets for data collection or analysis intended primarily for testing purposes. But probably the main explanation for the relative neglect of testing lies in the lack of continuity of research projects and of the associations of staff with them. If the development of a model takes three to five years, the testing requires another five years or longer, depending on whether economic events occurring in such a period present a sufficient challenge to the model. Academic research projects rarely run that long, and those that do are rarely able to retain individual staff members long enough to achieve the necessary continuity of interest. These circumstances go far toward explaining the fact that the literature contains so many more models than tested models.[1] In pondering the future of organized as distinct from individual economic research, the problems of how to provide for continuity in the testing of models therefore deserve particular attention. It may be desirable that this activity be pursued separately from model construction, provided that a full flow of information between builders and testers is not thereby inhibited.

The universities, and the private nonprofit research organizations formally or informally associated with universities, make favorable natural environments for research teams engaged in the development of structural models of the economy or its parts. At the same time, as pointed out by Richard Ruggles in Section IV of his perceptive essay on methodological developments[2] (of which the present Section 9 of this essay is largely an echo), the extent to which any one university can participate in organized economic research is limited by its primary organizational purpose of providing a subject-wise dispersed program of instruction. The task even of experimental model construction with economy-wide coverage and with full utilization of the new tools has therefore probably already grown beyond the capacities of any single academic research group. Cooperative projects distributed over several groups are likely to give a better chance of success to such work in the future.

[1] An exception is found in the field of agricultural economics, where the Department of Agriculture and research groups supported by it have kept a continuing check on estimated supply and demand relationships. See, for instance, Karl Fox, *The Analysis of Demand for Farm Products*, U.S. Department of Agriculture, Technical Bulletin 1081, September 1953.

[2] Richard Ruggles, "Methodological Developments," chap. 10 in B. F. Haley (ed.), *A Survey of Contemporary Economics, Vol. II*, Irwin, Homewood, Ill., 1952.

It is not intended to suggest that developments in these desirable directions should be an exclusive trend of future economic research. It may have seemed as if our discussion neglects, or implies a disregard for, the role of the lone wolf of economic research. The principal reason why we have not been led to comment on his essential role lies in the fact that, with the exception of mathematics, his tools do not occur in our list of recent tool developments. His prime contributions have been made mainly through the casual but penetrating observation and the perception of its implications, through the broad historical view, through the probing of ideas and questioning of concepts, and through the spotting of new problems. He has originated virtually all the basic ideas that have subsequently found their way into formal model construction. At the same time, continued activity on his part is the main safeguard against the risk that an increase in the size of research ventures might impress too narrow or too uniform points of view on economic research in general. He can be depended on to challenge the ideas that guide organized research efforts, to bring to light their implicit assumptions, to suggest tests to be applied to their results, and to insist that they be applied.

Another reason why the role of the lone wolf has not called for discussion up to this point is that there is no serious, as-yet-unsolved problem of organization involved in enabling his activity to flourish—except possibly that of obtaining the attention of foundations for making grants small enough to meet his modest needs. The university environment favors the development of his talent; the recurrent tasks of teaching stimulate his critical sense. He will always be with us, going strong.

Really difficult problems of evaluation and organization arise in regard to the larger and more integrated research ventures. Foundations need to depend on professional opinion and evaluation in appraising projects and in choosing between alternatives. Methodological conservatism may well inhibit or delay ventures that should be tried and chances that should be taken. A wider professional discussion and evaluation of the models developed so far and of possible directions of further work will increase the chances of progress through the utilization of new tools. If the present essay should help stimulate such discussion, it will fully have served its purpose.

INDEX

Page references in **boldface** type indicate definitions or descriptions. References followed by "*n.*" indicate footnotes.